John McHugo is an Arabist, an international lawyer and a former academic researcher. His writing has been published on the BBC website, and in *History Today* and in Chatham House's *The World Today*, among other publications. He is a director of the Council for Arab British Understanding and of the British Egyptian Society, and Chair of the Liberal Democrat Friends of Palestine. McHugo's other publications include *Syria: From the Great War to Civil War*.

www.johnmchugo.com

'A lucid and highly readable history of the Arab peoples up to the present day. John McHugo has managed to show, with compassion, a good deal of humour and unerring historical judgement, the power of the ideas and the forces that have shaped what we now think of as the Arab world. In doing so, McHugo has provided a way of understanding this complex and ongoing story that will enlighten all who read it.' Charles Tripp, author of *The Power and the People: Paths of Resistance in the Middle East*

'This concise, brilliant and erudite book is the product of wide reading, hard thinking and years of direct experience of the Middle East. The author has managed to throw fresh light on 1,400 years of Arab history from the Prophet Muhammad to the Arab Spring. There are lively and informative insights on almost every page.' Patrick Seale, author of *Asad: The Struggle for the Middle East*

'Thrilling and poignant, woven with a layered texture of knowledge and empathy that deftly stitches familiar figures into the narrative in a fresh way.' D̲ _____ _ancial Times, and auth

John McHugo

A

CONCISE

HISTORY

OF THE

ARABS

SAQI

First published in hardback in Great Britain by Saqi Books 2013

This paperback edition published 2014

Copyright © John McHugo 2013 and 2014

ISBN 978 0 86356 742 1
eISBN 978 0 86356 894 7

Cover image: Illustration of a caravan by Yahya bin Mahmud al-Wasiti for
The Assemblies (al-Maqamat) of al-Hariri. Iraq, 13th century.

A full CIP record for this book is available from the British Library.

Printed and bound by CPI Mackays, Chatham ME5 8TD

Saqi Books
26 Westbourne Grove
London W2 5RH

www.saqibooks.co.uk

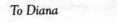

To Diana

CONTENTS

List of Maps		8
Glossary		9
Preface		13
ONE	When History Changed Direction	19
TWO	Growing Apart	49
THREE	The West Takes Control	77
FOUR	Sharing an Indigestible Cake	111
FIVE	Secularism and Islamism	150
SIX	The West Seems to Retreat	168
SEVEN	The Six Day War and its Consequences	215
EIGHT	Iraq, Israel, Militancy and Terrorism	228
NINE	The Age of the Autocrats and the Rise of Islamism	265
Conclusion: Something Snaps – The Arab Spring and Beyond		293
Acknowledgements		323
Notes		325
Bibliography		337
Suggestions for Further Reading		347
Index		351

LIST OF MAPS

Western Arabia with the Byzantine and Persian Empires on
the Eve of the Arab Conquests   21

The Arab Conquests under the Rashidun and the Umayyads   48

The Crusader States and the Mongol Conquests   65

The Ottoman Empire at its Maximum Extent   72

The Arab World in 1914   110

The League of Nations Mandates for the
Arabic-speaking Ottoman Provinces   117

The Partition of Palestine and the 1949 Armistice Lines   178

The Arab World at the Beginning of 1967   214

The Arab World on the Eve of the Arab Spring   294

GLOSSARY

Alawi: a member of a secretive Muslim sect which dates from the eleventh century and predominates in the mountains above Lattakia in Syria and in parts of the Orontes valley further east. There are also Alawis in Turkey.

Azhar: founded in Cairo during the 970s, the most influential teaching institution of Sunni Islam

Banu (or *Bani*): 'sons' or 'children', often part of the name of a tribe

Bey: an Ottoman title

Copt: a member of an ancient Egyptian Christian community which traces itself back to the preaching of St Mark in Alexandria in the first century AD. Today Copts constitute perhaps 10 per cent of the Egyptian population.

Druze: a member of a secretive sect which is an offshoot of Islam. They are numerous in parts of Lebanon and the Hawran plateau, south-east of Damascus. There is also a Druze community in Israel.

Fellah (pl. *fellahin*): peasant

Fitna: civil disturbance or discord

Hadith: the sayings or traditions ascribed to the Prophet Muhammad

Halal: permissible for Muslims according to the teaching of Islam. In everyday speech it often approximates to 'moral' but the concept is distinct. There may be nothing immoral as such about eating at noon during the fasting month of Ramadan, but for a Muslim it is not *halal*.

Haram: forbidden for Muslims according to the teaching of Islam. The word is not used for 'forbidden' in other contexts. Parking your car in breach of traffic regulations may be forbidden, but it is not *haram*.

Hijra: emigration

Ijtihad: independent judgement, especially in a legal or theological context

Imam: a religious leader. The word may mean no more than a prayer leader or preacher but for Shi'ites the word is used for the divinely inspired and infallible teacher whom all Muslims are bound to follow.

Jahiliyya: literally, 'the age of Ignorance', the age before the preaching of Islam

Jihad: literally, 'expenditure of effort' or 'endeavour'. Jihad is the struggle a Muslim should wage against his ego and for his religion. This can involve religious war.

Majlis: a place, or occasion, of sitting. A *majlis* can also be a hall or large room where guests are received.

Mamluk: a slave soldier usually brought as a boy from a distant country and brought up to be a member of a military elite

Maronite: a member of an ancient Christian community which has been in communion with the Roman Catholic Church since the Crusades. It is predominant in parts of Lebanon.

Millet: a religious sect or denomination

Mufti: a religious scholar of sufficient eminence to give opinions on questions of Islamic law which it is reasonable for other Muslims to decide to follow

Mujahid: literally, 'someone who struggles' or 'someone who fights in a jihad' but can also be used in a secular context

Mukhabarat: the intelligence or security services of a modern Arab state

Muwaatinoon: citizens or nationals of a country

Pasha: an Ottoman title, generally superior to a *bey*; also used in the Egyptian, Iraqi and Jordanian monarchies in the twentieth century

Rashidun: the first four caliphs, Abu Bakr, Umar, Uthman and Ali, who are accepted by Sunni Muslims

Salaf: ancestors, predecessors

Salafi: adjective from *salaf*; in the twentieth and twenty-first centuries the word is generally used to indicate a devout Muslim who believes Muslims should rigidly emulate the conduct of the Prophet and his companions down to the tiniest details of behaviour.

Sharia: the religious, or canonical, law of Islam

Shaykh: literally, 'old man'. The term denotes respect and is used of a tribal or religious elder or leader. A man who learns the entire Qur'an by heart is automatically a shaykh whatever his age.

Shi'ite: a follower of Shi'ite Islam, the second largest Muslim sect

Shirk: polytheism, idolatry

Sunna: habitual practice or custom, specifically that of the Prophet Muhammad which came to be regarded as legally binding precedent

Sunni: a follower of Sunni Islam, the largest Muslim sect

Taabi'oon: followers

Takfir: declaring another Muslim to have betrayed the faith by apostasy and to be worthy of death. Hence *takfiri*, a person who makes such declarations.

Tanzimat: a series of nineteenth-century Ottoman reforms

Umma: 'community', especially (but not necessarily) the Community of Muslims

Wahhabi: a spiritual follower of the Muslim puritanical movement started by Muhammad Ibn Abdul Wahhab in eighteenth-century Arabia. Wahhabism is the ideology governing Saudi Arabia.

Wasta: literally, 'intermediary-ness'. A colloquial expression used to refer to the reciprocal trading of favours up and down hierarchies of power, wealth and influence.

PREFACE

I

The upheavals which began as the Arab Spring cannot be understood unless they are put in the context of the long history of the Arabs. What are the origins of the confusions and complications that afflict our 'Western' understanding of the Arab world? How did this distinction we constantly draw between 'East' and 'West' begin, and how valid is it? Whose fault is it that things so often went wrong? Will the current upheavals exorcise any of the demons that have come between us? These are just some of the questions this book seeks to answer.

The Arab Spring found Arab autocrats complacent and in denial, despite their fearsome intelligence services with supposedly all-seeing eyes. It is therefore unsurprising that it caught European and American strategists, experts and commentators on the hop as they observed demonstrators in Arab countries calling for fair elections and human rights, the freedoms that we enjoy as a matter of course. But Europe and the USA had strategic interests to consider and cold calculations to make. As President Hosni Mubarak tottered in Egypt, there were fears about the Suez Canal. The price of oil became a worry once Libya descended into civil war, while Europeans feared uncontrolled immigration as thousands desperately took to the sea to escape from the turmoil. And what if the unrest were to spread to Saudi Arabia, far and away the world's largest oil exporter? Six Arab countries are among the top fifteen oil-exporting states, making the Arab region as a whole vital for the rest of the world. These were merely extra worries for policy-makers in the West, who already suffered headaches caused by the region's unresolved baggage. It was where the seeds of Islamist terrorism had germinated in the late twentieth century. Chaos and instability would give networks like al-Qa'ida the opportunity to reorganise and expand. There were also two major international issues which refused to go away: the unfinished business between Israelis and Arabs which had been a destabilising factor for decades, and the growing strife between Sunni and Shi'ite Muslims.

Hope was therefore tinged with nervousness and bafflement as governments across the world responded inconsistently to events in each country, and one crisis followed another. Revolutions have a life of their own. They can descend into civil war. This happened in Syria when the regime learned the lessons of Tunisia and Egypt and refused to relinquish control. The best organised forces, not necessarily the most popular or democratic ones, often triumph in the end. None of the uprisings started in the name of Islam, but Islamist politicians seemed to be the beneficiaries of the first truly democratic elections held in Arab countries for decades. Even before 9/11, there had been loose talk of a 'clash of civilisations'.[1] For many people, this put Islam – and therefore the Arab world – in existential opposition to the democracies of the West.

We are now going to find out, once and for all, whether this clash really exists. I believe that history shows that it does not. Civilised cultures influence and benefit each other. If they do not, they are quite simply not civilised. The expression 'clash of civilisations' has come to be used almost as a slogan. The 'clash' has a resonance for people with a certain attitude of mind – and a certain view of history. It has become an intellectually lazy way of helping them believe what they want to believe, of confirming their prejudices, and explaining things away without making an effort to understand them properly.

Since at least the October 1973 War between Israel and its Arab neighbours, the USA has been the predominant power in the Middle East. After the collapse of the Soviet Union, it enjoyed near hegemony. Yet imposing its will was at a huge cost, which was often self-defeating. The intrusion of domestic politics on its freedom of action in foreign affairs made it like a drunken man playing with a Rubik's Cube. However hard it tried, however much energy it exerted, the coloured squares obstinately refused to line up, and it periodically lost its concentration. The problem was that, as with Britain and France in an earlier period, American good intentions were regularly sacrificed on the altar of political expediency.

The reasons behind this failure are not hard to find. All too frequently, Europeans and Americans have created their own image of the Arabic-speaking countries of the Middle East and Islam. They have then proceeded to deal with the image rather than the reality. Memory distorts the pictures it builds, but we normally do our best to correct those pictures once we become aware of the distortion. Yet sometimes emotion plays a trump card and the mind finds ways to reject whatever conflicts with the ideal we have constructed. The Arab world and Islam are contentious issues in Western cultural wars, and narratives of history have been built accordingly. In some circles, the attitudes somebody displays to the Arab world and to Islam may be seen as a litmus test about his or her view of Western civilisation itself. There are even people for whom a negative or hostile picture of Arabs and Muslims seems to have become necessary for their own positive image of the West.

This book is intended to introduce Western readers who are unfamiliar with the topic to the history of the Arabs for the first time. It assumes no background knowledge and is written with a non-specialist audience in mind. It is a concise, not a definitive, history. I have therefore had to take difficult decisions about what to leave out. Some suggestions for further reading are included at the end.

It aims to show that what has happened over the decades – and, indeed, the centuries – is not a clash of civilisations but a concatenation of historical events, misguided policies and wilful ignorance which have opened an ever-deepening rift between Europe and the USA on one side, and the Arab world on the other. As a result, the door has sometimes been opened to a moral nihilism in which dubious means have been used to achieve the desired result. When this has happened, cycles of deepening hostility have been created. It is therefore vital to understand how the Arab world has arrived where it is today, and that can only be done by learning about its history. If we do not do so, we cannot heal the rifts between us.

The Arabs originally came from the Arabian Peninsula which is now divided into the sovereign states of Saudi Arabia, Yemen, Oman, the United Arab Emirates (the UAE), Qatar, Bahrain and Kuwait. Yet in many ways it is Egypt (the Arab world's most populous country) and the lands of the Fertile Crescent (Iraq, Syria, Lebanon, Jordan and what was Palestine before the Arab–Israeli War of 1947–9) that have formed the historic centre of the Arab world. I have concentrated on the political history of these central Arab lands because of their key role in the early history of Islam and the Middle Ages as well as in the encounter with the West in the modern era. This has inevitably meant saying less about other parts of the Arab world. Arabic is spoken all the way along the Mediterranean coast to the Atlantic Ocean and deep into the Sahara. It is the language of the majority of people in Morocco, Algeria, Tunisia, Libya and Sudan, and of many people in Mauritania and Tchad. I regret that I have been unable to devote much space to these countries (or to the countries of the Arabian Peninsula) except when developments in them are essential for the book's argument.

There are other matters about which I have not had the space to say very much. There are many ethnic minorities scattered across the Arab world. I have only been able to deal with them when it has been necessary for my wider purpose. Thus, a few words have been included about the Kurds of Iraq and Syria but almost nothing about the Amazigh, or Berbers, of North Africa who are particularly numerous in Morocco and Algeria, or the Nubians who are split between Egypt and Sudan. These are proud ancient peoples. It is important to acknowledge the existence of their separate identities, which are likely to become more important in the future.

It must also be stressed that this is not a history of Islam or of Muslims, although it would be ridiculous to try to tell the story of the Arabs without explaining what Islam is and its relationship to Christianity and Judaism. Material about Islam is therefore presented with these aims in mind. The history of Islam in other parts of the world, including Iran and other areas conquered by the Arabs but where Arabic did not eventually become the native tongue, is not covered. Nor is this book a cultural or sociological history. When I touch on cultural or sociological matters (such as the position of women), it is in order to explain a particular point.

The history of the Arabs has not been made by the Arabs alone. Some chapters of this book therefore include material concerning non-Arab actors. Elements of the history of Ottoman Turkey are included in Chapters 2 and 3 while the Arab encounter with the West from 1798 onwards dominates many of the subsequent chapters. It is no accident that almost all the boundaries of modern Arab states were first drawn by officials in Paris, London and (to a lesser extent) Istanbul (when it was Constantinople) and Rome. The major exceptions are in the Arabian Peninsula, where many boundaries were only drawn for the first time after the end of the colonial era. Since 1948, there has also been a non-Arab state situated in the heart of the Arab world. This book is not a history of Israel and the Zionist project, but aspects of the history of Israel are mentioned in some detail because they are essential to understanding the modern Arab world today.

Some Notes on Terminology

I find the concept 'fundamentalism' confusing when applied to Islam, and the word occurs just once in this book, whilst 'fundamentalist' does not appear at all. When I refer to Muslims who rely on the literal meaning of a sentence from the Qur'an without accepting that it needs to be considered in the light of the context in which it occurs or the traditional methodologies of interpretation developed by Muslim scholars, I speak of 'literalists' and 'literalism'. By 'Islamist', I mean anyone who has a political agenda purportedly based on Islam. 'Islamist' thus includes those who advance such an agenda by exclusively peaceful and democratic means, as well as those who believe it may be advanced by violence. 'Extremist' and 'extremism' require no comment. The meaning of 'terrorism' is discussed in Chapter 8. When I speak of 'secularism' or use the word 'secular', I am referring to the idea that religious affiliations should be irrelevant. I do not use these words to refer to ideologies that are hostile to religion as such, which I describe as 'atheistic' (although not all atheists are hostile to religion).

By 'Greater Syria' I intend the entire area from the Sinai desert up to Cilicia in modern Turkey. It consists of the areas east of the Mediterranean, south of the Taurus Mountains and north and west of the deserts and steppes of the Arabian Peninsula. Today, this essentially means modern Syria, Lebanon, Israel, the Occupied Palestinian Territory and Jordan, as well as an area which has remained inside Turkey. Use of the expression 'Greater Syria' helps prevent discussion of this area being obscured by political divisions which were only established in the twentieth century.

John McHugo
January, 2014

CHAPTER ONE

WHEN HISTORY CHANGED DIRECTION

I

To try to reach the spot where sunrise or sunset occurs is as futile as chasing the rainbow, since our movement towards it makes its location change. 'West' and 'East' should always be seen as relative terms. Universal creeds like Christianity and Islam therefore do not – or should not – conceive of themselves as Western or Eastern. How and why, then, have so many of us in Europe and North America come to see ourselves as 'Western', and decided that Arabs and Muslims are 'Eastern' in a way that, for far too many people, establishes a crude pair of irreconcilable opposites called 'us' and 'them'? A fault line has appeared, so it is scarcely surprising if it occasionally triggers earthquakes.

Let us begin at the beginning, before either the Arab world or the West existed. For Westerners today there is something unique about the central lands of the Middle East which are now predominantly Arabic-speaking: Egypt, Greater Syria and Iraq. This is because the origins of the West can be traced back to these countries. They gave us writing, mathematics, architecture, science, the seven-day week and much else. A European who visits the ruins of pagan sites such as Palmyra and Ba'lbek, or Christian ones like Qala'at Sima'an and Qalb Lozeh, sees architecture which seems familiar. It reminds him of Greece and Rome, and is closely related to his own heritage. The same might almost be said of the porticoes, columns and urns weird-ly hewn from the multi-coloured rock of Petra. There was a unity of design and ornamentation in the architecture, statuary and mosaics of the Graeco-Roman world which stretched from York in the prov-ince of Britannia to Palmyra in the Syrian desert. Nothing similar would be seen throughout the Mediterranean until Western styles, which themselves were largely based on classical models, began to re-appear in cities on its southern and eastern shores in the nineteenth century.

Columns and capitals, colonnades and domes, were similar everywhere. Mosaics showing scenes from Graeco-Roman mythology and statues with their easily recognisable classical drapery could be found all around the Mediterranean. Every self-respecting city had its own amphitheatre. The now ruined basilica of St Simeon Stylites in the hills outside Aleppo and the Umayyad Mosque in Damascus – which owes the architecture of the basilica a considerable debt – show how Syrians have as much justification as anyone for claiming their country was where Romanesque architecture originated, even though today we think of Romanesque as the glory of early medieval Europe and the forerunner of Gothic, that quintessentially European style. How many Europeans today are aware that soldiers from Greater Syria once served on Hadrian's Wall and the Roman forts along the Rhine? Or that both Greater Syria and North Africa gave Rome emperors and popes, that Egypt and Tunisia provided Rome with its wheat, and that Constantine, who built the new Roman capital of Constantinople – now Istanbul – was first proclaimed emperor in York?

As the central Arabic-speaking lands of today were once part of what was to become the West, they hold a special place in the West-ern psyche. After all, Judaism and Christianity both originated in Palestine. Yet what we think of today as 'the West' only came into be-ing long after Christianity had conquered the Mediterranean world, which itself only occurred after Judaism had also spread across it. We

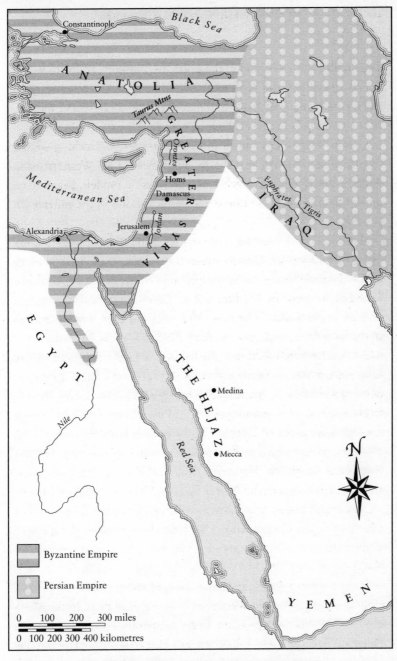

WESTERN ARABIA WITH THE BYZANTINE
AND PERSIAN EMPIRES ON THE EVE OF THE ARAB CONQUESTS

think of our ancestors, the Greeks and the Romans, as 'Westerners' because of subsequent history. In many respects the Romans were more interested in the rich provinces they acquired to their east than in the uncouth Celts and Germans who lived to the north and west where the heartland of Western civilisation would later emerge. They even identified themselves as descendants of Trojan refugees who had fled their home in Asia Minor.

The greatest dangers the Romans faced were not in the east but on the Rhine and Danube. It was Alaric the Visigoth, a European barbarian, who sacked Rome in AD 410. Even when the Sasanian Persians unsuccessfully besieged Constantinople in 626, it was their Avar allies from the Danube valley who surrounded the city walls on the landward side. By that time, the Roman Empire had ceased to exist in the West, but its eastern half, which today we usually call the Byzantine Empire, survived until the fifteenth century.

That Persian attack in 626 did not change the course of history. What did change it was the sudden emergence of Islam from the Arabian Peninsula a few years later. Western Christendom, which would still use Latin as its principal written language for a thousand years after the Western Roman Empire fell to pieces, was left staring fearfully and suspiciously at a new world facing it in the Mediterranean and extending far beyond.

II

Muhammad was born in about AD 570 and grew up in the remote oasis city of Mecca in the deserts of western Arabia. Mecca was of little interest to the Byzantine Empire which still ruled the eastern and southern Mediterranean, or to Persia, which included what is now Iraq as well as Iran. The Christian Byzantines disdainfully tolerated Judaism but not the ancient, pagan cults of Greece and Rome. The state religion of the Persian Empire was Zoroastrianism, but

Christianity and Judaism were also well represented in its territories, and there was hope among Byzantines that it would eventually be converted to Christianity.

The tribal confederations that lived in and around Mecca prospered from their trade with Greater Syria to the north and Yemen to the south. Mecca's dominant tribe of the Koreish also had a second source of wealth: religion. Although belief in one God was understood and people were at least vaguely familiar with Christianity and Judaism, the focal point of Arab religion was the Ka'aba, a black, cube-shaped shrine in Mecca, of which the Koreish were official guardians. Three hundred and sixty idols surrounded the Ka'aba, and others had been placed inside. The individual deities were essentially local and concerned themselves with particular needs. Thus, the god Hubal, whose name the Koreish called upon in battle, was also the god of rain. Mecca was the destination for an annual pilgrimage from many parts of Arabia which coincided with an important market and helped fill the city's coffers. The followers of the cults of Mecca and western Arabia put up considerable resistance to Muhammad's new religion, which shows that the old ways still had some appeal.

Muhammad was from the Koreish, but not from a leading family. He lost his mother when he was 6, while his father had already died before he was born. He was brought up by his grandfather and then by his uncle, Abu Talib. As a young man he is said to have made his living as an agent taking caravan trains to Syria, and married one of his clients, Khadijah, a wealthy lady who was noticeably older than himself but bore him several children. One of these, his daughter Fatima, gave him grandchildren and passed on his bloodline. He had a reputation for honesty and fairness in his commercial dealings, as well as an ability to defuse disputes. He was also charismatic and energetic but at the same time had a reflective and solitary side. One night, he was meditating in a cave on a mountain outside Mecca when he had a vision in which a figure he subsequently believed to be the angel Gabriel appeared and terrified him out of his wits. The figure said:

Recite in the name of your Lord who created –
Created humanity from a blood clot;
Recite – your Lord is most generous.
He it was who taught with the pen –
Taught humanity what it did not know.[1]

As has been the case with many other visionaries, Muhammad's
experience filled him with confusion. He feared diabolical possession
and questioned his sanity. Nevertheless, he came to accept the
revelations, which were to continue for the rest of his life, and soon
had an unshakeable conviction that he was the Prophet of God and
a determination to carry out the task appointed for him: to impart
God's message to humanity. These revelations make up the Qur'an
which was compiled as a single volume after his death.

Muhammad lived for about twenty-three years after that first
occasion when he believed Gabriel visited him. After some years
preaching, initially to family and friends and then more publicly,
he was still making only a small impact in Mecca. His teaching
threatened the existing order and the wealth the city gained from
pilgrims to the Ka'aba. He suffered ridicule, ostracism and the risk
of assassination. Those of his followers who lacked the protection
of a powerful tribe which would avenge them if they were killed or
injured were in very real danger. In 622, he therefore took up an
invitation to go to Yathrib, a large oasis over two hundred miles to
the north, where he would use his skill at settling disputes to arbitrate
between the local tribes. He set out to establish a new society there
which would be based on his new religion. The city's name was
changed to Medina, an abbreviation of *al-madinah al-munawwarah*:
the illuminated, or enlightened, city.

Once Muhammad had settled down in Medina, a new set of
problems emerged. There were five tribes in the oasis. The two main
ones, the Aws and the Khazraj, converted to Islam. Although some
conversions were enthusiastic and zealous, others were only superficial

and expedient. Moreover, although the tribal leaders had accepted Islam at least outwardly, ultimate political power remained with them. Insincere conversions had never occurred while Muhammad was still in Mecca. The loyalty of the *munafiqun*, the 'Dissemblers' or 'Hypocrites', as the insincere converts came to be called, was suspect. They were likely to conspire with his Meccan enemies who could be expected to do their utmost to destabilise the polity he was now setting up.

The same applied to the other three tribes in the oasis. These were Jewish Arabs, the Nadir, the Qaynuqa' and the Qurayzah. They were under the protection of the Aws or Khazraj, and thus bound by the agreements those tribes had reached with Muhammad. A number of individuals converted, but for the most part they followed their rabbis in rejecting the new religion. Although Muhammad accepted that their religion was a true path to God, they were among the factions opposed to him and were potential traitors to his new polity. In due course, two of the tribes were exiled. The Qurayzah, the third tribe, suffered a worse fate. It was believed to have planned to betray Medina at a crucial moment in the struggle with Mecca which could have led to the fall of the oasis. The adult males, except for two who opted to convert to Islam, were executed and the women and children made slaves.

The struggle with Mecca had developed a military element soon after Muhammad's arrival in Medina. This started with an initiative by Muhammad and his followers who began raiding Meccan trading caravans. He and his followers had lost their property in Mecca, and on one level this military element may just have been customary tribal raiding. Nevertheless, it also indicated that Muhammad believed the Meccans were determined to extinguish his new faith or at least stop it spreading, and that armed conflict with them was therefore inevitable.

The first major encounter was the battle at the wells of Badr. In early 624, Mecca learned that a raiding party from Medina was trying to intercept an important caravan returning from Syria.

Although the caravan changed its route and escaped, a relief force from Mecca met a much smaller Muslim army and battle was joined. Despite their superiority in numbers, the Meccans were roundly defeated. The victory of Badr marked the start of the Muslim martial tradition, and Muhammad received a revelation that he and his followers were aided by legions of angels. Politically, it greatly enhanced his prestige and at the same time laid down a challenge to the Meccans, who now had to avenge their defeat and crush Muhammad. To Muslims ever since, Badr has been an inspiration when they are at war.

The Meccans had partial revenge at the battle of Uhud the following year. Muhammad himself was wounded and feared dead at one point. The defeat strengthened the reputation of the Meccans, but it did not lead to the dissolution of Muhammad's new polity. The Meccans needed to make one final push and assembled a vast coalition to do so.

The third and final battle is known as the battle of the Ditch, or the Trench (al-khandaq). Having some idea of the size of the forces that might be marching against him, Muhammad and his followers prepared for a siege. Defensive ditches were dug at various points around the oasis to make it impossible for cavalry to cross. The tactic worked, and the Muslims were able to repel the assaults. When the weather turned cold and wet, the Meccan coalition broke up due to supply problems and discontent among tribes which had come in the hope of pillage when Medina fell.

Muhammad now seems to have had the upper hand. He announced that he wished to perform the pilgrimage to the sanctuary of the Ka'aba which, according to local tradition, Abraham had originally built with the help of his son Ishmael as a temple to the one true God. After negotiations, it was agreed that Muhammad and the Muslims would postpone their pilgrimage by one year, but that the following year the Meccans would evacuate the city for three days in order to enable the Muslims to enter without fear of strife.

The postponement involved an additional painful concession by Muhammad who agreed to return any Meccans who came to him as converts to Islam during this intervening period. He needed all his authority and charisma to persuade some of his followers to accept what looked like a setback, but he was skilful in the negotiations.[2] Soon after the Muslims had made their pilgrimage to Mecca, he took advantage of a breach of the armistice by the Koreish. When he marched on Mecca, opposition collapsed and he was able to enter the city in triumph.

Arabian polytheism was now suppressed and the Ka'aba cleansed of its idols. Shrines in neighbouring towns were also dismantled, sometimes after resistance. Muhammad's conditions for capitulation always involved the adoption of the new faith. Armies and emissaries from Medina persuaded tribal confederacies and rulers over most of Arabia to recognise him as the Prophet of God, although they often had no clear idea of what this entailed. Medina remained his capital, but his reform of the pre-Islamic pilgrimage rites had ensured that Mecca would be the focal point of the new religion. In 632, the last year of his life, he performed the pilgrimage with a large gathering of his followers. He was ageing, and may have been conscious that he did not have long to live. If this was the case, it is striking that he made no universally accepted arrangements for the community after his death.

III

The new religion lay broadly within 'the same universe of thought'[3] as Christianity and Judaism. All three faiths share core beliefs such as the transcendence and oneness of God, the forgiveness of sins following true repentance, the Last Judgement, the resurrection of the body, Heaven and Hell. As Sidney Griffith has recently written, the Qur'an itself:

in its origins obviously participated in a dialogue of the scriptures, with the Torah, the Psalms, the Prophets and the Gospel named in the Qur'an as the partners of record in the conversation. . . . [It] presumes in its audience a familiarity with biblical narratives, as well as with other aspects of Jewish and Christian lore, faith and practice. In short, the Qur'an and early Islam are literally unthinkable outside the Judeo-Christian milieu in which Islam was born and grew to its maturity.[4]

The influence of both Christianity and Judaism on Islam is immense. This is not just a question of the many hidden borrowings, such as teachings from the Gospels and the Torah restated in the Qur'an and Sunna, which Muslims see as instances in which the revelation to Muhammad confirmed earlier revelations. There are also openly acknowledged borrowings from Christian and Jewish sources. Christian monks seem to have been held in particularly high esteem by Muslim scholars, who often quoted their spiritual insights with approval. Some monks may have reciprocated this. Sections of the pastoral writings of Ghazali, the great twelfth-century Muslim theologian, were adapted by monks for Christian audiences.[5]

Nevertheless, despite the very considerable overlap of its teachings with the two religions which are ancestral to the modern West, Islam is not always easy for a Westerner to understand. Many non-Muslims who approach the Qur'an in a genuine spirit of enquiry find it a difficult text, particularly if they can only read it in translation. As is the case with the Bible, it is intended to be listened to or read by people who already accept it as divine revelation, and who therefore do so in a spirit of reverence, opening their hearts and accepting whatever it may say to them.

Because for Muslims the Qur'an is the Eternal Word of God, its compilers deliberately made the minimum editorial amendment to the text, and merely arranged the chapters in order of length after a brief opening prayer, the *Fatiha*. This means that it does not really have a beginning, middle or end. But it has refrains and cadences that are repeated, unifying it and making it sink into the reader's heart on a subliminal level. These cannot be conveyed in translation. The tone can change abruptly. Irshad Manji, the Muslim gad-fly and would-be reformer, has written about the shifts of mood in the text of the Qur'an, something that any Christian or Jew who is familiar with the Psalms should be able to understand. But the core of its message is already implicit in the earliest verses to be revealed: God is One, the Creator of all. Passage after passage in the Qur'an shows loathing of polytheism, which the Qur'an calls the sin of *shirk*, 'the attributing of partners to God'. Nothing exists except through God, and humanity's task is to submit (*islam*) to His decrees by following the message He revealed to Muhammad.

The God we meet in the Qur'an is thus like the God of the Bible. He created everything from nothing, and *'There is not like Him any thing'*.[6] The gods of the Arabian pantheon could thus only be figments of the imagination or beings created by God. Muhammad's hostility towards them is no different from St Paul's loathing for Diana of the Ephesians or Elijah's hatred for the cult of Baal, which led him to put its priests to death. The Arabian gods were dangerous distractions from the faith of the believer. Worshipping them was delusional, selfish and perverted, as well as bound to incur God's wrath.

The Qur'an calls upon Muslims to live a life of honesty, generosity and fairness in a way that the old paganism did not. Cruel practices which pagan custom tolerated were unacceptable. The Qur'an, like the Bible, uses fear of God to instil a moral system that is more caring and scrupulous than what went before. Thus, it uses understated menace to attack the practice of burying unwanted baby girls by parents who had hoped for a son:

> When the buried baby girl is asked
> For what sin she was killed ...
> Each soul will know what it has presented.[7]

Fear of the Lord lies at the root of all monotheism. The Qur'an – again, like the Bible – balances this by its emphasis on God's unlimited mercy. Every chapter of the Qur'an except one opens with the words 'In the name of God, the Compassionate, the Merciful'. God's compassion and mercy are stressed repeatedly, and realisation of this percolates into the listener or reader at a deep level. Humanity is called to live according to the laws God lays down. This involves putting trust in Him (rather than, say, asking the Meccan god Hubal to conjure rainfall), and implies solidarity among believers and care for one's neighbour, not merely an obligation towards the members of one's own tribe and those under its protection, as had been the case before. This solidarity seems to have been something new, in fact revolutionary, in terms of seventh-century Arabia, although Islam would not displace tribalism from Arabian society.

There are no sayings attributed to Muhammad similar to those of Jesus in the Gospels which led Christians to conclude that Jesus was God incarnated in Man. Muhammad claimed he had an extraordinary mission, but was otherwise an ordinary mortal who sinned and repented like anyone else. When the Meccans were left in possession of the battlefield of Uhud, they mutilated some of the Muslim dead. Hind, the wife of Abu Sufyan, the Meccan leader, even ate a piece of the liver of Hamza, the prophet's slain uncle, in order to fulfil a vow of revenge for her kinsfolk slain at Badr. Furious beyond measure, Muhammad swore to mutilate the corpses of thirty Meccan dead in retaliation the next time God granted him a victory over them. Yet shortly thereafter he realised that this would be wrong. He therefore renounced his oath, repented and forbade the mutilation of corpses. It should not be forgotten that he was also a political leader. Although he very often showed mercy to opponents – something which it was generally expedient to do – there were executions of a man who had abandoned Islam and a satirist who had mocked him after he took Mecca.

After the establishment of the polity in Medina, Qur'anic passages were revealed which increasingly regulated the lives of the believers. These were amplified by Muhammad's edicts and everyday practice. After his death, the memory of the community began to fade as the immediate descendants of those who had contact with him gradually passed away. It became necessary to establish a guiding tradition so that the community could emulate the way he lived his life. This tradition has been preserved in the sayings attributed to him or his companions, which came to be known as his Sunna, or custom. The Sunna includes what we would consider legal topics, such as the rules of marriage, divorce and inheritance, the validity of contracts, and punishments prescribed for crimes. It also includes other topics which most Westerners would not necessarily consider to be 'legal', such as the rules for the ways devotions are to be performed, dietary and hygiene requirements, and dress codes.

Like the God of Christians and Jews, the God of Muslims sees into our hearts. He will judge believers according to the sincerity with which they perform their actions, and will always show mercy to those who sincerely repent and try to make amends for their misdeeds. Nevertheless, Islam is not solely a private matter for a believer. The main rituals of Muslim worship intrude into the public domain in a very obvious fashion. Muslims are enjoined to carry out brief, formal prayers five times a day at specified times: dawn, noon, mid-afternoon, dusk and after dinner. These must be said facing the direction of the Ka'aba at Mecca. There is ritual purification beforehand, and the body moves through the postures of standing, bowing, kneeling and touching the ground with the forehead. The sight of men praying in the street at midday on Friday is so common in Arab countries that it is unremarkable. Throughout Muslim history, this mass congregating on Fridays has provided a dangerous moment for unpopular governments. This is still so, as recent developments in Arab countries have shown.

The fast of Ramadan involves total abstinence from food, drink and sexual activity from dawn to dusk for a whole month, although children, the sick, pregnant women and travellers are exempt and fasting can be postponed if there is an overriding need. In a predominantly Muslim society, Ramadan turns life upside down, especially when the month falls during a roasting Middle Eastern summer. The discipline of the fast is stern and disrupts the natural cycle of life. The Muslim year consists of twelve lunar months, eleven days less than a solar year. Ramadan, the feast days and time of pilgrimage revolve through the seasons approximately three times a century – that is, perhaps two and a half times in an average life span. During this topsy-turvy month night is almost turned into day, and is a time for feasting and jollity. It is the season for families and, above all, for making a fuss of children. Like other forms of worship which have a communal element, the fast is intended to bring believers closer to each other as well as to God.

Another key element of Muslim religious ritual is the Hajj, the pilgrimage to Mecca. The rites centre on the Qur'anic account of the story of God's command to Abraham to sacrifice his son. Muslims see the Qur'an as restoring the original truth of God's revelations to earlier prophets such as Abraham, Noah, Moses and Jesus, and therefore consider Islam not to so much a new religion as the correction and perfection of Judaism and Christianity. The simple pilgrimage garbs which are prescribed for male and female pilgrims underline the overarching equality of all believers before God, despite the different status Sharia (the religious law of Islam) gives to free men, free women and slaves. The fact that the rituals can only be performed on five prescribed days in the Muslim month of Dhu'l-Hijjah adds an extra rhythm to the Muslim year.

In a sense the Hajj also adds a rhythm to the life of a Muslim, since all able-bodied believers who can afford to do so – and who can also arrange for their families to be looked after while they are away – must perform it at least once. Today, thanks to air travel and modern organisation, some three million believers congregate to perform it every year. Throughout history, it has provided a huge coming together for Muslims, a focus of unity and brotherhood that has no true parallel in Christianity or Judaism. It also gives the ruler who controls the Holy Places immense prestige.

IV

Although the Muslims built an empire within decades of Muhammad's death, they did not achieve his hope that they would live together as brothers. Once the Prophet was in his grave, many tribes assumed that they were now at liberty to revert to their old ways. Sometimes they had not even made the formal profession of faith to convert to the new religion, and their treaty relations with Medina had been entered into by one faction of the tribe despite the opposition of others. Abu Bakr, who was acknowledged as the leader of the Muslim community after Muhammad's death, had the task of bringing them back into the fold. He was the *khalifa*, or 'caliph', a word which can mean either successor or deputy. The title thus had a certain ambiguity. Although the caliph was not a prophet, he was the ruler of the community and had a spiritual authority.

Abu Bakr had been a friend of Muhammad before his revelations began and was one of the first converts. After the death of the Prophet's wife Khadijah, Abu Bakr's daughter Aisha was betrothed to the Prophet as a child and went on to become his best known and most influential wife, many of whose wise sayings have been cherished by Sunni Muslims ever since. Abu Bakr showed the steely firmness not altogether unusual in people with a gentle disposition who are nevertheless convinced that what they have to do is right and necessary. He was also practical, and turned to those in the community with proven military expertise.

This often meant that Meccans who had converted to Islam rather late in the day, like Khalid Ibn al Waleed who had led the successful Meccan cavalry charge against the Muslims at Uhud, played leading roles in putting down the insurrections that followed Muhammad's death and the great conquests that followed. Bloody vengeance was exacted on the ringleaders of insurgencies, although in most cases ordinary tribesmen were treated more leniently. With the rebellions crushed, Abu Bakr sent the armies further afield. He ruled for two years and lived just long enough to hear of the first major victories against the Byzantines and Persians.

Umar Ibn al Khattab, another early convert, was chosen by the Prophet's companions as his successor. Umar had a very different temperament from Abu Bakr. He was hot-headed and obstinate, but as devoted to Muhammad as his predecessor. When he was assassinated in 644 by an angry prisoner who had been sold as a slave, the Persian Empire had been virtually destroyed and its core provinces occupied. Greater Syria and Egypt, which at that time were overwhelmingly Christian countries, had also been snatched from Byzantium.

The Byzantines had not had a chance to consolidate their position in these territories after they expelled the Persian invaders at the end of an exhausting conflict which had removed them from Byzantine control for a generation. That war had only ended a few years before the Arab conquerors arrived. Greater Syria had already suffered an economic decline and seen its population severely reduced by bubonic plague before the Persian invasion. The emperor Heraclius who had now regained this important province did not give it up lightly. But after Damascus had fallen to the Arabs, very possibly for the second time, and two large field armies had been destroyed in battle, he had little alternative to retiring behind the natural frontier of the Taurus mountains in the east of Anatolia.

The emissaries sent by the Arab armies offered three choices when they came to a new province or town. These were acceptance of Islam, acknowledgement of Muslim rule and payment of tribute, or war to the death. Few took the option of conversion, but people were always free to convert at a later stage. Acknowledgement of Muslim rule meant that the local Christian and Jewish population would be free to continue worshipping in their own way. They would retain their existing churches and synagogues, although they often lost the right to build new ones. They would pay extra taxes, were generally not allowed to bear arms and needed to recognise the superiority of Muslims. The status of those who submitted was similar to that which the Byzantines themselves accorded to religious minorities.

The choice between these three options did not compare unfavourably with what would have been on offer from other conquerors. The Byzantine Empire itself paid tribute to marauders when occasion demanded, and its taxes were higher than those of the new conquerors. Throughout antiquity, the Middle Ages and until considerably later, everyone knew that a city which resisted an invader would be delivered over to slaughter, rape and pillage if it fell to an assault. During the Persian invasion of Byzantine territory most cities had surrendered on terms, and a bloody example had been made of Jerusalem in 614 when it resisted. The Arabs replaced the Byzantines as rulers and often seemed an improvement. Nevertheless, the importance of booty for many of the conquerors should not be overlooked, nor should it be forgotten that there were areas, such as the province of Fayoum in Egypt, in which the Arabs were reported as behaving as savagely as any other barbarian invaders.

In some places, the surrender terms granted the Muslims the right to use part of a church for prayer, sharing it with the Christian worshippers. In Homs, a quarter of the church of St John was set aside for Muslim prayers, while a veil was placed down the middle of Damascus cathedral so that Christians and Muslims would worship on separate sides of it.[8] Over time, the number and proportion of Muslims gradually increased. Sixty years after the taking of Damascus, when the city had become the capital of the vast Arab empire, the caliph decided the city needed a main mosque as its focal point. The Christians had to surrender their cathedral, but in return they were compensated and the future of other churches was guaranteed. Christians were involved in building the mosque, and the Byzantine emperor sent craftsmen to decorate it with mosaics in the kind of courteous gesture rulers have shown to each other throughout history.

When the Arab warriors of the caliphs invaded Greater Syria in the 630s, it is far from certain that their Byzantine opponents initially realised they were dealing with a new religion. A few years before, Heraclius had used Christianity as a rallying cry against the Persian foe. Yet there is no indication from the admittedly sparse historical sources that he did the same against the Muslims.[9] Very possibly the idea did not even seem worthwhile. A number of Arab Christian tribes joined in the conquests, not seeing why they should miss out on the opportunities for plunder. Although many of them were later to convert to Islam, others did not. There are also stories from the Arab chronicles which, if true, suggest the invaders received assistance from local Christian and Jewish communities. At first, Islam was viewed by many Christians as a heresy, and was still being listed as such by the great Christian theologian St John of Damascus approximately a century after the Arab conquest of Syria.

St John wrote in Greek, the language of the Byzantine elite in Greater Syria and Egypt, but it was not spoken by the bulk of the population. Coptic was the language of the people of Egypt, and was a simplified version of the tongue of the Pharaohs. In the nineteenth century, Jean-François Champollion's knowledge of Coptic would play a key role in enabling him to decipher the Rosetta Stone and unlock the secrets of the Ancient Egyptian hieroglyphs. To this day Egypt's ancient Christian community are known as Copts – the name is a variant of 'Egyptian' – and they trace the establishment of their church back to St Mark, the Gospel writer, who preached in Alexandria. Syriac was the native language throughout Greater Syria and much of Iraq. In the seventh century the speakers of this language were predominantly Christian but many of them followed forms of Christianity deemed heretical by Constantinople, as did the Copts. It was in vain that Heraclius worked with the ecclesiastical authorities to devise formulations of faith which he hoped would reconcile all his Christian subjects. If he was trying to build a shared, Christian-based identity with which they could jointly confront the Arab invaders, it was a conspicuous failure.

Although Christian writers in the conquered lands refer to Islam as the religion of the Beast in the Book of Revelations, those who were not Orthodox did not necessarily see the state-imposed religion of the Byzantines as much better. Monks writing in their cells looked forward to an apocalyptic end to Muslim rule which would be brought about by divine intervention. They saw the victories of the Arabs as divine punishment for the sins of the Byzantines. Once the conquests had been consolidated, local Christian writers praised individual Muslim rulers whose reigns brought peace and who treated the Christians well.

V

The first two caliphs lived a simple lifestyle in Medina, despite the fabulous riches that were their share of the plunder and tribute from the conquered territories. They did not spend this on themselves but used it for purposes of state. There are stories of messengers stopping to ask directions from an old man walking along the road in the dust or dozing under a palm tree in the afternoon heat. They needed to find out where the caliph was so they could inform him of a great victory or deliver a chest of priceless jewels as his prescribed share of war booty. It was only later, when they were ushered into the presence of the caliph, that they realised he was the same old man. Abu Bakr continued to milk his family's goats, whilst Umar had a penchant for spending his evenings personally delivering sacks of flour to poor widows when there was a famine. He was also prepared to listen to complaints from soldiers against their leaders. If he suspected wrongdoing, he was prepared to remove them from power. In this way, he may have unwittingly encouraged a culture of insubordination.

Yet if the caliphs maintained an example worthy of a radical new religion, the same did not apply to all the army. Abu Bakr had forbidden tribesmen who had tried to secede after the death of the Prophet from taking part in the raiding into Syria and Iraq which evolved into the campaigns of conquest. Umar reversed this policy. His decision worked wonders for the manpower needs of the conquering armies, but was yet another step away from the purity of the original Muslim community which had defied pagan Mecca. Because Christian tribes joined in, the conquests were not even entirely Muslim. And what of the majority of the conquerors who were Muslims? Where did the urge to spread the faith, desire for glory and greed for plunder lie in the order of motives of the conquerors? According to later Arab chroniclers, vast wealth was accumulated by some leading Muslims as a result of the conquests. There was also another major factor behind the conquests: the need to preserve the unity of the new Muslim polity. This required that the traditional raiding which Arab tribes had conducted against each other should now be directed against outsiders.

By the time of the accession of the third caliph, Uthman, in 644, a mere twenty-two years after Muhammad's emigration to Medina and twelve years after his death, tensions in the highly successful Muslim empire were increasing to the point at which they threatened to tear it apart. These may have been aggravated by temporary reverses on the battlefield. Uthman was from the Bani Umayya, the branch of the Koreish tribe that was senior to the Bani Hashim from which the Prophet had come, and was wealthy in his own right. Despite his piety – remembered today because he ordered the editing of the canonical text of the Qur'an – he had to cope with resentment at the fact that so much of the leadership of the community was now drawn from the Koreish.

Until Muhammad's triumphant entry into Mecca, Uthman's

uncle, Abu Sufyan, who was the leader of the Koreish oligarchy, had strongly opposed Muhammad. Yet after Mecca opened its gates to the Prophet, both Abu Sufyan and his wife Hind converted and were treated well. Abu Sufyan was made governor of Yemen, while Hind lived to cheer on the Muslim warriors at the battle of the Yarmouk, the key battle in the conquest of Greater Syria, just as she had cheered on the Meccans at Uhud. Their son Mu'awiya, who was Uthman's cousin, became the Prophet's secretary. Umar appointed him as governor of Syria. Many early converts noted the rapid promotion for the son of people who had loathed the Prophet up to the moment when their own cause was lost.

Uthman's answer to the increasing tensions and indiscipline was to try to centralise administration, not least by establishing more effective financial control over the conquered provinces. Umar's policy had been to link seniority in the new elite to the time at which Muslims had originally converted to the new faith, and to how close they had been to the Prophet. Uthman, perhaps inevitably as the original community began to age, reverted to traditional methods of clan rule under the leadership of his own tribe, Koreish. This caused resentment, especially as it meant many Muslims who had taken part in the first waves of conquests were likely to lose out. His appointment of members of his family to key positions would have been unremarkable for any other ruler at that time, yet it seemed to go directly against the spirit of the new faith, which had seemed to promise the equality of believers.

Grievances in the army increased in Egypt and the military cantonments of Kufa and Basra in Iraq. Only Syria, under Mu'awiya, remained quiet. Disaffected soldiers began to meet and confer. Eventually groups of mutineers from Egypt went to Medina to demand the caliph satisfy their grievances. Under pressure, Uthman yielded. While the mutineers were returning home, they captured a messenger who overtook them. He was allegedly carrying a letter from Uthman asking the governor of Egypt to deal with them severely.

The group went angrily back to Medina and besieged Uthman in his house. He denied writing or giving instructions for the writing of the letter and refused to resign. Eventually, a group in which a son of the deceased caliph Abu Bakr was involved stormed the house and killed him.

This was a 'loss of innocence' moment if ever there was one. Not only had the successor of the Prophet been murdered by mutineers from among his own people, but it seemed that none of the companions of the Prophet in Medina had been prepared to stand up to them, not even Ali ibn Abi Talib, the Prophet's cousin and son-in-law who was one of the very first converts. There were questions which sprang immediately to mind as news of the murder spread. Were the companions indifferent to Uthman's fate? Did they secretly desire it? And were they – or some of them – secretly in league with the mutineers? History cannot give us conclusive answers to these questions.

VI

The chaos that followed led to civil wars which might well have broken up the new empire had it not been for Mu'awiya. He was already arguably the most powerful player on the stage, and demanded what no one could deny was his right: justice for the murder of his kinsman, Uthman. Ali ibn Abu Talib was elected caliph by the now elderly surviving companions of the Prophet, but there was a weakness in his position. He risked being perceived as sympathetic to the mutineers, some of whom were among his strongest supporters, and from whom it was virtually impossible for him to withdraw his protection. He was also associated with groups such as the Ansar, the devout Muslims of Medina who had loyally supported the Prophet and fought for him, but did not have the same interests as Koreish and had been largely overlooked by the new elite that was now governing the empire. When Ali requested that Mu'awiya offer him allegiance, the latter refused. This left Ali with no practical alternative to preparing an army to send against him. At the same time, a revolt broke out under the leadership of two companions of the Prophet who were backed by powerful moral support from the Prophet's widow Aisha, though Ali was able to defeat it.

The unthinkable was now happening: Muslims fighting Muslims in bloody battles but considering themselves entitled to the benefits of Paradise which came from death fighting unbelievers, whilst their comrades in the same army shouted tribal war cries from pre-Islamic days at their fellow Muslim opponents. Members of tribes could find themselves on opposite sides, because some tribes were now split between the military cantonments in Syria, Iraq and Egypt, whilst devout men could be found in each and every party.

A battle between the forces of Ali and Mu'awiya at Siffeen in the Euphrates valley is said to have ended in a dramatic stalemate after two days of bloody fighting when Mu'awiya's forces tied copies of Qur'anic verses to their lances and called 'Let God decide'. The cry was also taken up by Ali's men and both armies refused to fight further. Any chance of Ali achieving a military victory and consolidating his position as caliph was lost at that point and he was outmanoeuvred in the negotiations that followed. Soon Mu'awiya also proclaimed himself caliph, and the two rivals were including curses on the other and his supporters in the Friday prayers. While Mu'awiya's support stood firm, revolts against Ali's authority began to occur. Some of these were by former supporters who saw the attempt to negotiate a settlement at Siffeen as compromising an important matter of principle: the succession was a matter to be decided by God, not for negotiation by the believers.

The idea of a caliphate purer than that which could be provided by a dynasty took hold among a number of those who abandoned Ali's cause. According to this group, it should not matter whether the caliph came from this or that tribe or how closely he was connected to the Prophet, who had now been dead for some thirty years. The only factor in his selection should be the strength of his faith and the devoutness with which he lived his life. The group became known as the Kharijites, those who had 'left' or 'walked out', and separated themselves from Ali. By doing this, they rejected the main community as apostates. In 661, a Kharijite assassinated Ali while he was leading the Friday prayers.

The murder of Uthman had been a story of hot anger and mob violence. That of Ali was a tale of cold premeditation by someone working in secrecy and isolation. It was even more shocking because Ali had been very dear to the Prophet and was the father of his grandsons, Hassan and Hussein. Like many other fanatics throughout history, the assassin achieved something he did not intend. He reunited the empire under Mu'awiya.

Mu'awiya is arguably the most controversial figure in Islamic history. His admirers can point out that he saved the polity Muhammad had established from disintegration, and was able to stabilise it as a vast empire which began a new period of expansion for Islam. His detractors argue in reply that he did this by turning the Muslim polity into an Arab kingdom ruled by a secular dynasty. They allege that he did this by perverting his religious authority as caliph – to which many believed he was not entitled – and thereby betraying the ideals for which the Prophet and his companions had fought.

VII

The reigns of the first four caliphs, Abu Bakr, Umar, Uthman and Ali, are known to history collectively as the period of the Rashidun, the 'rightly guided' or 'patriarchal' caliphs. This glosses over the strife during Uthman's reign and the fact that Ali failed to achieve universal recognition by the faithful. The earliest surviving sources which tell us about the period were written down much later, and the writers had their own agendas (though these are not always easy to discern today). It would be roughly another three hundred years before the crystallisation of Muslims into incompatible sects known to history as Sunnis and Shi'ites was completed,[10] but their different attitudes to the Rashidun is one of the major points of contention between them. The expression 'the Rashidun' is only used by Sunnis, the majority grouping of Muslims in both the Arab world and Islam as a whole, who believe that whatever may have happened in the past has to be accepted, since the most important thing is for Muslims to live in peace and harmony. Caliphs in the centuries after the Rashidun should also be accepted as legitimate, even if they did not always rule well or justly. The only proviso was that they must have acted in a way that did not go against the basic teachings of Islam. Authority, even if flawed, is better than *fitna*, civil strife, of which the Muslim community had already seen enough.

The teaching of Shi'ism, which is the second largest grouping in Islam, starts from the assumption that Ali and his descendants were always intended to lead the community. This was because he was the cousin and son-in-law of the Prophet, and it was only through his marriage to Fatima that the line of the Prophet survived. Ali seems to have delayed six months before accepting the primacy of Abu Bakr, which might be interpreted to suggest that Abu Bakr assumed an office which rightfully belonged to Ali.

According to Shi'ite tradition which is also found in authoritative Sunni collections of the *hadith*, the sayings attributed to the Prophet, Ali accompanied the Prophet back to Medina after the farewell pilgrimage. The caravan halted at the pool of Ghadir Khumm, where Muhammad asked his followers whether he was closer to them than they were to themselves. The crowd enthusiastically agreed that he was. He had taken Ali by the hand, and now said, '*man kuntu mawlaahu fa-'Ali mawlaahu*', which means 'Ali is also the *mawlaa* of those for whom I am the *mawlaa*'. The most likely meaning of *mawlaa* is 'patron', but the word is also connected to the word for 'closer', *awlaa*, which Muhammad had used in the question he had just put to the assembled gathering. In Arabic, this made an elegant pun, and means that the earlier sentence would have been in the forefront of the minds of the listeners when they heard what Muhammad said about himself and Ali. Shi'ites interpret the words at Ghadir Khumm as a clear statement that Muhammad intended Ali to lead the community after his death, while Sunnis argue that it meant no more than that Muslims should have a high regard and affection for Ali. On the night the Prophet died, Ali was absent from the deliberations that led to the decision that Abu Bakr would be the first caliph. But the reason for this could be argued to indicate his pre-eminence: he was occupied washing the Prophet's body and preparing the funeral rites.

For Shi'ites, Abu Bakr, Umar and Uthman are thus usurpers and falsifiers of history. But because of the veneration in which the Rashidun are held by Sunnis, the difference between Sunnis and Shi'ites rises above the level of a mere disagreement about what happened in those first, crucial years of Islam. It is also exacerbated by the story of Ali's sons, the grandsons the Prophet had dangled on his knee when they were tiny. Hassan, the elder, chose not to resist Mu'awiya. Years later he was poisoned in his harem, and the assertion that Mu'awiya instigated this cannot be disproved.

The fate of Hussein, Hassan's younger brother, is poignant. When Mu'awiya died peacefully in his bed in 680 at the age of seventy-eight, he was succeeded by his son, Yezid. This showed beyond any lingering doubt that his tribe the Banu Umayya (better known to history as the Umayyads) wanted a dynastic right to rule. Their government was also regarded as oppressive by many, especially in Iraq which had been the centre of Ali's support. Hussein was invited to the garrison town of Kufa, where many might have rallied to his standard. Yet it was not to be. After crossing the Arabian desert, he and his party were caught by the authorities and killed at Kerbala just before they reached the Euphrates. The incident shocked all

Muslims and weakened the legitimacy of Umayyad rule.

The martyrdom of Hussein caused further discord between the parties that were to develop into Sunnis and Shi'ites. Shi'ites now commemorate the events at Karbala with the penitential rites of Ashura as atonement for the failure of the men of Kufa to go to Hussein's aid on that fateful day. For them, the history and the true meaning of the faith have diverged. In Shi'ism there has therefore been a concentration on a hidden or inner meaning of the teachings of Islam. Each faction which identifies itself as Shi'ite claims to follow an *imam* or 'leader' descended from the Prophet and Ali, who was the first imam. Over the course of history, some claimants founded new dynasties, while others preached a 'hidden imam' who is out of contact with the main body of believers until he reappears at the end of time.

Muslim millenarian movements have often been Shi'ite and appeared among the marginalised and dispossessed. Today the overwhelming majority of Shi'ites are 'Twelvers', those who believe that the twelfth Imam, Muhammad al-Mahdi, who disappeared in 874, was the last. Since then he has only appeared to his followers secretly or in dreams, but one day he will come to usher in justice throughout the Earth. In the meantime, Shi'ites have developed their own schools of law and theology in parallel with those of Sunni Islam, but are noticeably different both in the detail of Sharia and in their methodology.

Over in Byzantium, there had been relief when the Arabs paused after the murder of Uthman to fight among themselves. Praise was duly given to God for this breathing space which enabled the empire to regroup and survive. But the Byzantines were never to win back Greater Syria and Egypt. These lands, like the other territories conquered by the Arabs, were to be ruled by Muslims and now had new chapters of history which the rest of the old Roman world would not share. For well over a millennium, few in Byzantium or Western Europe would study this history, while the history of Europe would be virtually unknown in Arab lands. This difference lies at the root of why the West and the Arab world each have such separate historical consciousnesses today.

Deep-rooted cultural differences also evolved. In contrast to Islam, Christianity forbids polygamy and preaches the indissolubility of marriage. The position of women and the family in the West and the Arab world will be touched upon in the final chapters of this book. Another major difference concerned attitudes to representation of the human form in art. Although neither the Qur'an nor the New Testament forbids representational art, provided that it is not intended for idol worship, the making of 'graven images' is explicitly forbidden in the Book of Exodus and there are many sayings ascribed to Muhammad in which he condemned the making of pictures of the human form or animals. The triumphant figure of the Caliph Abdul Malik appeared on the first known Islamic gold coins in 697. Within a year, they were succeeded by a new issue which pointedly only carried inscriptions, including a text which occurs almost at the very end of the Qur'an:

Say - He is God, the One,
God the Eternal
He did not beget and He was not born.[11]

It would not be until the twentieth century that the images of the rulers of some Muslim lands would regularly appear on coins. In the meantime, figurative art would be a distinguishing feature of Western civilisation, while its absence would almost characterise the world of Islam - at least in Arabic speaking lands. Yet perhaps this cultural difference was not inevitable. There was a major theological controversy in Orthodox Christianity over the representational art of icons, which led to a complete prohibition on them in the Byzantine Empire for a century and a half. This started at almost exactly the time when Abdul Malik removed his picture from his coins. St John of Damascus was then a young man. He would become one of the great defenders of the icons and his writings led to a reversal of this policy at the Byzantine court. He wrote his treatises from a Syrian monastery in the domains of the caliphs.

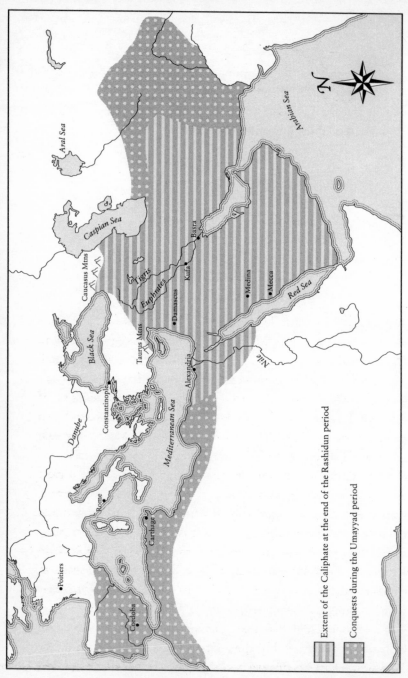

THE ARAB CONQUESTS UNDER THE RASHIDUN AND THE UMAYYADS

CHAPTER TWO

GROWING APART

I

The period of the Rashidun was followed by the Umayyad Caliphate which lasted until 750. Mu'awiya and his successors ruled from Damascus with their strong Syrian army behind them, although Iraq was the wealthiest and most fractious part of the empire. Mu'awiya's government has been described as 'almost a confederation of different leaderships acknowledging one overall authority'.[1] His model of rule was that of the trading alliances of Mecca, at which his family had excelled before they converted to Islam. However, this was an inherently unstable structure for what was now a great empire. Abdul Malik, who came to power in 685, only some four years after Mu'awiya's death, centralised the state. As well as minting the first coins of the caliphate, he made Arabic the official language of administration and commissioned the Dome of the Rock in Jerusalem, the first great mosque designed to rival the Christian churches of the conquered lands. These policies had a message: Islam and the Arabs were here to stay.

The conquests resumed. Determined attempts to take Constantinople failed, but the Arabs pushed across North Africa into the western Mediterranean. This was a region where political authority was weak and divided. Many saw opportunities in the coming of the Arabs. In North Africa, the conquerors met resistance at first but important tribal confederations of the predominant Berber population soon converted to Islam. In 711, the first Muslim foray into Spain took place. Less than twenty years later, the forces of the caliphate had penetrated deep into what is now France. Their presence in the southern half of the country may already have been weakening before they were finally checked by Charles ('the Hammer') Martel at Poitiers in 732, exactly a hundred years after Muhammad's death. That particular battle was probably a minor event when seen from the perspective of Damascus, but the Arab invasion across the Pyrenees still echoes deep in the European psyche, a half-remembered shock from the distant past which some scholars see as triggering what became the European or Western sense of identity.[2] This invasion was but the first of many such psychological shocks Muslims and Westerners have given each other.

Nevertheless, the great Arab conquests had certain things in common with other 'barbarian' invasions which are all but forgotten today. Some of these had been almost as remarkable as those of the Arab conquerors in terms of speed, distance covered and successful military campaigning. The Vandals crossed the Rhine in 406, the Pyrenees only three years later, and the Straits of Gibraltar in 429. After another ten years, they reached Carthage, the metropolis of Roman Africa, then went on to seize Sicily and the Balearic islands. In 455 they took Rome itself, neatly just under half a century after first entering the empire. Nor was their appearance a bright light that immediately burned itself out. Their North African kingdom endured for a century, and the Vandals gave their name to Andalucia, the southern part of Spain.

The fundamental difference between the Vandals and the Arabs was that the Vandals, like the other peoples that crossed the Rhine or Danube, were assimilated into the culture of their new world. These barbarians would request permission to live within the empire and to serve it. They aspired to become part of it. It tended to be when permission was refused, generally because there was no empty land or no money to pay for their services, that they became Rome's mortal enemies. Even so, many of them adopted the language of the country they conquered. This is how the Germanic Franks came to speak French and their Lombard cousins Italian. Even those who retained their original languages gradually became assimilated, although it might take generations for them to adopt Christianity. The old distinction between 'Roman' and 'barbarian' became irrelevant and was gradually forgotten.

This was not the case in the new Arabic-speaking world and marked a major cultural difference as the centuries passed. The Arabs retained a language and an identity with which they recreated the countries in which they settled, except where they were themselves conquered at a later stage. They saw themselves from the start as conquerors who had come to replace the old order with their new one called Islam. The overwhelming majority of Arabs were illiterate (like most other peoples at that time), but their language was already written – something which was generally not the case with the languages of the barbarians who crossed the Rhine or Danube. This, greatly strengthened by the fact that Arabic was also the language of their religion, meant that they had no need to adopt the alphabet, let alone the culturally dominant language, of areas they conquered. The Arabs who settled in Greater Syria, Egypt and the lands to the west were relatively few in number, although there were other periods during which Arab tribes migrated into the conquered territories, and a sizeable part of the population of Greater Syria and Iraq was already Arab before Islam arrived. Gradually, over several centuries, Arabic became the native tongue – something that did not happen in the lands the Arabs conquered to the east of Iraq – and most, or sometimes all, of the native people became Muslims.

The spread of the Arabic language and conversion to Islam by the bulk, or sometimes the entirety, of the Christian population in countries which today are Arabic-speaking is still being unravelled by scholars. The histories of Christians and Jews in predominantly Muslim lands are not scarred to the same extent by tales of official persecution and irrational outbursts of popular violence as those which sometimes broke out against Jews in pre-modern Christian Europe. Indeed, some Jews – as well as some Christian dissidents – migrated to Muslim lands to escape oppression. There seems to have been little migratory traffic in the other direction before the last decades of the twentieth century. Nor were there blanket expulsions of Christians or Jews from Muslim territory to compare with those expulsions of Muslims which took place in Spain and Sicily after reconquest by Christian monarchs.[3]

We know that some Christians began writing in Arabic and using it as an ecclesiastical language by the last third of the eighth century[4] and that the practice spread. Conversion to Islam seems often to have been a gradual process, although there were periods when large sections of the population moved across to Islam. Episodes of persecution also played a role, especially those which occurred as a reaction to the Mongol depredations in the thirteenth century and because some Mongol rulers had favoured Christians.

Yet possibly more significant than these episodes or the disabilities Sharia placed upon non-Muslims was the fact that Islam was the dominant culture of the public sphere. As the centuries passed, divisions between Muslims and the other 'Peoples of the Book' became more rigid and access to the public sphere for Jews and Christians was reduced. It made good sense to become Muslim, and in many areas Muslims may well have become the majority over the course of the tenth century. The similarities between the faiths may have made conversion quite an easy step to take, particularly at any time when a Christian community was in internal disarray because of war, famine, plague or factional strife. When this is taken into consideration, the surprising thing is not that the bulk of the population became Muslim but that substantial Christian and Jewish communities survived in so many places. Religious minorities in pre-modern Europe were much less successful in surviving and maintaining their identity.

II

There were many revolts and civil wars during the Umayyad period. Some were about local grievances, but the most serious concerned the caliphate itself. 'The Caliph of God' (*khalifatu' llah*) was seen as having a religious authority over the community of believers on matters of law and practice. Who became caliph therefore mattered, and the argument that membership of the Umayyad family should not be an overriding qualification for the office seemed perfectly fair. It gained particular traction in Iraq, where the dynasty was widely hated. The Umayyads often appeared to be primarily a secular dynasty, and used the title of caliph less than that of 'Commander of the Faithful', which stressed their military authority. Yet the purpose of the caliph was to ensure that the community lived according to the Qur'an and Sunna. After the killing of Hussein, the feeling never went away that kinship with the Prophet was needed to provide the authority for this. Indeed, it grew steadily.

Eventually, in 750, some ninety years after the assassination of Ali, rebels who united behind this principle crushed the armies of the last Umayyad caliph. A new caliphate was born, that of the Abbasid dynasty who claimed descent from the Prophet's uncle, Abbas. Damascus ceased to be the centre of power and a new capital was founded in Iraq at Baghdad in 762. The supporters of the Abbasids included many converts to Islam who considered that the Umayyads had failed to accept them as equal to the original, Arab believers. Yet the Abbasids were not direct descendants of the Prophet, and soon found that they needed to look nervously over their shoulders at supporters of the blood-line of Ali, who would evolve into what we now call Shi'ites.

The Abbasid Revolution, as it is often called, led to the final splitting of the Muslim polity which has never been restored as a single unit. Before the Abbasids could stamp their authority on Spain a survivor of the Umayyads established his own kingdom based on Cordoba, which one of his successors was to proclaim a separate caliphate. Fragmentation of the Abbasid Caliphate itself soon began. Yet whenever the caliphate lost control of a province to its governor or a local rebellion, its rulers remained Muslim. Unless they were Shi'ite, they also continued to acknowledge the caliph as the source of legitimate rule by praying for him in the Friday prayers. This fragmentation often led to the founding of powerful states which were vigorous for a generation or two and sometimes extended the frontiers of Islam yet further. Thus, the Aghlabids of Tunisia added Sicily to their domains over the course of the ninth century.

An important development around this time was the increasing recruitment of soldiers from peoples on the margins of the Muslim world. These included Berbers, black Africans, Greeks, Slavs, the peoples of the Caucasus and, above all, Turks. Such recruitment continued on an institutionalised basis for centuries in a way that had no real parallel in Europe. The military in many Muslim states thus came to have different languages, customs and interests from those of the population. They were often slaves, and formed castes which replenished themselves from foreign sources rather than being gradually assimilated. They expected the country to be run for their benefit, and could be prone to very destructive fighting among themselves. This situation continued in many Arab countries for a thousand years, in some cases into the early years of the nineteenth century. The first loyalty of the soldiers was to their own leaders and to themselves as a group. Very often their leaders ended up taking effective control of the government. In this way, as early as the 860s, Ahmed Ibn Tulun, the Abbasid governor of Egypt, became the first Turkish prince to establish control over a country in the Muslim world.

Wars and bad administration led to economic decline. By the early tenth century, all outlying provinces had been lost and the caliphate was unable to pay its Turkish soldiers while the once prosperous agriculture around Baghdad had been devastated. In 945, the caliph was forced to allow Ahmed Ibn Buwayh, the leader of an Iranian confederation, into the capital and ask him to become his chief military officer. This was a humiliation, since the Buwayhid family inclined to Shi'ism which they eventually adopted, although they did not suppress the Abbasids in favour of a caliph from the family of Ali. It was bankruptcy, not defeat on the battlefield, that sucked the political power from the Abbasid Caliphate.

Meanwhile, another Shi'ite dynasty, the Fatimids, had proclaimed their own caliphate in Tunisia in 909. Within a few years they had seized the rest of north-west Africa, then conquered Egypt, where they founded a new capital for themselves at Cairo in 969. Towards the end of the tenth century the Fatimid Caliphate reached its maximum extent, as Damascus, the Hejaz and Yemen acknowledged its control. This interlude during which Shi'ite rulers dominated the heartlands of Islam ended with the appearance of a major new Sunni power, the Seljuk Turks, who drove the last Buwayhid from Baghdad in 1055. Yet, although they recognised the nominal authority of the Abbasid Caliph, the Seljuks kept real power in their own hands.

III

It was during the Abbasid era that Islam was systematised as the religion that has come down to us over the centuries. The scholars who contributed to this process came from all over the lands of Islam and wrote in Arabic, even when this was not their native language. Baghdad played a pivotal role. Although there were many other centres of learning, it was here more than anywhere that the intellectual elites of the religious and secular sciences met, shared their ideas and wrote their books.

Historians wrote down the biography of the Prophet and the chronicles of Islam, while the *hadith* or sayings attributed to the Prophet were compiled and tested for their accuracy by examining the trustworthiness of the transmitters. Scholars studied grammar, philology and early poetry, so as better to understand and comment on the Qur'an. All this made possible and encouraged the elaboration of Sharia, the religious law of Islam, so that it could be applied among Muslims everywhere, depending, of course, on which sect they belonged to and which rite they followed. At the same time, theologians pondered the Unity of God, the distinction between His essence and attributes, and questions of freewill and predestination. There was an acrimonious debate over whether the Qur'an was created by God or was an eternal manifestation of His attribute of speech. The latter view prevailed and has become a defining feature of Islam for most Sunni Muslims ever since.

The differences between Sunnis and Shi'ites were finally formulated to make them incompatible sects. Twelver Shi'ites began publicly cursing the memory of the caliphs Abu Bakr, Umar and Uthman, as well as the Prophet's widow Aisha. In 964, they publicly celebrated for the first time the Prophet's words at Ghadir Khumm, which they deemed had established Ali as his rightful successor.[5] This went well beyond the reverence for the memory of Ali which non-Shi'ites could share.

Simultaneously, the thoughts of the Sufis, which sometimes included heterodox notions, were systematised and annotated by commentators. Sufism began as an ascetic and mystical tendency which grew as Islam put down roots in the conquered lands and often straddled the emerging Sunni–Shi'ite divide. The word Sufi probably means 'wearer of wool', since threadbare woollen gowns, like those of Christian ascetics, were the characteristic dress of the wandering fakirs or dervishes (both words mean 'poor' and became synonymous with Sufi). Sufis played a major role in the conversion of non-Muslim populations to the new religion, and often adapted Christian and other non-Muslim customs and practices to Islam. Pointing this out should not obscure the fact that Sufism was always intended to be a way of life for devout Muslims, and that its origins and core lay in meditation on the Qur'an and love for the Prophet. Under the Abbasids, Sufis composed insightful psychological treatises dealing with the nature of the soul and its path towards God. Some wrote compendia of the deeds and sayings of saints who provided models of the love of God and tried to put into words the ineffable nature of experience of the divine. Occasionally, a Sufi would make ecstatic utterances that shocked the devout because these words seemed to indicate that the mystic was claiming to be God. This sometimes led to the martyrdom of an enthusiast, the best known example being Hussein bin Mansour al-Hallaj who was executed in Baghdad in 922.

It was also during the era of the Abbasid Caliphate that the theory of jihad was developed. Warfare in Islam goes back to the battle of Badr and the Prophet's struggle with Mecca. The calls for the use of the sword in the Qur'an were instrumental in opening up a vast area to Muslim domination and proselytisation, and creating an empire stretching from Spain to Central Asia within a century of Muhammad's death. However, once the rush of conquest finally came to an end in the eighth century, the emphasis in the Muslim martial tradition shifted to defence. There were to be further offensive jihads, like that in Central Asia during the tenth and eleventh centuries against still pagan Turks, but the jihad on the Byzantine marches in a period of Byzantine resurgence which ended with the battle of Manzikert in 1071 and the jihad against the Crusaders in Greater Syria and neighbouring territories were essentially defensive.[6]

'Crusade' and 'jihad' have uncanny resonances of each other, although this is not a case of the overlapping of traditions, and the two concepts cannot be traced to a common source. In modern Arabic idiom, it would be as unremarkable to use the word 'jihad' in a phrase like 'the jihad against poverty' or 'the jihad against climate change', as it would be in English to speak of 'the crusade against poverty' or 'the crusade against climate change'. Neither crusade nor jihad would necessarily have any religious sense in either of these examples, although in each tradition, when the word is used strictly, the concept includes spiritual preparation as well as the violence implicit in 'Holy War'. Idealism and self-sacrifice, indeed love, lie behind this recourse to violence. Jihad is also a boy's name used by Arab Muslims and Christians alike. It is not entirely mischievous to suggest that the two terms 'crusade' and 'jihad' could be used to translate each other when they are being used loosely.

Jihad is frequently translated into English as 'Holy War', although a literal rendering of the words 'Holy War' into Arabic would not produce 'jihad' but an expression alien to the ears of an Arabic speaker. The plain meaning of the word is 'struggle', 'endeavour' or 'expenditure of effort'. The 'struggle' against unbelievers ('the lesser jihad') followed on from the 'greater jihad' which a Muslim must first conduct against his own lower nature. Jihad in a military sense was considered to be an obligation on the Muslim community as a whole to repel invaders of Muslims lands, but only a voluntary commitment – which an individual Muslim may or may not choose to make and which was not binding on the community as a whole – in an offensive war to force non-Muslim rulers to submit to Muslim authority and allow Islam to be preached. It was also accepted that Muslim rulers could make temporary truces if this was for the benefit of the Muslim community, although in theory these could not become a permanent peace.

IV

What had once been the Graeco-Roman world was now divided culturally into three blocs: that of Latin Christianity in Western Europe, that of Greek Christianity based on the Byzantine Empire, and that of Islam which was centred on the Abbasid Caliphate and extended far beyond Rome's onetime eastern frontiers – right across Iran and into the Indian subcontinent and Central Asia. Latin, Greek and Arabic were the respective languages of high culture in these three blocks. For a period of well over five hundred years starting roughly with the Abbasid Revolution in 750, Arabic learning outstripped that which was produced in Latin or Greek. The Arab world and the eastern lands of the Caliphate, not Europe, became the intellectual dynamo of human civilisation.

Arabic secular literature flourished and was produced by Muslims and non-Muslims alike. Science and philosophy took root in Arabic, building on learning which had been written in Greek, although Syriac, the language of the Christians of Greater Syria and Iraq, also had a major role, particularly as some works were translated by Christians first into Syriac and then from Syriac into Arabic. There were also important translations from Persian and Sanskrit, the language of learning in India. Indeed, in Baghdad the movement to translate ancient knowledge into Arabic seems to have begun with Persian texts. The first philosophical Greek text to be translated was Aristotle's *Topics*, a treatise on logic and argumentation which would aid Muslims in religious debate especially with members of other religions, such as Christians, Jews and Manichaeans, as well as with other Muslims and materialists. A tradition of clear, rational thought based on the Greek writers of antiquity took root in Arabic and was shared by Muslims, Christians and Jews. Before long, Muslim scholars were penning essays on the hierarchies of knowledge, the concept of the ideal ruler and the relationship between reason and revelation. This has influenced Arabic prose style to this day. In everyday speech, people all over the Arab world still use the same expressions for 'in general' (*bi-siffah 'aammah*) and 'in particular' (*bi-siffah khaassah*) that the medieval Arabic philosophers had used when they learned of this basic logical distinction from translations of Aristotle. Arabic scholarship broke much new ground, and preserved and developed the thought of the ancient world. It was also important because of what it absorbed from other civilisations further east such as China (the manufacture and use of paper) and India (the decimal system for writing numbers).

What is remarkable about Arabic philosophy and science in this period is the sheer intellectual curiosity and thirst for knowledge for its own sake that it exhibited, and which belie the fact that the initial impulse to study was often for a practical reason. There was something very systematic about the evidence-based approach many Arabic scientists took to their work, anticipating the development of the 'scientific method' in Western Europe hundreds of years later. Arabic was the language in which the principles of algebra were first set out and the first systematic textbook of ophthalmology was written. It thus comes as no surprise that in the ninth century Muslim Cordoba had the greatest library in Europe, or that the essayist al-Jahiz of Basra could mock the Byzantines, arguing tendentiously that Christianity had stifled their rational thought and creativity and produced a civilisation of mere artisans and imitators of the ancient Greeks.[7]

In due course, much of the new knowledge produced in Arabic was transmitted to the Latin West after being translated into Latin. The prime centre for this was Spain, where translations were often carried out by Jews, particularly after key seats of Muslim learning such as Toledo were reconquered by Christian monarchs. The philosophical debates held in Iraq, Spain and elsewhere in the lands of Islam were to continue in the Latin-speaking universities of the European Middle Ages and later. Astronomical tables produced to help calculate the Muslim prayer times would one day provide the raw data that enabled Copernicus to develop a scientific hypothesis to suggest that the Earth did indeed revolve around the Sun. Similarly, the thirteenth-century Syrian doctor Ibn al-Nafis discovered pulmonary transit and this discovery was transmitted to Europe. Harvey's discovery of the circulation of the blood some four hundred years later was built on this essential foundation.

Why did this golden age end? Why did Arabic metaphorically hand the torch of learning over to Latin and then the modern tongues of Western Europe? These are not easy questions to answer. Jim Al-Khalili considers several commonly given reasons, but argues persuasively that none of them is completely satisfactory when taken on its own. He also shows that the decline in Arabic science and thought was less precipitous than scholars had once believed. The slowness of Muslims in adopting the printing press for Arabic (which only occurred on a wide scale as late as the nineteenth century) was probably a contributory factor, but a decline in scientific research written in Arabic can already be seen through the thirteenth to sixteenth centuries before printing first appeared in Western Europe. Nor does it appear credible that the sack of Baghdad by the Mongols in 1258 which finally ended the Abbasid Caliphate could have been the cause. Apart from anything else, by then Baghdad was a shadow of what it had once been and there were other centres of learning and research that escaped the savagery of Hulagu. Nevertheless, as will be seen later in this chapter, the final destruction of the Abbasid Caliphate may well have had something to do with it – even if only indirectly.

V

The eleventh and twelfth centuries saw the disintegration of the Umayyad Caliphate of Cordoba into petty, localised states and the expansion of the Christian kingdoms in the north of the Iberian peninsula which won back much territory from the Muslims. At the same time, the Normans reconquered Sicily and ended Muslim rule. These were among the first of a series of territorial changes which were to reshape the boundaries between the worlds of Christendom and Islam. Arabic-language chronicles written by Muslim historians contemporary with the Crusades recognised crusading as a western

Christian form of jihad, and saw the eruption of the Crusaders into Greater Syria as connected with the slightly earlier Christian 'jihads' in Sicily and Spain.

The territorial changes reflected the steady build-up of pressure by two forces which were to have a huge impact on the course of history. The first was the increasing power of Latin Christendom, the forerunner of the modern West. The other was the impact of peoples speaking Turkish languages from the steppes of Central Asia, who converted to Islam and provided the roots for a prodigious number of Muslim empires: the Seljuks, Mamluks, Ottomans, Timurids, Safavids and Mughals.

For it was not only Muslim power in the western Mediterranean that was in long-term decline. After the Seljuks defeated the Byzantines at Manzikert in 1071, Turkish tribes began the settlement of Anatolia. This led to appeals for help against these successful Muslim invaders. In Western Europe there was increasing unease over Muslim control of the Holy Land after the Church of the Holy Sepulchre in Jerusalem was demolished in 1009–10 by the Fatimid Caliph al-Hakim, who persecuted his Christian subjects. Later in the century news filtered back of Muslim rulers in Anatolia and Syria making the transit of pilgrims hazardous.[8] Such incidents combined with a new Western assertiveness against Islam. This had really begun with the Norman reconquest of Muslim Sicily and successful Christian campaigns in Spain. Then, in 1095, Pope Urban II launched what has become known as the First Crusade, when he called on the chivalry of Western Europe to march to Jerusalem *ad liberandam ecclesiam Dei*, 'to liberate the Church of God' from Muslim domination.[9]

The Crusaders reached Greater Syria in the last few years of the eleventh century and remained there almost two hundred years before they were expelled from the mainland altogether. Their role in the Middle East has been described as 'transient but unforgettable'.[10] A map of the Crusader States at their maximum extent shows that, with the exception of the short-lived County of Edessa and the extension of the Kingdom of Jerusalem south-east of the Dead Sea into the mountains of Moab, they never established themselves far from the coast and the protective line of mountains behind it. They were unable to take the inland cities such as Damascus, Aleppo and Homs. If there had not been a political vacuum in the Levant caused by the splitting of the Muslim states into petty principalities, the Crusaders would probably never have been able to set themselves up along the coast of Greater Syria at all. Short of manpower, badly coordinated and given to infighting among themselves, the Crusaders relied on fortifications. They were unable to make their small states viable propositions without support from Western Europe.

The contemporary laws of war were harsh, but a righteous fanaticism infected many Crusaders who seem to have seen it their duty to subdue all that was not Latin Christian (one almost wonders whether one could say 'was not Western'), and use whatever brutality was required in the process. It may well have been such attitudes that eventually united the Sunni Muslims of the area against them. When the Crusaders took Jerusalem they carried out frightful massacres and the mosques were seized and turned into churches or put to other uses. Some Crusaders had a casual attitude to honouring agreements with other parties who were not Latin Christian. The main victims, however, were arguably the Byzantine Greeks. In 1204, a Crusader army which had become embroiled in intrigues over the imperial throne sacked Constantinople, desecrating the Cathedral of Hagia Sophia itself and carrying the loot they seized back to Western Europe. This left a lasting wound among Orthodox Christians that has remained open over the centuries, a wound much deeper than that which it inflicted on the Muslim and Arab psyches at the time. It is unsurprising that modern historians see the whole crusading enterprise as increasing xenophobia in Europe.

Nevertheless, the Crusaders who settled in the Latin principalities and those born there learned something of the lands in which they lived. Trade was carried on, Muslims and Franks alike charging the merchants of other religions a toll to pass through their territory. The status of Muslims under Christian rule frequently resembled that of Christians in Muslim ones. The semi-independent principalities which the Crusaders encountered when they first arrived must have reminded them in certain respects of the fiefdoms of Western European knights and barons. Franks and Muslims often forged alliances with each other against common opponents of either faith.

The Crusaders were helped by the split between Sunni and Shi'ite rulers. Shi'ites would not listen to Sunni calls for the mounting of a jihad to repel the Crusaders, and the extreme Shi'ite grouping known to history as the Assassins saw the Sunnis, not the Crusaders, as their real enemies. It would take nearly a century after the Crusader principalities were first established before Nur al-Din Zangi, a Sunni ruler, gained control of both Egypt and the Syrian hinterland, including Damascus and Aleppo. These cities had been in a perpetual state of feud and perfectly prepared to seek Crusader allies against each other. It was only then that jihad was preached effectively in reaction to the Crusaders. Jerusalem was retaken after Nur al-Din's nephew and successor Saladin destroyed the Crusader army at Hittin west of the Sea of Galilee in 1187, although the position stabilised after this. Fresh divisions emerged on the Muslim side after Saladin's death and Jerusalem was even demilitarised and ceded back to the Crusaders for a while, but the Crusader States remained exposed. Some subsequent Crusader expeditions tried to conquer Egypt. This would have given the Crusaders strategic depth and transferred its large revenues from a Muslim to a Frankish power, but such attempts failed.

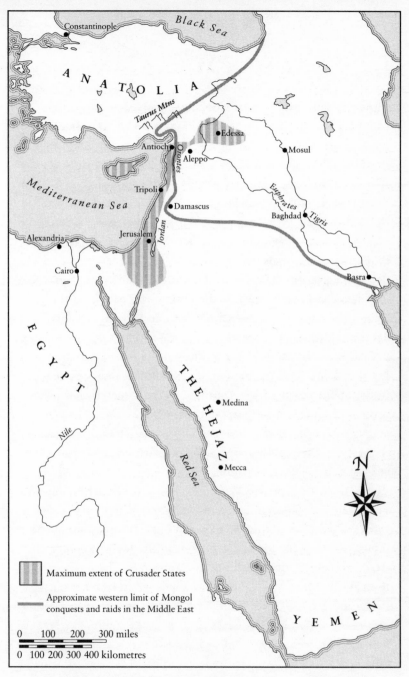

THE CRUSADER STATES AND THE MONGOL CONQUESTS

VI

Three small and inward-looking Arabic-speaking religious communities which still play important roles in the Middle East today can be traced back to the era of the political disintegration of the Abbasid Caliphate and the Crusades. The first of these are the Alawis or Nusayris, a splinter group which emerged from Shi'ism during the theological ferment of ninth- and tenth-century Baghdad but was rejected by mainstream Shi'ites.[11] The Alawi teaching was preached at Lattakia in north-west Syria in the eleventh century at a time when it was under the Byzantines. The sect has remained the dominant group in the mountains of the city's hinterland ever since.

The second community are the Druze, who date from the early eleventh century. They deified the Fatimid Caliph al-Hakim, and are thus an offshoot of the Shi'ism of the Fatimids which has gone beyond the boundaries of Islam. The teaching was preached across Egypt and Greater Syria, but Druze communities only survive today in the Shouf mountains in Lebanon, the volcanic Hauran plateau south and south-east of Damascus, a few places elsewhere in Syria, and in the Galilee. Both Alawis and Druze have a tradition of *taqiyya*, the practice also found among Shi'ites of concealing their true beliefs when threatened by persecution.

The third group are the Maronite Christians. Originally followers of Maroun, a fifth-century saint who preached in the Orontes valley, they developed their own church institutions in the Lebanese mountains after the Muslim conquest. In the twelfth century, they threw in their lot with the Crusaders and united themselves to the Roman Catholic Church. They have remained in communion with Rome more or less ever since, and Catholicism is an important part of their identity. Their heartland is in the mountains behind Beirut, but there are also scattered Maronite communities in many other parts of Greater Syria and in Cyprus. Like the Armenians and Georgians, the martial Christian peoples of the Caucasus, the Maronites in their rocky fastnesses could ignore many of the restrictions that were meant to be placed on Christians by Sharia. Their elite rode horses and carried weapons, and on occasion even welcomed Muslims who openly converted to this locally dominant sect, as their Ottoman governor Bashir II did in the early nineteenth century. Until they fell out with their Druze neighbours in the 1830s, the two communities had often cooperated together against central authority. In 1772, they even joined forces to occupy Damascus and ransack the city.

Despite the diversity of their beliefs, these three communities have retained characteristics in common from the Middle Ages to the present day. Each is a minority sect with a strong sense of identity which has enabled it to survive as a distinctive little island in the great sea of Sunni Islam which surrounds it. It is no coincidence that their principal centres are in remote and mountainous areas, nor that they are composed of tough and clannish farming folk who have shown themselves to be fierce fighters when their community is at war.

VII

The Crusaders in the eastern Mediterranean turned out to be never more than a local threat to Islam, but a much more serious threat appeared during the twilight years of the Crusader States of Greater Syria. This was the Mongol invasion of the thirteenth century. The Mongols overran Muslim Central Asia and Iran. They stormed Baghdad and executed the last Abbasid Caliph in 1258, then took Damascus and Aleppo. Over time, the Mongols saw it expedient to convert to Islam, but this was after they had left a trail of devastation that was of a far greater order than the ravages of the Crusaders.

Two years after the sack of Baghdad the Mongols were stopped at Ayn Jalut in Syria by the Mamluks of Egypt, a Turkish-speaking caste of military slaves who were brought from the Caucasus as boys to be trained as soldiers and provide a standing army, but who eventually took over the government. The spirit of jihad, which had declined once again after Nur al-Din and Saladin, was revived to repel the invaders. No longer could the Crusader principalities along the coast of Greater Syria be allowed to pose a strategic threat, particularly as there were diplomatic contacts and attempts to form alliances between Mongols and Franks. The Mamluks methodically and brutally eradicated the last Crusader strongholds in Greater Syria with an exceptional savagery which equalled that of the Crusaders when they took Jerusalem.[12] They also persecuted their Christian subjects and conquered the Christian kingdom of Nubia to the south of Aswan.

With the expulsion of the Crusaders and the assimilation of the Mongols, the Muslim world had survived a trauma which seems to have caused a new defensiveness among Sunni Muslims. There was a greater suspicion of local Christians, who had probably still constituted the majority of the population in large parts of Greater Syria and other significant areas when the Crusaders arrived. A good example of this defensiveness occurred in 1123–24 when the cathedral of St Helena and other churches in Aleppo were seized and converted into mosques in anger at the Crusaders who were at the city's gates and showing their contempt for Islam by desecrating cemeteries. During these times of trouble the preservation of Islam and life lived according to Sharia was shown to be the most potent rallying cry against invaders. Preachers attacked laxity and innovations which might subvert Islam. The drinking of alcohol seems to have been widespread in medieval Muslim societies,[13] but armies which were motivated by jihad against Crusaders and Mongols forswore alcohol and all other loose-living in favour of prayer.

When Mongol rulers converted to Islam they often retained Mongol traditions and laws. To some Muslims, it seemed they were picking and choosing what they would take from Islam and what they would not. One thirteenth-century thinker, Ibn Taymiyya, possibly responding to the destruction of the Caliphate, developed the theory that the power of the state was needed to enforce Sharia by following the Qur'anic injunction 'to command the good and forbid the wrong'. Such enforcement should be the touchstone of legitimate rule and a constraint upon those charged with government. Bitterly hostile to Shi'ism and especially so to Alawism, Ibn Taymiyya also set out to refute Christianity and to circumscribe the position of Christians under the most rigorous interpretations of Sharia, sometimes even arguing that Christians and Jews should only be tolerated in Muslim-dominated lands when there was a need for their services.[14] In earlier centuries, there had been a rich tradition of Arabic Christian literature aimed at defending Christianity against Muslim preaching and polemic, even quoting the Qur'an back at Muslims to justify Christian doctrines like the Incarnation. This seems to have just faded away, and the thirteenth and fourteenth centuries saw widespread conversions by Christians to Islam in many Arabic-speaking countries.

This was the end of the half-millennium of *convivencia* in the central Arab lands during which, as Sydney Griffith puts it, relations between Muslims and Christians had been 'constant, often intellectually and culturally complementary, mutually comprehensible, but both confrontational and co-operative at the same time'.[15] Despite plenty of differences and much dislike, there had been sufficient respect by Christians and Muslims for each other for them to be willing to accept others on their own terms, and to listen to what they might have to say. It is hard not to see a connection between the end of this *convivencia* and the decline in science and philosophy written in Arabic. If the shock caused by the end of the caliphate and assaults on the citadels of Islam by Mongols and Crusaders provided the immediate context, there was also a wider one. Islamic law had become increasingly restrictive as it developed. Although the text of the Qur'an had always reigned supreme, early judges had considerable discretion to exercise their own *rai'*, 'opinion' which might sometimes even prevail against a saying attributed to the Prophet. Yet under the Abbasids in the early ninth century, a solid hierarchy of the sources of law was established by the jurist al-Shafi'i. This consisted of the Qur'an, the Sunna (as contained in the *hadith*), the consensus of the community and finally (and as a last resort) reasoning by analogy that was known as *qiyas*, and was a form of *ijtihad*, the exercise of independent judgement. A *hadith* researched from compilations assembled by respected scholars was used to plug the gap whenever there was no relevant text in the Qur'an on which to found a judicial decision. This had the consequence that the field open to *ijtihad* shrank steadily and the law became ossified. This cannot have been conducive to the encouragement of scientific enquiry. It also led to the rigid and literalist streak in Islam with which we are so familiar in the twenty-first century.

VIII

Until the fifteenth century, the Latin Christian bloc in the west, the Orthodox Christian bloc originally centred on the Byzantine Empire, and the Muslim bloc to the south, jointly made up the Mediterranean world. They overlapped and cross-fertilised, but each existed separately. Wars continued among and between Christians and Muslims, and saw some shifting in the land surfaces of the blocs. In the east, a new Sunni Muslim power arose, the Ottoman Turks, who used cannon to breach the great land walls of Constantinople in 1453. In the west, the newly united Spanish kingdom of Castille and Aragon took Granada, the last Arab state in the Iberian Peninsula, in 1492.

These two conquests were traumatic for both the victims and their co-religionists elsewhere, and did much to reinforce the existing mutual fear and suspicion between Muslims and Christians.

In Spain, the use of Catholicism to forge a national identity ended religious toleration for the Muslim and Jewish inhabitants, despite the pledges of the conquerors. The mentality of the Crusading period survived for a while, and played a significant role in the first European voyages of discovery. Columbus had the ambition to regain Jerusalem, while the first Portuguese entering the Indian Ocean looked for allies against Islam. Yet they soon found that, as had been the case during the Crusades and the reconquest of Iberia, the most convenient allies were often Muslims or other infidels with whom they could cooperate against their fellow Europeans who soon followed them round the Cape of Good Hope.

If the *Reconquista* and the appearance of Western Europeans in the Indian Ocean were traumatic for the Muslim world, the fall of Constantinople in 1453 and conquest of the Balkans matched or exceeded these traumas for Christendom. The last Byzantine emperor disappeared in the fighting as he heroically led the defenders against the Turks streaming into the city. Sultan Mehmet II, known as Mehmet the Conqueror, delivered it over to the Ottoman soldiery for the customary three days of pillage before re-establishing order. Its principal churches, including the Hagia Sophia, were converted into mosques, something that was paralleled by the transformation of Spanish mosques into churches. In fact, by now it had long become the general practice that the principal church or mosque of a city that fell or was ceded to a ruler who belonged to the other faith would be converted to serve the conqueror's religion.

The defence and expansion of Islam were key elements of the ideology of the Ottoman Empire, the greatest ever Muslim power, but a glance at a map of the Empire at its maximum extent shows that it expanded into Muslim and Christian lands alike. During its first three centuries, the Empire faced greater threats from other Muslim powers than from Christian ones, and the struggle for preeminence within the Muslim world has been described as 'every bit as contentious as the rivalry between Christian and Muslim states'.[16]

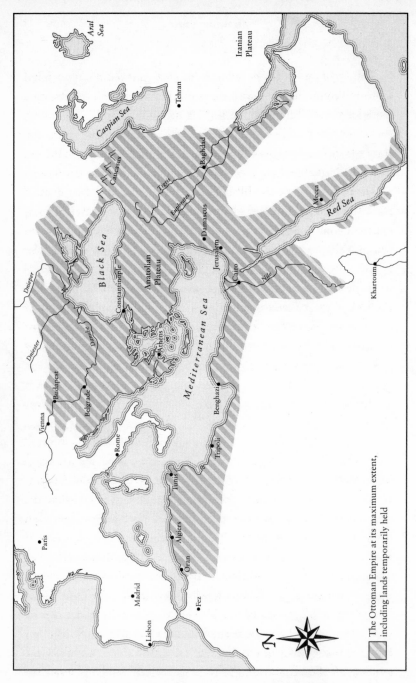

THE OTTOMAN EMPIRE AT ITS MAXIMUM EXTENT

The Empire's armies and fleets set out from its capital Constantinople towards all points of the compass: into the rich lands of the Balkans and up the Danube towards Vienna (which they besieged in 1529 and 1683); into the Caucasus and north-west Iran; to Greater Syria and Egypt (which they conquered in 1516-18); to other Arabic-speaking lands as far south as Yemen and as far west as Algeria; and across the Black Sea to the Crimea and the valleys of the Dnieper and Dniester. The order the Ottomans established was appreciated by many who were not Muslim. Christians and Jews as well as Muslims would sometimes offer prayers for the success of the Sultan's armies.[17] Many – sometimes the majority – of the soldiers in those armies were Christian levies, vassals and allies. This was probably even the case during the Ottoman siege of Vienna in 1683 which nearly succeeded. Until the failure of that siege and their loss of Hungary in the campaign that followed, the Turks were the terror of Europe.

IX

Even while Europe remained under threat from the Turks, changes were taking place there which had no counterpart in the Arab or Muslim world. The Reformation ended its religious unity, while the spoken languages of the European peoples were increasingly used for written communication rather than Latin, paving the way for the modern nation state. The sixteenth and seventeenth centuries saw Catholics and Protestants fight some of the most vicious religious wars ever to take place, the most terrible of which was the Thirty Years War (1618-48). This caused the death of up to half the population of Germany, but the Peace of Westphalia which ended it provided the building blocks of the modern state system: the recognition of the sovereignty of each state and its right to political self-determination, the equality of all states, and the principle of non-intervention by one state in the affairs of another. It was hoped that the balance of power would deter parties from making unjust wars and lead to a more peaceful world. Europe's brutal wars aimed at religious conversion came to an end, but in the process of time the continent would give birth to even more terrible wars caused by more modern weaponry deployed in the causes of nationalism and secular ideologies.

There were many other crucial developments in what we must now call Western Europe that led, by many twisting and turning paths, from the mindsets of the medieval to the modern world. Religious reformers tried to return to the roots of their faith, while intellectuals set out to rediscover the learning of ancient Greece and Rome, rejecting accepted authorities and the received wisdom that had been transmitted and embellished by commentators. At the same time, technological advances and experiments led to scientific discoveries that could not be explained within the framework of the theories of Aristotle and other ancient writers who had been venerated throughout the medieval period in the lands of Latin Christianity, Orthodox Christianity and Islam alike. Earlier civilisations had made staggering advances, but in Europe a kind of virtuous circle was now created which made the new scientific and technological gains irreversible and provided spurs to further progress. It was increasingly felt that it was possible to understand and master the world in which we live. By the eighteenth century intellectual currents were at work that sidelined the God of the revealed religions and shared the optimistic conclusion that reason and scientific method could explain the human condition.

Constitutional forms of government began to evolve in some states, and were admired by influential people in others. Writers like Locke and Montesquieu[18] formulated theories such as the separation of the three powers of the state: the executive, the legislative and the judicial. These should not be allowed to fall into a single pair of hands lest this led to tyranny, and therefore checks and balances are required. They would be taken into account when new constitutional settlements were devised, the first being that of the United States of America which enshrined many of the ideas of the Enlightenment, including democracy and secularism. This also demonstrated how 'the West' was spreading out of Europe to lands across the oceans which Europeans had settled.

Freethinkers felt able to reject publicly beliefs which were fundamental to Christianity. The diffusion of such ideas beyond an intellectual elite was a slow process, and religious faith remained the bedrock of society. Yet it meant that when, at the end of the eighteenth century, the next great encounter in the Mediterranean between the West and the Arabic-speaking world began, one could no longer talk of Europe as being primarily Christian in its intellectual apparatus. Instead, the predominantly Muslim world that lay on the southern and eastern shores of the Mediterranean would be confronted by European rationalist ideas as well as the Christianity of the ancestral, Frankish foe.

Baroque architecture came to Constantinople, and even baroque mosques like the Nuru Osmaniye were built. The Ottoman astronomer Uthman bin Abd al-Mannan wrote that the Earth did indeed seem to revolve around the Sun, since it was more logical to barbecue meat by turning the skewer over a fire than by making the fire revolve round the skewer.[19] Nevertheless, many of the new European intellectual and scientific ideas hardly reached the Ottoman Empire, although it was receptive to military technologies from the West. As has been seen, at an earlier stage, the world of Islam had forged ahead in its interest in science. Those in the Ottoman world who paid attention to ideas of the kind that Locke and Montesquieu were formulating seem to have been few and isolated. Nevertheless, after their crushing defeat before Vienna in 1683 and loss of Hungary, the Ottomans became aware that there was more than a gap in technological expertise between themselves and the Europeans.

The Empire was becoming economically weaker. Although its finances had ups as well as downs, whenever the coffers were empty the likely result was a mutiny by the army which could result in bloody insurrection and the deposition of the Sultan. Life-time tax farming was introduced in the 1690s. When this coincided with an economic boom brought about by a revival of trade, the result was the emergence of a wealthy new elite composed chiefly of bureaucrats, soldiers and religious scholars who sought to enrich themselves further. Far from strengthening the state, this new class set out to increase its own privileges at the expense of central authority.

A cold wind was blowing through the palaces of the Ottoman elite as the eighteenth century drew to a close. Not only had they lost the initiative to the European powers to the north and west, but those states were now constantly gaining in strength while the Ottomans were not.

CHAPTER THREE

THE WEST TAKES CONTROL

I

In the final decades of the eighteenth century, every country where Arabic was spoken lay within the Ottoman Empire, save for Morocco, the Sudan and the central, southern and eastern parts of the Arabian Peninsula. But the Empire was now in decline, and its chief preoccupations were Austria and Russia which were rolling back its frontiers in the Balkans and along the Black Sea littoral. At the same time, the Empire was weakened by the increasing strength of the commanders of the local Mamluk garrisons and notable provincial families on which it depended to collect taxes and administer authority in the name of the Sultan. Local governors and tax farmers would often build up their own armed strength. This happened in Cairo, in Damascus and Acre in Greater Syria, in Baghdad and Basra in the valleys of the Tigris and Euphrates, and along the North African coast in Tripoli, Tunis and Algiers. Constantinople was often reduced to negotiating its control by playing them off against each other and sometimes faced open revolt. At the same time, the gap between the major European powers and the Ottomans was growing rapidly wider. The Empire was about to receive a very rude shock.

Napoleon's conquest of Egypt in 1798[1] showed there was no longer any doubting the technological, military and organisational superiority of the West. He had no difficulty defeating the local Mamluks. The Sultan was manifestly unable to dislodge him. The lion's share of this task was therefore entrusted to France's rival, a willing Britain. It proved not to be too difficult once the French fleet had been sunk by Nelson and Napoleon had returned to France for greater things, leaving his army stranded in a hostile environment. If the East had been humiliated at the hands of the West it had thus been a double humiliation.

The French Revolution was settling down by the time of Napoleon's invasion. With the restoration of order it looked as though France might now be able to put the ideals of the Enlightenment into practice. Well-meaning scholars and experts who accompanied Napoleon's expedition intended to do just that in Egypt. They studied everything about the country from its architecture to its ornithology, collected statistics, put forward ideas to improve its agriculture, infrastructure and public health, and unearthed half-buried ruins of the country's glorious past. They also gave Egypt its first Arabic-language printing press and the secret ballot, which was used in new administrative councils Napoleon established. But what would Egyptians make of the fact that Napoleon had an Arabic proclamation produced on his printing press in which he announced that the French had come to save them from oppression by their rulers, and even suggested that the French might be Muslims themselves?

Napoleon's proclamation was intended to reassure the population that he had not come to refight the Crusades. This was true, and the Egyptian historian Jabarti, who wrote an account of the times in a manner that had not changed since the medieval Arabic chroniclers, disdainfully observed that French soldiers who converted to Islam to marry Muslim women tended to have no religious faith of their own, something that made their conversions meaningless. But the French were unable to pacify the country despite brutal reprisals, and it was obvious that they were not Muslims in any real sense. Napoleon's proclamation that the French had come to bring freedom and equality and should be considered as fellow Muslims was worse than condescending because it showed he did not appreciate what Islam was.

The French displayed a naivety and willingness to deceive that were an insult to Egyptian intelligence, since the expedition's propaganda was premised on a lie. Napoleon had seized Egypt for its strategic value. In the eighteenth century France had lost most of its overseas possessions to Britain. By securing Egypt, Napoleon hoped to reverse this. He wished to strike at British trade and threaten Britain's position in India. Everything was incidental to this greater purpose and would be ruthlessly sacrificed when the time came. In the meantime, Talleyrand, his foreign minister, worked hard and mendaciously to persuade the world that France was acting for the benefit of Egypt, and even of the Ottoman Sultan.

II

There are myths in the West about Napoleon's occupation of Egypt which die hard. He is not entitled to acknowledgment in some vague way as the initiator of the modern Egyptian state. What he and his soldiers and scientists did contribute, however, was example: there was a more efficient, more modern, 'Western' way of doing things that produced results.

The person who set out to put this example into practice was Muhammad Ali Pasha, an ethnic Albanian soldier and tobacco merchant from Macedonia who fought in the returning Ottoman army. He seized control of Egypt in the first few years of the nineteenth century and ruled almost until his death in 1849. He was acknowledged by Constantinople as governor of the country, and consolidated his power by slaughtering the Mamluk elite after inviting them to a reception, thus disposing of any potential rivals. After a largely unsuccessful attempt to build an army of Sudanese troops, he recruited soldiers from the Egyptian peasantry: the first ruler to do this for hundreds if not thousands of years.

He seized all private landholdings and created monopolies of production and trade. Yet he did not believe in state monopoly for any ideological reason, and made land grants to members of his family and others who would be expected to use it productively. Irrigation and drainage systems were improved, ports were built at Alexandria and Suez, and silted up canals reopened to water-borne transport. He was unsuccessful in an attempt to build a government-run industrial base, but cotton production was expanded as a major cash crop. Engineering and medical schools were established in Cairo and a house for Egyptian students of technical subjects maintained in Paris. He set up Egypt's first ever ministry of education and a translation institute to introduce European technical knowledge to Egypt. But there was a price to be paid. Peasants were brutally conscripted into his army and public-work programmes, thereby lighting a slow-burning fuse of resentment against his dynasty.

Muhammad Ali's principal concern was the country's armed forces, which he reorganised with the help of Europeans. He responded to a request from Constantinople to conquer the troublesome Wahhabis in central Arabia. His army accomplished this after a campaign which involved the logistical nightmare of supplying an army in the midst of the Arabian desert. He helped the Ottomans against the rebels in the conflict that became the Greek War of Independence in return for a promise that he could add southern Greece to his dominions. When this venture ended in failure, he extended his authority over Greater Syria in the way that other powerful Egyptian rulers had done ever since the days of the Pharoahs. There were strategic reasons for this. Greater Syria had always been a vital area for Egypt and its main source of food whenever the Nile flood failed. But his ambitions were greater still. His army marched into Anatolia and it looked for a moment as though he might take over the Ottoman Empire itself. It was only under European pressure that his troops were withdrawn to the frontiers of Egypt in exchange for a concession by the Sultan which made his vice-royalty of Egypt hereditary.

These adventures in Greece, Greater Syria and Anatolia show that Muhammad Ali was not an Egyptian nationalist. His building works in Cairo reflect Ottoman tastes. His huge mosque that dominates Cairo's citadel is, very unusually for Cairo, in the style of Constantinople, as is his summer palace at Shoubra. The kiosks, drinking fountains and edifices of piety he endowed were often inlaid with inscriptions in Ottoman Turkish, something that had been rare or unknown among his predecessors. Yet, paradoxically, he set Egypt on the path to modern nationhood by creating in embryonic form the institutions that would become the hallmarks of nationalist governments in Europe and elsewhere: military service and a system of national education.

III

Muhammad Ali's grandson Ismail, who ruled from 1863 to 1879, built a new capital on European lines between the walled city of medieval Cairo and the Nile. He gave the country one of the first developed railway systems outside Europe and North America (although the key line from Cairo to Alexandria had been opened as early as 1854), a modern postal service and, most importantly of all, the Suez Canal. Ismail increased his power at the expense of the Sultan in Constantinople. He was awarded the honorific title of Khedive to give him precedence over the governors of other Ottoman provinces, and even acquired the right to execute treaties and raise loans like a sovereign state.

For a brief moment Ismail could almost pretend that his country, which now had an indirectly elected Assembly of Deputies (albeit with minuscule powers) and a press with a fair degree of freedom, was part of Europe. Egypt even had its own colonial empire stretching south to cover the Sudan and the African coast of the Red Sea, and he sent out expeditions to suppress the slave trade like a good European liberal. His moment of triumph and recognition came in 1869 when the Suez Canal was opened and he hosted a magnificent party which representatives of many European royal families attended, treating Ismail virtually as an equal. Yet such equality was illusory. Within little more than a decade, the country was under foreign military occupation – this time by Britain. What had gone wrong?

When Ismail came to power, the temporary disappearance of cotton produced by the southern states of the USA from the world market as a result of the American Civil War had led to a cotton boom in Egypt. This helped lure him and his ministers into a fool's paradise when they calculated how much money they could afford to borrow. European banks and finance houses were beginning to search for deals in Egypt where they could lend at higher rates of interest than in Europe. Loans were granted on the security of specific government revenues, but the distinction between the property of Egypt as a semi-independent state and that of the Khedive was frequently unclear. There was a general failure to keep expenditure under control, and bad bargains and conflicts of interest abounded. Not for the first or last time in history, bankers rushed to lend at rates which borrowers could not afford to repay. Scandalous incidents occurred in which the Egyptian government played the role of dupe or accomplice, and the financing of the Suez Canal and other projects gave a good return to the European investors but turned out to be very expensive for the Egyptian treasury. Not for nothing has Eugene Rogan pointed out that European bankers provided a greater danger than European armies.[2] In addition, large sums were spent on unsuccessful military campaigns in the African interior and extravagance by Ismail and his circle. When Ismail was unable to reschedule his debts, he had no alternative but to sell his shares in the Suez Canal to the British government.

The military and financial superiority of countries like Britain and France was now such that the main restraint on their freedom of action against Turkey or Egypt was the European balance of power. Yet when the powers had common interests they could make their demands jointly, and it was very difficult for an Egyptian or Ottoman ruler to withstand them. In 1876, Egypt was put into receivership by Britain and France as it slid towards bankruptcy. Commissioners appointed from both countries took control of every aspect of government revenue. Ismail had to acquiesce in the appointment of a British minister of finance and a French minister of public works. He was also obliged to transfer his family's landed property to the state.

The changes of the last fifty years had had a slow but incremental effect on Egyptian society. Turkish was in retreat as the language of government, its place now officially taken by Arabic, while windows were opening into the European world as French became a lingua franca for the educated and English was also used. Learning European languages exposed an increasing number of Egyptians to Western ideas. The officer corps was no longer exclusively extracted from the old, Turkish-speaking elite descended from Mamluks. Ismail's goal, like that of Muhammad Ali, had been to free himself from Ottoman rule. He could no more be considered an Egyptian nationalist than a contemporary Habsburg was an Austrian nationalist, but popular feeling against the way in which the country seemed to be run for the benefit of foreign interests was something he may have felt he could harness to defend his own position.

He was perceived as being behind a demonstration by army officers that mobbed the prime minister and minister of finance in February 1879 to protest at the reduction of their pay as part of a programme to cut government expenditure. He dismissed the government and appointed a new one composed entirely of Egyptian ministers, leading to a clash which showed where power now lay. British and French diplomatic pressure in Constantinople led to a decree in June that year in which the Sultan removed Ismail as Khedive and replaced him with his son Tawfiq. The same decree reduced the size of the Egyptian army. Britain and France had taken advantage of a fundamental weakness in the Egyptian position. Despite all the achievements of Muhammad Ali and Ismail, Egypt was not an independent sovereign state.

Egyptians knew that much of the money with which Egypt was now indebted had gone in fees and commissions, and had never reached the country. They could not help but notice the increasing number of well-paid Europeans working for the government. There was also disquiet at the growth of the power of foreign communities. These, especially the Greeks, Italians, Ashkenazi and Ottoman Jews and Christian Syrians, had been arriving in the country in search of opportunity ever since Muhammad Ali had opened Egypt up to the world. Under Ismail, the new arrivals had become a flood. Although their industry added to the wealth of the country, treaty arrangements known as the Capitulations gave those of them who were citizens of European countries a privileged status. They were not subject to the same courts as ordinary Egyptians and had massive tax exemptions. Perhaps what was worst was that a foreign national could only be arrested in the presence of his consul – something that was frequently abused and led to a culture of impunity. Such privileges bred resentment.

Discontent simmered in the army, and demands for a constitution increased. Pressure led to the appointment of Urabi Pasha, an ethnically Egyptian army officer with a talent for making rousing speeches, as minister for war. At the same time, the European financial controllers continued to insist that there should be no Egyptian say over any part of the country's budget, even that which was not devoted to repaying the debts incurred during Ismail's reign. A breach opened between the new Khedive Tawfiq, backed by Britain, France and Turkey, and his own government. Rioting broke out in Alexandria, where poorer members of the foreign communities were concentrated, and where Tawfiq fled. British warships in the harbour bombarded the city and a British expeditionary force occupied the country, easily defeating the Egyptian army. Egypt thus came under British occupation.

Like Napoleon, the British had some good intentions when they came to Egypt. They also arrived reluctantly, nervous about what commitments and expenditure they might be taking on. Nevertheless, they were there for their own purposes and this time there was a major difference: they had come with the authority or at least the complicity of the international community. They would stay as long as they themselves deemed necessary. It was to be seventy-two years before the last British troops left Egypt.

IV

The Ottoman Empire's problems were greater than Egypt's because of its diversity. In the early nineteenth century it still contained the peoples of the southern Balkans, most of whom were Orthodox Christian but spoke a great variety of languages, the Anatolian peninsula, which was predominantly Turkish when taken as a whole, but also had large communities of Kurds, Armenians and Greeks, and Greater Syria and Iraq, which were largely Arabic-speaking but had very substantial numbers of Shi'ites and Christians. Although, as we have seen, Egypt was a semi-independent province, to its west were Cyrenaica and Tripolitania (now Libya) which were under direct control from Constantinople. Algeria and Tunisia also started the nineteenth century as Ottoman provinces with a large measure of independence under local governors, although Algeria was soon lost to France.

As was the case in Egypt, Ottoman students were sent to the West to learn the new skills and technologies. Western books were translated and military reforms carried out. Inevitably, liberal and other Western ideas now began to percolate into the Empire's elite. Previously, there had been no concept of equality before the law. In the early nineteenth century, the Ottoman Empire and all other states with Muslim rulers still saw their subjects as owing allegiance on the basis of the rights and obligations of the members of the particular religious community, or *millet*, to which they belonged. There were extra taxes for Christians and Jews which had existed throughout the history of Islam, although Muhammad Ali abolished these in Egypt. On the other hand, Christians and Jews were free from the threat of military service. Originally, the Ottoman army had been dominated by a slave elite of soldiers raised by a levy of boys and young men who were taken from certain Christian communities and ordered to convert to Islam. This practice had gradually come to an end, and Ottoman soldiers were now Muslim-born.

There was a feeling among many Ottoman Muslims that it was only fair for the Christians and Jews to pay more tax, because the duty of defending the Empire fell upon its Muslims. Obstacles in the way of reform thus included not only the unchanging ways of the centuries but practical ones concerned with tax revenues and the risk of stirring up sectarian tensions. Nevertheless, Turkish reformers wished to enact a constitution which removed these religious-based distinctions and created a single Ottoman citizenship. The hope was that this would lead to an Ottoman patriotism which would be felt among the Empire's non-Muslim inhabitants as well as the Muslims, and the Empire would become a liberal state like some of its European neighbours. If modern education, taxation and military skills on the European model were not adopted, the Empire was doomed.

Root and branch reforms known collectively as the *tanzimat* were therefore attempted. Laws that had obliged Ottomans to dress in different ways depending on their religious faith and status had been periodically reasserted, the last such occasion being as late as 1814. Now these were abolished. Western dress was encouraged, and the fez was introduced as a symbol of Ottomanism to replace the traditional turbans. In a solemn moment in 1839, a decree was promulgated to end the old forms of tax, as well as tax farming, and replace them with a system under which every individual would be registered as a taxpayer. The conditions for military service were to be regulated to make them less arbitrary and to spread the burden among all subjects of the Empire, irrespective of their religion. The administration would be cleaned up and reformed, and monopolies abolished.

Unsurprisingly, implementation of the reforms proved difficult. The reasons included poor communications and widespread illiteracy everywhere, but the old taxes could not be abolished overnight because the revenue was needed. Many Muslims resented new taxes that were applicable to them for the first time, while there were cases of Christians fleeing to the newly independent Greek state to avoid military service or producing papers from European consuls asserting that they were exempt.

Further boosts to reform came after the Crimean War in the 1850s. Distinctions based on 'religion, language or race' were to be 'forever effaced from administrative protocol'. Members of all creeds became eligible for employment in the administration, which had previously been dominated by Muslims. There were also provisions intended to lead to modernisation of the infrastructure of the state. It was expressly stated that ways should be found 'to profit by the science, the art and the funds of Europe'.[3] Many Muslims resented the reforms, which were to a large extent imposed through pressure from the European powers.

Ottoman reformers themselves doubted whether they should all be instituted at once. The theory was that all subjects of the Empire would benefit, but it soon proved that they could lead to an increase in sectarian tension. Nationalism among the Christian peoples of the Balkans proved too strong for the new concept of 'Ottomanism' to succeed. Wedges were driven between Muslims and non-Muslims. At one point it seems 120,000 Greek subjects of the Empire could benefit from Russian protection, while another 260,000 Christians in what would become Romania could claim protection from Austria. Among the advantages that flowed from such protection was freedom from Ottoman taxes. Economic activity with the West was dominated by Christians and Jews, and Muslims had little share in it. A kind of balance had existed because of the Muslim dominance in political power. The reforms threatened to end this without changing the Christian and Jewish domination of the economy.

In the 1870s Ottoman Turkey had a financial crisis similar to that of Egypt. The government finances were out of control as a result of borrowing from European financial institutions. This was aggravated by incomplete and badly administered tax reforms. Revolts broke out in the Balkans, and Western opinion was outraged at massacres of Christians, especially in Bulgaria. Russia invaded, seeing itself as the champion of the Empire's Orthodox Christians and of Slav peoples everywhere. Russian troops advanced almost to the gates of Constantinople. Although pressure from the other European powers forced a diplomatic solution in which Russia withdrew from most of the territory it had occupied, it imposed a crippling war indemnity on Turkey. Most of the Ottoman Balkans, including some of the Empire's richest lands, now became fully or virtually independent.

This changed the balance between Muslims and Christians in the Empire. For the first time in the long Ottoman history, Muslims were an overwhelming majority. It was not surprising, therefore, that Abdul Hamid II, the new Sultan who came to power in 1876 and reigned until he was deposed in 1909, stressed his role as caliph in a way no previous Ottoman ruler had done. Ever since Selim the Grim had conquered the Mamluks of Egypt and Greater Syria 350 years earlier and brought the relics of the Prophet to Constantinople, Ottoman sultans had adorned themselves with this title. It had not been considered to be much more than an honour, and it was also used by various other Muslim rulers. As an institution with some claim to allegiance from all Sunni Muslims the caliphate had ended with the sack of Baghdad and execution of the last Abbasid caliph in 1258, but the Mamluk sultans in Cairo had appointed a member of the Abbasid dynasty as a puppet caliph who attended their court. He had no power himself, but invested each new sultan with his authority. This had a certain moral force as it appeared to guarantee legitimacy and was a bulwark against Shi'ism. Now, it was publicly proclaimed, the last puppet caliph of the Mamluks had transferred his functions to Selim the Grim and girded him with the sword of the Caliph Umar.

In fact, as a political institution the Ottoman Caliphate was a face-saving eighteenth-century device to enable the Sultan to pose as having spiritual authority over Muslims in the Russian Empire as a counterweight to Russian claims to be the protectors of Orthodox Christians in the Ottoman Empire. There were also limits to the recognition of the Ottoman 'Caliphate' within the Empire itself. Even though religious scholars in an outlying province like Egypt looked to the Sultan as the protector of Sunni Islam on a practical level, they did not generally concede that he could acquire a special religious status in this way.[4]

Abdul Hamid suspended the recently introduced constitution and attempted to use Islam as glue to keep the Empire together instead of the failed Ottomanism. He hoped this would make Turkey unique as a European power, and give him a central role for Sunni Muslims the world over, notably in the European colonial empires. Yet this policy also failed. The Albanians had constituted one of the Empire's most loyal communities, and over two-thirds of them were Muslim. Nevertheless, nationalist feeling began to spread among them as well.

For the time being, Turkey was saved from occupation or partition by European powers because the risk of war between them was too great. Instead, the Empire suffered the death of a thousand cuts while European pressure stifled its diminishing freedom of action. When it could, a European power would grab a piece of the Empire from under the noses of the others. Yet these losses, even when added together, were less than those it suffered because of the growth of nationalism among its peoples. The beginning of the nineteenth century had seen the Ottoman frontiers in Europe still reaching the edges of the plain of Hungary and the valley of the Dniester. By 1914, all that remained to Turkey in Europe was Constantinople and eastern Thrace, the area that is still part of Turkey today.

V

Compared with this general picture of dismal decline, the Ottoman record in Greater Syria and Iraq in the decades immediately before the First World War reads almost like a success story, although this was certainly not true in Greater Syria during the period leading up to 1860, as will be seen. The Ottomans were able to re-establish direct control of all the major cities and link them by telegraph to Istanbul. Even though railway development was slow, in 1908 a line from Damascus to Medina joined the Hejaz to the rest of the empire, and the initiation of the Berlin–Baghdad rail project promised that it would soon be possible to travel by train all the way from Constantinople to Basra. There was even some colonial expansion on the British and French model. Control of a sort was re-established in Yemen, and Britain and Turkey signed treaties in 1913 and 1914 to carve up the Arabian Peninsula into spheres of influence.

Yet in many areas Ottoman control still depended on negotiation with local interests and tribal leaders for the collection of taxes and the enforcement of authority. Ottoman administration was only gradually improved. As late as 1901 Ja'far al-Askari, a sixteen-year-old officer cadet who would one day play a role in establishing an independent Iraq and have the unhappy distinction of being the first man to be killed in a military coup in an Arab country, travelled from Baghdad to Constantinople to attend the military academy. The journey took him forty-four days: riding to the Mediterranean port of Iskenderun by horse and mule, and thence by sea. Until the Young Turk Revolution of 1908, he found that soldiers only received their pay for a few months in the year, although thereafter the situation improved. To survive, and to compensate themselves, it was common practice for them to extort money when they collected taxes.

Paradoxically, Ottomanism provided a spur to what would become Arab nationalism. The middle years of the nineteenth century were a bad time for relations between Muslims and Christians in Greater Syria. The sectarian divide had worsened. Catholic missionaries from France and Italy and their Protestant counterparts from Britain and the USA were by now having a growing effect on the Empire's Christian communities. Many of their members were receiving a Western education and developing links with Europe, something that gave them a distinct commercial advantage over most of their Muslim peers. Particularly influential were the increasing numbers of Arab Catholics. These included not just the Maronites, but the 'Uniates': Orthodox and other Christians who entered into union with Rome on condition that they were allowed to keep their ancestral forms of worship and traditions. A prosperous and confident Uniate bourgeoisie emerged in Aleppo, Greater Syria's commercial capital. Many Uniates insisted on the rights given to them by the *tanzimat* reforms which they interpreted as allowing them to display their religion publicly. This included events such as public Good Friday processions in which crosses were carried, while Christians stopped showing Muslims the deference that had been expected from them for centuries. For conservative Muslims, such things were unprecedented and deeply shocking. Fear, too, was mingled in with surprise and dismay. In 1821, twenty years after the French occupation of Egypt had ended, the revolt that became the Greek War of Independence had brought military and naval support from the Christian powers of Europe to Christians rebelling against the Sultan. In 1830, the French colonisation of Algeria had begun. It was perfectly rational for a Syrian Muslim to fear that something similar might be about to happen in his own country.

In 1860, war broke out on Mount Lebanon between Maronites and Druze. Tensions between the communities had been growing, especially as the Maronites had taken advantage of the Egyptian occupation of Greater Syria by Muhammad Ali's forces in the 1830s to better their position at the expense of the Druze. The Mountain had been a tinder box ever since. The fighting happened at a time of Maronite disunity, which is probably why it proved an unequal contest. The key towns of Zahle and Dair al-Qamar as well as at least 200 villages were sacked in what has been called a war of extermination.[5] Worse was to come, as Druze bands attacked Christian villages around Damascus, and the Christian area of the city was flooded with destitute refugees. A Muslim mob, much of which had come into the city from the countryside, worked itself up at grievances which included hostility to the *tanzimat* reforms and the ending of Muslim superiority, jealousy at the commercial success of many Christians and the widespread (and partially justified) perception that the Christians had supported the unpopular Egyptian occupation of the 1830s. These motives merged with a naked desire for loot and fear that Christians might be about to seek retribution, sparking eight days of anti-Christian riots which constituted the worst communal violence the city had seen since the Middle Ages. Although areas where Muslims and Christians lived side by side and poorer Christian areas escaped, and many Muslims sheltered Christians, the estimates of the dead vary up to ten thousand.

Europe had always been sensitive to news of the persecution of defenceless Christians by the Ottomans (although much less inclined to notice reports of Christians attacking defenceless Muslims), and the threat of Western intervention loomed large. Religion was by far the most potent marker of identity in the Ottoman Empire, and the Damascus 'events' widened the chasm, making it harder for the members of both communities to see any role for themselves save that of victims and refracting all reports of violence 'through the prism of religious identity', as Bruce Masters has put it.[6] If riots and massacres are to be weighed in a balance of victimhood, then the 'events' should be set against Christian massacres of Muslims during the Greek War of Independence and in ethnic fighting on Crete. The central Ottoman authorities realised that their only hope to avoid the loss of Greater Syria to European control was a vigorous restoration of order, which they duly carried out. The governor of Damascus was sentenced to death, scores of public hangings of Muslim looters from all sections of society took place, Ottoman soldiers who had joined in the riots faced firing squads, and tribunals for the assessment of compensation claims were set up. By the time a French expeditionary force arrived to restore order, there was no need for it to take any action.

Before the *tanzimat* reforms began to introduce the modern world to Damascus, the city had been remote and isolated compared with the relative sophistication of Aleppo. Aleppo, too, had been touched by anti-Christian riots in 1850 but the authorities had learned their lesson and this time they nipped any possibility of unrest in the bud. Henceforth, a firm hand would be the model. Over the last half century before the First World War, a degree of stability and prosperity led to Muslims and Christians in Greater Syria gradually becoming less guarded in their approach to one another.

Production of raw materials for export, such as cotton, tobacco and wheat, created many newly prosperous Muslims and they, like the Christian merchant class, had an interest in stability. Uniate and Protestant churches often used Arabic, rather than Syriac or Greek, as the language of liturgy, and some Christians even began to refer to the Sultan as 'our king' and observed that Constantinople was genuinely having some success at making positions in the Empire's bureaucracy open to all: something from which Arabic-speaking Muslims also benefited. Modern education in newly opened government schools began, and an increasing number of Muslims, too, were exposed to European ideas. A literary renaissance, now known to history as the Nahda, took place among the Arabic speakers of Greater Syria. Many of its leading lights were Christian intellectuals. Some, including members of the clergy, played a notable part in reviving the glories of classical Arabic literature. At the same time, many Christian laymen broke new ground as secular thinkers who used Arabic to convey the new thought of Europe to a widening public. They established and edited newspapers and aimed to make Arabic a language in which modern thought could be expressed as easily as it was in English or French. This wish to acquire the best from Europe, and to seek a new identity that was not based exclusively on religion and was hostile to the narrow religious identities fostered by powerful church leaders, combined easily with a new pride in their heritage as Arabs. It also fitted well with the aims of the *tanzimat* reformers, so long as it did not begin to lead down the road to separatism.

At first, these new Arab patriots thought in terms of Ottomanism (at least in public). They wished to improve the role of Arabs within the Empire, and sought official status for Arabic alongside Turkish. If they had succeeded, the Ottoman Empire might have evolved into a dual monarchy on the lines of the Austro-Hungarian Empire, or home rule might have been introduced for the Arab provinces. But Turkish national feeling was developing at the same time. In 1908, a group of officers who became known as the 'Young Turks' revolted and took power. Although they saw themselves as constitutionalists and secularists, they soon travelled down the road of Turkish national identity. This strained relations with the Arab population of the Empire (as it did with the other minorities), and shadowy secret societies which recruited their members among army officers were the beneficiaries. By the time the First World War began, calls for Arab independence had begun to find a resonance among the elite of Greater Syria.

'The nation is a soul, a spiritual principle,' wrote Renan, the French nineteenth-century religious and political thinker. '[It] consists of two things. One is the common legacy of rich memories from the past. The other is the present consensus, the will to live together . . .'[7] He knew there was a dark side to this, since he also wrote, more cynically, 'a nation is a group of people united in a mistaken view about the past and a hatred of their neighbours.'[8] A shared language and a shared religion are commonplace components of national identity, while a feeling of belonging to a homeland is an essential one. For some Maronites, such as the secularist Butrus al-Bustani who was uneasy at the threat of political and cultural domination by Western countries, Greater Syria as a whole was the homeland, but for many of his co-religionists a sense of a separate Maronite nationhood was developing. Inspired by a proud self-identification with the ancient Phoenicians who had first brought the alphabet to Europe, they considered Lebanon rightfully a part of the West. Their Catholicism reinforced this feeling, and their powerful church was as central to Maronite identity as Catholicism was to that of some peoples in Europe, such as the Poles, the Catholic Irish, the Bavarians, the Bretons and the Basques. When, during the dark days of the First World War, the Ottomans hanged suspected Arab nationalists in Damascus and Beirut, not all those who swung from the gallows were men who had dreamed of a pan-Arab state comprising all the Arabic-speaking areas of the Empire, or even of a separate state for Greater Syria. Some were partisans of an independent, Maronite Lebanon with close ties to France.

VI

Between Napoleon's landfall in Alexandria and the start of the British occupation of Egypt in 1882, the world changed at a speed that had no precedent. On the seas, sail was steadily giving way to steam and Alexandria, Beirut and other eastern Mediterranean ports were now linked to Europe by steamship services. The railway and the electric telegraph were shrinking the world beyond recognition. The industrial revolution had spread beyond the British Isles across much of Western Europe and to the United States. The countries of the Middle East were already being drawn into a new pattern of trade before the nineteenth century began. Local manufacturing was in decline as factory-produced European goods, financed by modern European credit instruments provided by new European finance houses, dominated markets. As the century progressed, the European powers were granted treaties which opened eastern markets to their traders. In the case of the Ottoman Empire, this meant that these goods were often free of internal customs duties which were still imposed on local competition.

This was the era of supreme self-confidence among Westerners, the time of 'Manifest Destiny', the *Mission Civilisatrice*, and 'the three C's: Christianity, Commerce and Civilisation' which should transform the African interior. It was the age when European blue-water colonial empires spread through Africa and much of Asia and the Pacific, while the United States and Russia expanded across vast continents. Its final decades and the years leading up to the First World War were the high noon of European imperialism, the time of jingoism, the planning of impossibly grandiose projects, and a sensation of cultural and racial superiority which produced a hubris that would meet its nemesis in the two World Wars. By 1914, European powers had replaced the Ottoman Turks as overlords all the way along the African shore of the Mediterranean, while the West had also become economically dominant except in the remotest places.

The rivalry between the European powers intensified as the century progressed. Britain's indirect rule in the Persian Gulf was put on an increasingly formal basis and was extended to include Kuwait. East of the Black Sea, Russia expanded into land that had been thought of as largely Muslim or, if Christian, as under Muslim domination. In the western Mediterranean, the French conquest of Algeria began in 1830. By 1860, the towns along the coast had predominantly European settler populations and French control had expanded into the interior. France also gained a protectorate over Tunisia in 1881 and over the greater part of Morocco in 1912 (Spain was recognised as controlling an area in the north of the country). In a striking example of a democracy mounting a war of undisguised aggression, Italy seized Libya from Turkey in 1911 and occupied most of the Turkish islands in the Aegean. Even in the Arabian desert, Britain and Turkey drew provisional frontier lines to mark their spheres of influence which cut right across the peninsula, leaving to Britain its colony of Aden and the small sultanates in the hinterland of Aden, together with Oman, Bahrain and the shaykhdoms that now make up the United Arab Emirates. Turkey's sphere covered most of what is now Saudi Arabia, Qatar and north Yemen.

The cockpit of European imperial rivalry in the Arab world was Egypt. The man put in by Britain to sort out the country's treasury, Evelyn Baring, later Earl of Cromer, was determined, efficient and confident. By the early 1890s he had restored the country's finances. Because of this, and his efforts in public works, irrigation and administration, he did much good. Unfortunately, however, there was another side to his role and that of Britain which made the contradictions plain. Britain gradually decided it wanted to stay in Egypt for strategic reasons and to keep out France and other European powers. However, once the purpose for which Britain had come there had been achieved, what need was there for the occupation – which was financed by the Egyptian treasury – to continue?

France did its best to create mischief for Britain in Egypt. A good example was the Fashoda incident in 1898. A British-led army, acting on behalf of Egypt, reconquered the Sudan which had been overrun by an indigenous religious movement led by the Mahdi. As it penetrated south, it encountered a small force which had advanced out of the French colonies to the west and claimed the area for France. One of France's motives was to use its claim as a bargaining chip to pressurise Britain into withdrawal from Egypt. The ploy failed, but in 1904 Britain and France agreed to a secret trade-off which left Britain control of Egypt in return for giving France a free hand in Morocco.

Sudan rubbed salt into the wound in the relationship between Britain and Egypt. Two-thirds of the troops in the reconquest had been Egyptian, and they suffered more than two-thirds of the casualties. Likewise two-thirds of the financial costs were borne by the Egyptian government, which was faced with paying the bills for the Sudan for years to come. To Egyptian nationalists, it was obvious that Britain's motive was to add the Sudan to its empire, and to take control of what rightfully belonged to Egypt.

At the turn of the twentieth century there were three main sources of power in Egypt which were to remain in varying forms until after the Second World War. The first was the British Agency, later High Commission and then Embassy, whose grip on the country's government was still tending to increase as the nineteenth century drew to a close. Cromer and many other British officials saw themselves as the true friends of the Egyptian *fellahin* or peasantry, whose lives benefited from the rationalised tax system as well as the improved irrigation and drainage which they introduced. They believed they were the defenders of the *fellahin* against extortion, corruption and a state of virtual slavery.

The second source of power was the Khedive and those around him, still largely the old Turkish-Mamluk aristocracy, in fact precisely that landowning class that Cromer and his colleagues saw as the cause of the peasantry's woes. Here there was another contradiction, since the task of Cromer and his colleagues was meant to be to prepare Egypt to be returned to its legitimate government – in other words, to the Khedive.

The third source could be called public opinion: the still embryonic nationalist movement which included constitutionalists and liberals as well as those who still looked to the Sultan-Caliph in Turkey as the legitimate source of authority, and who were known as pan-Islamists. In the late nineteenth century these different groups were still weak. Both the British and Khedivial authorities were essentially unsympathetic to them all except when it suited their purposes, but public opinion became steadily more important as time went on. In a remark that was by no means untypical and is more revealing about the mindset of the writer than of the people he was writing about, Kitchener, the British general who had reconquered the Sudan and performed Cromer's role in Cairo in the run-up to the First World War, wrote in 1912 that 'The Egyptians are not a nation ... They are a fortuitous agglomeration of miscellaneous and hybrid elements.'[9]

Discontent at the British role grew. A *cause célèbre* was provided in 1906 when a party of British officers went pigeon shooting in the village of Dinshaway in the Delta, unaware of or indifferent to the fact that the birds were an important part of the village's food supply. A *fellah* woman was shot by accident. Violence followed in which two of the officers were injured. One of them died later of heat stroke. A court composed of Egyptian judges was rapidly convened. Four *fellahin* were sentenced to death, another four to life imprisonment, and a further seventeen to lesser terms of imprisonment and floggings. The sentences were carried out promptly and without any appeals.

The Dinshaway incident led to parliamentary criticism in London and to the resignation of Cromer, whose health was declining. In his farewell speech in Cairo, he warned strongly against the dangers of introducing parliamentary democracy in Egypt and asserted that British rule should continue for the foreseeable future. Although a Legislative Council and General Assembly had been instituted by the British authorities soon after the occupation began, their powers were so small – the Legislative Council could not even initiate legislation – that the government could effectively ignore them, particularly as many of their members were appointed rather than elected.

Yet by now Egyptian nationalist sentiment was gaining a hold on the educated classes. After the Dinshaway incident, it united with popular feeling. The incident has parallels with the much bloodier Amritsar massacre in India in 1919 in joining urban intellectuals and peasants together in their anger and strengthening nationalist sentiment. Competing brands of Egyptian nationalism now existed and were represented by political parties. These varied from those which saw Egypt progressing in stages to complete independence and a modern constitution to more firebrand versions. The constitutionalists and liberals were a tiny minority of intellectuals who could not control the nationalist emotions aroused in the masses. These often expressed themselves in pan-Islamic terms: support for Turkey when it was at war with European states, and even to some extent in a dispute over the frontier between Ottoman Greater Syria and Egypt itself. There was also emerging a common 'Eastern' identity which had nothing to do with either a territorial-based nationalism or pan-Islamism. This was a form of solidarity which would one day evolve into the anti-colonial movement, and for the time being was able to take delight at Russia's humiliation by Japan in the Russo-Japanese War of 1904-05.

The elected politicians lacked the confidence to confront the government, something that became apparent when they hesitated to oppose proposals to limit press freedom which were backed by the Khedive and the British Agency. Divisions in society prevented the nationalist movement from developing the moral authority which it needed if it was to succeed. The wealthier classes shied away from supporting what they feared would degenerate into mob rule, while Copts were alienated and frightened by the trend to articulate nationalism in terms of Islam. But things would change. When the First World War had ended, Britain would discover that Egypt had become a very different place from the country it had first occupied in 1882.

VII

The spread of Western ideas such as nationalism and constitutionalism in Egypt was a gradual process, as it was in other Arab countries. Before they could be adopted, they needed to be measured critically against local values, especially those of Islam. Yet by 1914, there had been changes to Egyptian intellectual life that could never be reversed.

The Egyptians sent to study in Europe during the reign of Muhammad Ali included perceptive observers with enquiring minds. Rifa'a al-Tahtawi, who accompanied a party as their imam, praised the literate, freethinking Parisians for their openness to new ideas as well as the conviction with which they expressed their views. He was a religious shaykh from the Azhar, Egypt's ancient seat of Islamic scholarship which dated from the Fatimid era. It was an institution noted for its rigidity and rote learning, but had offered almost the only intellectual training available for ordinary Egyptian Muslims. Tahtawi showed no hint of sensing any looming danger in European political ambitions in the Middle East, even though he praised the Algerians who resisted France as heroes. He became a pioneer of Western education, including for girls. His main work was translating French technical works and literature, but he also encouraged the printing of classical Arabic works to make them accessible to a wider audience. He seems to have found no contradiction between taking what he passionately felt was beneficial from the West, and remaining secure in his own heritage.

His time in Paris coincided with the excitement caused by the great advances in Egyptology made as a result of Champollion deciphering the hieroglyphs, and he returned to Egypt fired with enthusiasm for the past of his native land and its future destiny. Although Mamluk histories had included descriptions of the ancient Egyptian monuments about which Egyptians had always been intensely curious, it was Tahtawi who formulated pride in the history and continuity of Egyptian civilisation. He felt that Egyptians had been essentially the same people since the days of the Pharoahs and that their ancestral values had been degraded by Mamluk misrule. His pride extended equally to the heritage of Islam and the Arabs, and he may have been the first Arabic-speaking intellectual to argue that modern European science was a development of the achievements of medieval scientists in the Middle Ages who wrote in Arabic.[10]

It was also Tahtawi, more than anyone, who introduced the ideas of the Enlightenment to Egypt. Some of these fitted naturally into a Muslim framework: man is a social being, man's fulfilment lies in society, and society should be governed by justice which a ruler is responsible to ensure. Others were new: laws should reflect the circumstances of the time and be adapted accordingly. There should be active participation in government by the people, which requires the institution of systematic education, including education in politics.

Yet the reasoning which brought Tahtawi to these daring thoughts was still traditional. He saw Sharia and Ottoman law as circumscribing the unfettered power of the ruler, and used Montesquieu's doctrine of the separation of powers to support this contention. Sharia needed to cope with the circumstances of the modern world. A wise ruler would consult with doctors, engineers and scientists who had state of the art knowledge, as well as the specialists on Sharia who themselves needed and deserved a modern education. Although he was concerned that Sharia should be observed, he believed it should be informed by conceptions of the public benefit or common good, and interpreted in a way favourable to material progress.[11] His concept of love of country involved all who lived there: non-Muslims as well as Muslims. This thought was new in a Muslim context, and provided a kernel for secular nationalism which would show the first signs of germination in Egypt within years of his death in 1873.

Nationalism developed slowly. Understandably, it was among those most exposed to Western ideas that nationalist ideas took root. As we have seen, in the Arabic-speaking provinces of the Ottoman Empire many early nationalists were Christian. In the case of Egypt, one of the first was a Jew.

Ya'qoub Sanu', also known as James Sanua, was born in Cairo in 1839 and sent to Italy to study as a young man. He fell under the spell of both nationalism and the theatre while in Europe, and achieved fame in Cairo as a pioneer writer and producer of plays in colloquial Egyptian Arabic. Comedy was his stock in trade, although at one stage he also produced plays with themes such as love of country, freedom and independence. Using Moliere as one of his inspirations, Sanu' produced successful operettas and comedies that satirised Egyptian society. His targets included religious hypocrisy (he produced a Muslim adaptation of *Tartuffe*), gullibility, the unseemliness of old men marrying young girls, the aping of Western ways by the emerging middle class (especially by women), and the practice of polygamy among the wealthy. This may have lost him the patronage of the Khedive Ismail, who was the last ruler of Egypt to maintain a harem. As well as falling out with the Khedive, he upset the increasingly powerful British representatives in Egypt. He also set up a political salon where liberal ideas were debated and some army officers, including Urabi Pasha, attended meetings.[12]

When he was in the womb, his mother had feared a miscarriage and sought the prayers of a Muslim shaykh. Very unusually for a Jew (and against his father's wishes), he was raised learning the Qur'an as well as the Hebrew scriptures. Although he remained a Jew and was a fierce opponent of sectarianism, he used what we would now call Islamist rhetoric to appeal to peasants, army officers and religious scholars to unite against the Khedive, as well as to oppose Britain and the foreign communities, which he saw as milking Egypt. Sanu' turned his versatile talents to satirical journalism, using his ability to write Arabic in registers which resonated at every level of the language so as to catch the attention of ordinary people. His articles and sketches excoriated Britain and the Khedive in a way that captured the popular mood. This led to his exile to Paris in 1877, from where he continued to publish an Arabic newspaper which poured invective on the same targets. He clearly had contacts with the young officers who supported Urabi,[13] and his paper seems to have been distributed among Urabi's troops in 1882.[14]

At the same time, another reaction appeared among Egyptians as they found their country increasingly pressurised by foreign interests. It was natural for Muslims everywhere to feel solidarity for each other and to fight alongside fellow Muslims who were under attack by an officially Christian, colonial power. The advocates of pan-Islamism, like the peripatetic Jamal-al-Din al-Afghani, who was probably of Iranian or Afghani Shi'ite origin but spent most of the 1870s in Egypt, pointed out that there was no reason why Christian states should be inherently superior. Afghani saw Muslim divisions and decay as among the reasons for Western success and attributed a very large part of the blame to Muslim rulers themselves. Although he was not a constitutionalist by principle, he accepted that constitutions would be a good way to rein in their despotic powers and believed in the right of revolt against an unjust ruler. He saw the theatre as a way of awakening political consciousness among the Egyptian people, and encouraged Ya'qoub Sanu' in his activities. Ultimately Westerners had only taken advantage of weakness which Muslims should never have allowed to arise in the first place. What was needed was unity among Muslims, the setting aside of differences and the reform of social morality.

His goal was not a universal Muslim state. He believed that Muslim rulers should subordinate their own ambitions and privileges to the greater good of Islam by cooperating for the sake of the community, the *Umma*. He did not envisage a political function for a universal caliphate. If there was to be a caliphate, he saw it as having a spiritual role or being essentially a title of honour. He wanted rulers to serve Islam, not Islam to be used by them to further their own ambitions.

A key concept for Afghani and other reformers was social solidarity, which he recognised could stem from the bonds of a common religion or a natural relationship such as the use of the same language. He observed that in Europe the bonds of national solidarity are assumed to be good in themselves – a sentiment to which he also subscribed – and to lead to progress, whilst religious bonds were deemed always to lead to fanaticism. His answer was that this might well apply to Christianity. In Islam, on the other hand, he maintained that religious fanaticism had been rare while the kind of solidarity which is essential for progress was inherent to it.

Afghani's ideas for the reform of Islam were the beginning of a process that has continued to this day, and which was not confined to those who felt their pan-Islamic identity as Muslims should be deeper than their national one. The encounter with Western ideas and power, coupled with the honest admission that all was far from well in the house of Islam itself, led to much soul searching. What were the essential principles of Islam which must not be compromised? And how could European knowledge and techniques benefit Muslim peoples? The traditional schools which offered a rigid education with an emphasis on rote learning did not prepare their students for a modern world, while the new elite was educated in modern schools, many of which were foreign and even run by Christian missionaries. They therefore risked losing touch with their roots. He maintained that Islam now needed its Martin Luther. The door of *ijtihad*, the ability for a respected jurist to use independent reasoning to reinterpret Sharia in the light of new circumstances and discoveries, should be reopened, after having been closed since the great classical law schools of Sunni Islam were formulated in the eighth and ninth centuries.

Afghani's most influential disciple was Muhammad Abduh, the reformer who became chief mufti of Egypt in 1899. The starting point of his thought was the same perception of the decay which had occurred in the Muslim world. He could be scathing about the state of religious teaching. 'If I have a portion of true knowledge', he once said, 'I got it through ten years of sweeping the dirt of the Azhar from my brain, and to this day it is not as clean as I would like.'[15] The question he pondered was how to live in the modern world while remaining a good Muslim. If a way could not be found to do this, he wrote, there was a risk that the backwardness and ignorance of the religious scholars would cause Islam to be seen 'as a kind of *thobe* [an old-fashioned robe which was being discarded by educated Egyptians in favour of Western dress] in which it is embarrassing to appear'.[16] The gap between traditional Islam and the modern world, between those who had had an old-style education and those being educated in the new way, had to be bridged.

He made use of the old and fundamental distinction between acts of worship (*al-'ibaadaat*) and behaviour towards others (*al-mu'aamalat*). Whilst revelation lays down rules about how God wants to be worshipped, Abduh considered that it frequently only sets out general principles with regard to behaviour. These principles were the field for the modern Muslim jurist, who could reopen the door of *ijtihad* and at the same time reunite what was best in the different law schools. This was essential. Islam, by its very nature, had to be rational, and the use of the principle of *maslaha*, the rule that revelation should be interpreted in the way most conducive to the promotion of human welfare, should inform the literal text.[17] It had generally been assumed that the Qur'an, if interpreted literally, forbade the taking of interest on a loan irrespective of whether the rate was unconscionable and extortionate or not. Abduh, while fiercely condemning the rates of interest charged by the banks of his day, gave an opinion that there were cases in which interest could be justified on social grounds.[18]

For Muhammad Abduh, Islam was in its essence a principle which guided the believers so that they could distinguish what was good from what was bad. Islam ought, therefore, to produce a virtuous society that was confident, happy and prosperous. Then it would both respect itself and be respected by others. He believed such a society had existed in the golden age of the religion's forefathers, the *salaf*, who for him did not stop with the generations that had known the Prophet but included the great thinkers and systematisers of the Abbasid era. The reasons why this society had decayed included the adoption of non-Muslim ways by some and, at the other extreme, an over-rigid adherence to the letter of the religious law by others. He placed the blame for both tendencies at the door of the Turkish rulers of Egypt across the centuries.

Yet at the same time as Muhammad Abduh and others debated how to live as Muslims in the modern world, an unprecedented change in the intellectual life in a predominantly Muslim, Arabic-speaking country was happening. As the nineteenth century approached its end, debates among educated Egyptians were increasingly couched in Western terms. Concepts which had originally been Muslim subtly enlarged the senses in which they could be used to include new ideas introduced from Europe. Islam itself could even become identical with 'civilisation and activity, the norms of nineteenth-century social thought'.[19]

For some thinkers this subtly went from arguing that modern civilisation was compatible with Islam to suggesting that Islam was compatible with modern civilisation. This was an imperceptible shift of emphasis that betrayed a fundamental change of mindset. Sometimes what Albert Hourani called 'the Islamic scaffolding' collapsed. Arguments which had started with appeals to the right interpretation of the Qur'an and Sunna were continued in the new language of the nineteenth century and concepts like freedom, progress and civilisation.[20]

VIII

Napoleon had been worried that the soldiers he brought to Egypt would be perceived as Crusaders. Perhaps he need not have been troubled about this. At the time of his invasion, no word existed for 'Crusade' or 'Crusader' in Arabic, and Arabic-speaking intellectuals only learned these terms when, later in the nineteenth century, they first read Western histories of the Crusades which were translated into Arabic.

Before then, the Crusaders had just been thought of as *ifranj*, 'Franks', a word that was still widely used for a Western European – much in the way that Arabs and Muslims had been referred to as 'Moors' or 'Turks' in English. But once modern Arabs began to discover the Crusades through the prism of European scholarship, which was often written from the perspective of a Western nation with imperialist ambitions in the Middle East such as France, they learned of horrors which had not been recorded in the Arabic chronicles – such as the fact that starving Crusaders resorted to cannibalism after the fall of Ma'arrat Nu'man and ate the bodies of the Muslim slain. They also saw sinister parallels with the expansion of Europe across the Mediterranean in their own day.

How valid such parallels are is highly debateable, but it was natural for them to have an emotional resonance. The Ottoman Sultan Abdul Hamid II made full use of them as the final decades of the nineteenth century turned into the first years of the twentieth, claiming time and again that his Empire was the victim of a crusade by the European powers. Some Europeans acted in ways that suggested there might indeed be something in his rhetoric. In France, for instance, reimagined memories of the Crusades helped stir popular enthusiasm for the conquest of Algeria and later ventures in Greater Syria.

This transformation for Arabic speakers in the meaning of 'crusade' from a specific idea related to a long-vanished period of history into a terrifying one that fills the listener with dread and drags ancestral terrors up from the subconscious had its mirror image in Western perceptions of Islam as the violent creed of jihad. As explained in Chapter 2, jihad literally means 'expenditure of effort' or 'struggle', and when used as a religious term is a closely defined concept. It firmly forbids attacks on civilians. But jihad first appeared as a loan word in English at more or less the same time as a translation of 'crusade' was first appearing in Arabic. According to the *Oxford English Dictionary*, its earliest recorded use was in 1869, referring to

Muslim 'Holy War' preached in India. It rapidly entered figurative language and by 1886 an English newspaper was speaking of a jihad against the increasing numbers of deer in the New Forest. In English, it soon acquired overtones of fanaticism which are completely absent from the original Arabic, but which *salibi*, the modern Arabic word for crusader, certainly carries. Today, when speakers of English or another European language hear the word jihad, they are likely to be struck by a feeling of vague dread. The same applies to a modern Arabic speaker when he or she hears the word 'crusade'.

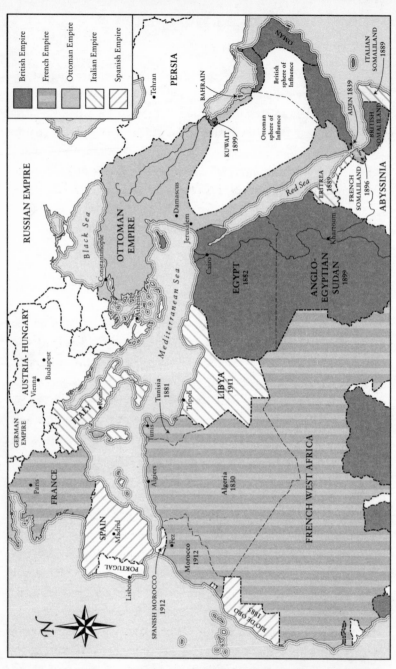

THE ARAB WORLD IN 1914
(DATES REFER TO YEAR OF ESTABLISHMENT OF EUROPEAN CONTROL)

CHAPTER FOUR

SHARING AN INDIGESTIBLE CAKE

I

The First World War was triggered when a Serb nationalist in Bosnia assassinated the heir to the Austro-Hungarian throne. This spark lit a fire in a European house crammed with highly combustible materials. With the hindsight of a century, we look back at the ensuing slaughter which included 'half the seed of Europe' and scratch our heads at how it ever started. The tragedy that unfolded had its own momentum which locked the opposing alliances in a combat to the death as the war took its juggernaut path. Today it seems sadly ironic that it was once known in Britain as 'The Great War for Civilisation'.[1]

The 1904 arrangement between Britain and France under which France allowed Britain a free hand in Egypt and the Sudan, while Britain gave the same to France in Morocco, was just a minor part of the agreement that had brought the two colonial rivals together to oppose imperial Germany. In the modern West this arrangement is an almost forgotten detail of the great alliance between Europe's two leading democracies, the Entente Cordiale. Yet it is hardly surprising that when war did break out in Europe, and Britain and France were fighting 'the tyranny of the Hun', their cause struck few chords among the peoples of the Arabic-speaking world. As was seen in the last chapter, virtually the whole of the Arab world was under the full or partial control of non-Arabs. In the Ottoman provinces, these were now the Young Turks who were imbued with a spirit of Turkish nationalism. In Egypt, the Sudan and much of the coastline of the Arabian Peninsula the dominant power was Britain. In North Africa it was France, save for Libya which was under Italy and small areas of Morocco which were under Spain. War came to the Middle East when Ottoman Turkey joined the side of Germany.

II

Britain, France and their ally Czarist Russia had ambitions in the Ottoman Empire which they wished to be reflected in the final peace settlement. When Russia withdrew from the war in 1917 after the October Revolution, it looked for a brief moment as though France and Britain would be left to agree on how to divide the Empire.

Britain had long accepted France as protector of the Maronite Christians of Mount Lebanon. France also wanted the area covered by the modern state of Syria, Mosul and a sizeable chunk of modern Turkey. For its part, Britain wanted control of a land route from the Egyptian border to the shores of the Persian Gulf, encompassing what is now Israel, the Palestinian territories, Jordan and the south-ern parts of Iraq. Arrangements between Britain and France were set out in the secret Sykes-Picot agreement of 1916.

Britain had two other debts to pay. It had already promised that the people of the Arabic-speaking Ottoman provinces would have independence if they joined the Allies against the Turks. This had led the semi-independent ruler of the Hejaz, the Sharif Hussein of Mecca, to cast in his lot with the Allies in 1916 and raise the standard of the Arab Revolt which was taken into Greater Syria by his son, Prince Faisal, with British help. The promises made to Hussein were inconsistent with the slightly later Sykes-Picot agreement with France. In the Western world, too, Britain had made a promise. This was the carefully worded Balfour Declaration in November 1917 which gave British support for 'a national home for the Jewish people' in Palestine.

Historians still discuss the extent of the commitments Britain made to the Sharif Hussein, the degree of inconsistency between these and the secret agreement with France, and precisely what the Balfour Declaration meant. In the context of the Middle East today, these are highly charged questions, as are many aspects of the historical record itself such as the extent of the military contribution the Arab Revolt made to the Allied cause.

The position is murkier because the various agencies of the British government frequently had different and even conflicting objectives, and there was often a lack of clarity of aims. Moreover, the holders of key cabinet posts had sometimes changed at the time when different pledges or 'engagements', as they were often called, were made. Scope for misunderstanding was immense, and it is often hard to tell where this ended and bad faith and deception began. When British officials spoke of Arabs achieving 'independence', they frequently meant limited independence similar to that then enjoyed by Bahrain, Kuwait and the emirates that now make up the UAE. These tiny states had delegated the conduct of their foreign affairs to Britain by treaty and relied on Britain for their external defence. Mutual trust was in danger of evaporating completely when the Russian Bolsheviks made public the Sykes-Picot agreement. This happened as Britain was issuing the Balfour Declaration with a fanfare to attract Jewish support all over the world.

The inconsistency of the engagements made by Britain under the stress of wartime conditions was admitted in a rather sheepish statement which Viscount Grey, who had been foreign minister at the time of the pledges to the Sharif Hussein, made in a speech in Parliament in March 1923:

I am sure that we cannot redeem our honour by covering up our engagements and pretending there is no inconsistency, if there really is inconsistency . . . I think we are placed in considerable difficulty by the Balfour Declaration itself . . . It promised a Zionist home without prejudice to the civil and religious rights of the population of Palestine. A Zionist home, my Lords, undoubtedly means or implies a Zionist Government over the district in which the home is placed, and if 93 per cent of the population are Arabs, I do not see how you can establish other than an Arab Government without prejudice to their civil rights . . . I do see that the situation is an exceedingly difficult one, when it is compared with the pledges which undoubtedly were given to the Arabs. It would be very desirable, from the point of view of honour, that all these various pledges should be set side by side, and then, I think, the most honourable thing to do would be to look at them fairly, see what inconsistencies there are between them, and, having regard to the nature of each pledge and the date at which it was given, with all the facts before us, consider what is the fair thing to be done.[2]

The latter stages of the war also saw the arrival of a potential new player, the United States. This was not quite America's first encounter with the Arabic-speaking world. Within a few years of independence, the young US navy had mounted retaliatory attacks along the coast of North Africa after pirates attacked American shipping. American marines had played a minor role at Alexandria in 1882, and American battleships had briefly appeared off the coast of Morocco in 1904 during a diplomatic incident when a man believed to be a US citizen was held to ransom by a tribe. Like their European counterparts, and frequently in advance of them, American missionaries had been active in the region for decades, offering modern education and healthcare in areas where little or none was provided.

The Arabic-speaking peoples had no reason to distrust the USA. Woodrow Wilson, the US President, spoke of the fate of the territories of the defeated Central Powers in terms of the self-determination of peoples. Many felt that a great power which might be worthy of trust had appeared in the region. In January 1918, he made a speech to the combined US Senate and House of Representatives in which he proposed Fourteen Points to provide a basis for the negotiation of peace treaties to bring the conflict to an end. Although America had never declared war on Turkey, Point 12 dealt with the Ottoman Empire and included the following: '[The non-Turkish] nationalities which are now under Turkish rule should be assured an undoubted security of life and an absolutely unmolested opportunity of autonomous development.'[3]

This was clearly inconsistent with the Anglo-French plan to partition the Arabic-speaking areas of the Turkish Empire. Needing to reassure the Arabs, Britain and France felt obliged to commit themselves to a similar approach. In the Anglo-French Declaration of 7 November 1918 they announced:

> The object aimed at by France and Great Britain in prosecuting in the East the War let loose by the ambition of Germany is the complete and definite emancipation of the peoples so long oppressed by the Turks and the establishment of national governments and administrations deriving their authority from the initiative and free choice of the indigenous populations.[4]

In theory, the new conception of self-determination had triumphed, and would now be embodied in the system of League of Nations Mandates. The League was the organisation of states established in the aftermath of the war with the intention of creating a new international order that would reduce the risk of future wars. It was based on another of President Wilson's Fourteen Points, but in the event Wilson fell from power and the United States decided not to join. A Mandate was a form of trusteeship granted to one or other of the members of the League to administer a former German or Turkish territory in the interests of its people and prepare it for independence. As Article 22 of the Covenant of the League of Nations put it:

To those colonies and territories which as a consequence of the late war have ceased to be under the sovereignty of States which formerly governed them and which are inhabited by peoples not yet able to stand by themselves under the strenuous conditions of the modern world, there should be applied the principle that the wellbeing and development of such peoples form a sacred trust of civilisation . . . The character of the mandate must differ according to the stage of development of the people, the geographical situation of the territory, its economic conditions and other similar circumstances . . .

It also stated specifically with regard to the former Turkish territories:

Certain communities formerly belonging to the Turkish Empire have reached a stage of development where their existence as independent nations can be provisionally recognised subject to the rendering of administrative advice and assistance by a Mandatory until such time as they are able to stand alone. The wishes of those communities must be a principal consideration in the selection of the Mandatory.[5]

There were different classes of Mandate, Class A being for those territories which were considered to be nearest to effective independence. All the predominantly Arabic-speaking Turkish provinces were placed in this category and became Mandates under Britain or France.

After some haggling, the boundaries between the territories which came under Mandates were fixed. These provide many of the frontiers of Middle Eastern states today. The modern states of Syria and Lebanon fell under French Mandate, Iraq and Palestine (all the land between the Mediterranean coast and the River Jordan as well as what is now the modern state of Jordan on the river's east bank) fell to Britain. The Mandate for Palestine incorporated the commitment Britain had made in the Balfour Declaration to facilitate a Jewish national home in the territory west of the River Jordan.

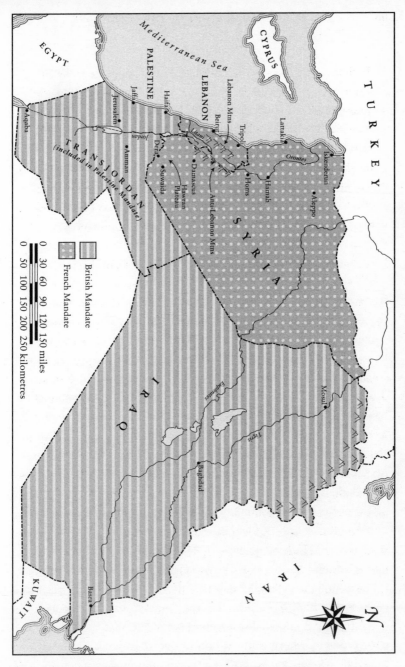

THE LEAGUE OF NATIONS MANDATES
FOR THE ARABIC-SPEAKING OTTOMAN PROVINCES

III

The division of the predominantly Arabic-speaking Ottoman provinces into British and French Mandates was always going to be unsatisfactory. Greater Syria and Iraq contained steppes, deserts and oases, river valleys with swamps and cultivated areas, mountain ranges with abundant rainfall and forests, and green coastal plains along the shore of the Mediterranean. There were strong local identities in many places as well as differences between people which had not yet crystallised into feelings of a separate consciousness, and there was no inevitability that in every case they would do so.

As elsewhere in the former Ottoman lands, towns and villages frequently belonged to a different ethnic or religious group from the community next door, while the cities contained quarters or neighbourhoods where each community could live according to its own customs and laws, and where those who came in from the countryside could make themselves at home among their own kind. There were pockets of Armenians, Turks, Circassians (Muslims who had fled or been driven out when the Russians conquered the lands to the north and east of the Black Sea) and Syriac speakers, while some Arabic speakers were left in Turkey. There were also semi-nomadic tribes with seasonal migration patterns which the new boundaries ignored.

By far the most substantial non-Arab ethnic group in these lands were the Kurds, most of whom were Sunni Muslim although there were also Shi'ite and some non-Muslim Kurds, including Jews, Christians and Yezidis. The life of most Kurdish tribes was centred on transhumance, the taking of their flocks from low-lying pastures up into the high mountains for the summer after the snow had melted. They dominated a large mountainous area spreading over what is now northern Iraq and south-eastern Turkey, and extending into Iran. There were also substantial communities in the plains of north-eastern Syria. Cities such as Damascus and Baghdad, contained large numbers of Kurds, many of whom were now Arabic-speaking. Because the Ottoman Empire categorised its subjects according to their religion, not their ethnic group, the Kurds had tended to be politically invisible. This was not helped by the fact that the Kurdish language was still unwritten and divided into very different dialects, or by the fact that Kurds were famed for their tribal divisions and disunity as well as their rebellious nature. The notables of the cities had always looked down on them as wild and unruly, but they were known to make good soldiers. Their leaders tended to be dervish holy men or the heads of tribal confederations who were often illiterate in both Arabic and Turkish. Half-hearted proposals for a Kurdish autonomous region were discussed at peace conferences. Ultimately, nothing came of them but the Kurds had their own culture and sense of identity which would not disappear.

The boundaries of the Mandates were drawn to meet the wishes of Britain and France. They disregarded existing administrative boundaries and did not necessarily reflect either physical or human geography. Thus, the Jezirah, the large 'island' between the Tigris and Euphrates before their courses run close to each other in central Iraq, was divided between the French Mandate of Syria and the British Mandate of Iraq, introducing an international frontier where none had existed. Perhaps most significantly, the boundaries did not always reflect ethnic divisions.

So-called natural frontiers, like the Jordan and Yarmouk rivers, could be misleading to bureaucrats in London or Paris who thought they would provide excellent boundaries for the British Mandate of Palestine and the French Mandate of Syria and Lebanon. This might look neat on a map, but there was often no intrinsic difference between the peoples who lived on either side of them. It was almost as absurd as a foreign power deciding the Thames formed a sensible natural boundary along which to partition southern England, or the Potomac to partition the USA. The political fragmentation caused by the Mandate system now made it impossible to go by rail from the Palestinian ports of Jaffa or Haifa to Iraq, or even to Amman, without changing trains in French-controlled territory. The railway from Aleppo to Mosul and Baghdad was chosen to demarcate a substantial section of the frontier between Turkey and the French Mandate of Syria, making it vulnerable to political uncertainties and threatening secure communications between Syria and Iraq. Once the Mandates were established, border controls and custom posts, which were completely arbitrary to the people of the territories, cemented the partition that had been imposed.

The armistice had left an 'Arab government' in loose and provisional control of Damascus and Aleppo, as well as most of the rest of the modern state of Syria, all of modern Jordan and much of modern Lebanon. It was headed by Prince Faisal, the son of the Sharif of Mecca, who proclaimed himself king in Damascus. Along the coast, Britain was in effective control of the territory west of the Jordan, while France controlled Beirut and the coastal districts of Lebanon as well as some areas to the north. Legally, all this was still occupied Turkish territory. Its future would depend on the peace treaty that was still to be agreed. There was a struggle for control on the ground, as French emissaries went inland and tried to persuade people, especially Christians, to back French rule, while Faisal's followers sent their own officials to Beirut and Palestine to seek local endorsements.

Something in the nature of a constitutional convention was held at Damascus in the summer of 1919. A Congress was selected by the surviving electors of the Ottoman parliament from Greater Syria. It claimed to represent Muslims, Christians and Jews and demanded absolute independence for Greater Syria as a single state. It prepared a programme that called for this state to be 'a democratic civil constitutional monarchy on broad decentralisation principles, safeguarding the rights of minorities'. If, for whatever reason, the great powers were not willing to concede this claim, then the Congress insisted that the country should be retained as a unity.

French claims were dismissed. If there had to be a Mandatory to supervise the country as it progressed to independence, then its preferred choice was the United States of America.

It also specifically rejected Zionist claims:

> We oppose the pretensions of the Zionists to create a Jewish commonwealth in the southern part of Syria, known as Palestine, and oppose Zionist migration to any part of our country; for we do not acknowledge their title, but consider them a grave peril to our people from the national, economical and political points of view. Our Jewish compatriots shall enjoy our common rights and assume the common responsibilities.[6]

Of course, questions can be raised about how much support Faisal actually possessed as the constitutional monarch of a Greater Syria which the Congress hoped to establish. Today, Syrian schoolchildren are taught that he had little or none, but that is a writing of history for a political purpose. What is certain is that the Congress could have been the start of a process of political self-determination for the people of Greater Syria. To the north, in the centre of the Turkish heartland of Anatolia, surviving deputies of the Ottoman parliament fled British-occupied Constantinople and congregated in a conference in Ankara, which was a crucial step on the road to the establishment of the Turkish republic and to ending the proposal by the victors in the war to partition Anatolia.

There were two crucial differences between the congresses in Ankara and Damascus. The Turkish conference had a strong and undisputed leader, Kemal Ataturk, the war hero who had won the Gallipoli campaign and now rallied the Turkish nation behind him. He also had the still very substantial remnants of the professional and battle-hardened Ottoman army to back up his claims. Faisal's authority and military resources were very limited by comparison. He therefore could not face down the Allies as Ataturk was to do.

Ataturk and his congress in Ankara saved what remained of Turkey from dismemberment. The Damascus Congress failed to save Greater Syria from the same fate. Britain and France had taken their decision and had the strength to implement their wishes in Syria, if not in Turkey. Britain wanted its Mandate over Palestine with the Balfour Declaration intact as well as Iraq and its land route to India. France wanted its share, too.

IV

Britain and France had sliced up the cake and shared it out, but it was indigestible. France took control of what are now the states of Lebanon and Syria. Faisal left, realising the futility of resistance and the prudence of not antagonising the Allies, but his defence minister, Yusuf al-Azma, insisted on confronting the French. At the battle of Maysaloun, the cavalry of the small, untrained and uncoordinated Syrian army fought with the gallantry of those who insist on dying for the sake of honour. The country was then occupied and split into a number of statelets. One was set up for the Lebanese Maronites, another for the Druze centred on the Hawran plateau around Suweida south-east of Damascus, and a third for the Alawis based on Lattakia and its mountainous hinterland. Yet another centred on Antakya where the population contained a large Turkish element. This was eventually ceded to Turkey as an inducement to support France against Hitler, but in breach of the terms of the Mandate.

This conception of statelets was flawed, because each contained large numbers of people who did not belong to the supposedly dominant group for which it had been created. The statelets were designed to separate the population on ethnic and sectarian lines as much as possible: a policy of divide and rule that conflicted with France's supposed sacred trust to prepare the country for independence. If the policy had succeeded, it would have had the effect of cutting

Syria's hinterland, including the great cities of Damascus, Aleppo and Homs, off from the sea, and might have been successful in forcing the country to need a permanent French presence.

Only one of the statelets, Lebanon, eventually became independent. The Maronite heartland on Mount Lebanon had been turned into an autonomous province under a Christian governor after the massacres of 1860, but it was not a naturally prosperous area or a viable independent state and in any case many Maronites lived outside its territory. Other areas were therefore added: the adjoining majority Druze areas in the mountains, Beirut and the Sunni port of Tripoli in the north, and the region around Tyre and Sidon in the south as well as the Beqa' valley, which had poor Shi'ite populations. On a physical map, Lebanon looks a compact little country, but this is deceptive. The frontier drawn with the rest of Syria was not always logical in terms of human geography. According to the 1931 census (the only one carried out) Maronites only made up 29 per cent of the total population of the Lebanese statelet while members of all the Christian sects when added together only came to 52 per cent. The Lebanese statelet deprived Syria of its remaining principal ports, after Haifa and Jaffa were lost to the British Mandate of Palestine.[7] It was very difficult for Syria to reconcile itself to the separation of Lebanon, which was also against the wishes of many Lebanese. At the root of the separation were the competing visions of a specifically Maronite identity, which saw Lebanon as essentially European and therefore specifically not 'Arab', and the Arab identity which was opposed to this, and to which most Lebanese Muslims and Druze, as well as Orthodox Christians, subscribed. The two countries would only agree to establish normal diplomatic relations in 2008.

The separation also stored up trouble for the future of the Lebanese themselves. The French introduced a constitution based on 'confessionalism', under which political power was intended to be divided between the different sects on a theoretically proportionate basis. As the sects increased naturally (and emigrated) at different rates, it was very difficult to implement in a way that was fair to all – which arguably was never the real intention as Lebanon was intended to be a predominantly 'Christian' state. Confessionalism had the effect of entrenching religious differences in the political life of the country in a dangerous way.

France encountered difficulties in Syria right from the start, but the great uprising in 1925 came as a complete surprise. What began as a local rebellion among the Druze of the remote Hawran plateau in the south turned into a revolt that shook the Mandate to its core. The French had overlooked the fact that their Druze statelet did not reflect either economic or wider cultural realities, and that the Druze farmers of the Hawran had strong links with Sunni merchants in Damascus to whom they sold their corn. Snubs to Druze leaders and unpopular policies, such as conscripting villagers to build roads, led to discontent which spilled over into premeditated and coordinated rebellion when demands were not met.

Some local Muslim and Christian villages joined the Druze, and nationalists stirred up activity elsewhere. The conservative Sunni city of Hama exploded into sudden revolt, and had to be crushed by punitive bombing by the French air force, but the insurgents only fled to the countryside and continued fighting. The revolt also gripped the Ghutah, the cultivated area around Damascus. The city itself rose. Realising that the capital had come under effective rebel control, the French army responded in the same way as in Hama and bombarded it indiscriminately, killing 1,500 people and causing an international outcry. Once again, this forced the rebels out into the countryside where they disrupted supply routes.

To their horror, the French found that Sunni Muslims were prepared to make common cause with the fierce and heretical Druze, while many Orthodox and some other Christians frequently gave them active support. The Mother Superior of the ancient convent of Saydnaya, for instance, organised collections to help the rebels, and fed the destitute among them. When it suited them, the rebels would appeal to Muslim martial sentiment, but on other occasions could use traditional Muslim epithets like *mujahid* (that is, someone who fights in a jihad) to mean a nationalist fighter for the Arab, Syrian nation. Arab and Syrian identity was the rallying cry behind which they set out to unite Syrians. The conceptions the rebels had of the independent Syria for which they were fighting probably varied considerably. They had not risen in revolt in response to a specific manifesto but to a mixture of local and Syria-wide grievances, as well as a gut feeling that the Mandate had no legitimacy and should never have been imposed. Yet the rebellion posed an awkward question for France: if Syrians of different faiths could unite against the occupier, what justification was there for the French to remain and hold the ring between them? In fact, it was the French rather than the rebels who exacerbated sectarian differences, not least by recruiting Christian Armenian refugees into units which terrorised the countryside.

Generally speaking, the urban elites held back from supporting the revolt, or were only dragged into going along with it by popular pressure. The leaders of the revolt were former Ottoman army officers with military experience from the First World War, earlier Ottoman wars in the Balkans and the campaign to resist the Italians in Libya in 1911-12. The intake of the Ottoman military academy had tended to come from less privileged backgrounds, which were often rural or tribal, while the urban notables had sent their sons to schools which would train them to be high-level administrators. The revolt was a revolt of peasants, tribes and young urban men who were destitute or had few prospects. It was only crushed by overwhelming military might shipped in from France and its colonies. The French then ruled in cooperation with moderate nationalists from the traditional notable families which had dominated life in Syria under the Ottomans. These figures were prepared to take a more gradualist approach to winning their country's freedom, and knew that not everything could be won at once. Yet the French were loath to abandon their divide and rule policy. Until 1935, they still hoped the Druze and Alawis statelets, like Lebanon, would be the way forward. Few Alawis had taken part in the great rebellion, and the French looked disproportionately to the minorities, Alawis, Druze and Christians, to provide them with troops to govern the Mandate.

The coming to power of the Popular Front government of Leon Blum in 1936 led to the negotiation of treaties with Syria and Lebanon which would have given them independence. However, the treaties were blocked in the French parliament until the Blum government was replaced by one in the grip of a conservative colonial lobby. Stalemate then ruled until the Second World War.

V

The people who lived in the area of the Palestine Mandate were often referred to as 'southern Syrians' until about the time of President Wilson's Fourteen Points.[8] They developed a separate consciousness gradually, although some historians see its origins as early as the resistance to the Egyptian army sent into Palestine by Muhammad Ali in the early nineteenth century. Damascus was the main cultural and administrative centre that had governed them, and was still the metropolis of the region. Today, other Arabs cannot tell the accents of some Syrians, Palestinians and Lebanese apart.

The Palestine Mandate was less diverse than the French Mandate over Lebanon and Syria or the British Mandate over Iraq. The entire indigenous population spoke Arabic and perhaps 80 per cent of them were Sunni Muslims (the Shi'ite element was tiny). There was a substantial Christian minority, with some Christian towns and many Christian villages. The relatively large Jewish community was predominantly urban, based in Jerusalem, Hebron, Safad and Tiberias. There were also a number of Druze villages and the ancient Samaritan community south of Nablus. More of the people of Palestine had the advantage of a modern education than elsewhere because of the numerous Christian missionary schools. The land between the Jordan and the Mediterranean should, in theory, have been the easiest Mandate to prepare for independence. Instead, it would turn out to be the hardest.

The reason for this was that there was a rival conception of Palestine. The idea that the Jews were a people with shared memories and customs predated the rise of nationalism by thousands of years. Nationalist feelings embodied in a movement called Zionism had begun to spread among some Jews in Central Europe as the nineteenth century wore on. Various ideas of establishing a Jewish homeland in a sparsely populated area of the world were considered, but there was no existing link between Jews and these places. On the other hand, there was a territory to which all Jews had a powerful emotional attachment because of their religion: Palestine. Settling Jews there and turning it into the homeland of the Jewish people became the Zionist goal. Like the Crusades, Zionism was a phenomenon in the history of the West which would play itself out in the Middle East.

From the 1880s onwards, Zionists began to go to Palestine with a view to colonising and building a Jewish homeland. At that time, the proportion of the population that was Jewish may not have been more than 3 per cent.[9] Despite the settlement of pioneers in agricultural colonies on land which often had to be reclaimed by back-breaking physical labour, most Zionist immigrants to Palestine ended up in the towns: particularly on the coastal plain or in Jerusalem, unconsciously mirroring the demographic pattern of the French colonisation of Algeria. By the time the First World War started, the Zionist immigrants as well as the old-established Jewish communities made up almost 10 per cent of the population, of whom perhaps half were Zionists from Europe and their children.

A tremendous boost was given to the Zionist movement in November 1917 when the British Foreign Secretary, Arthur Balfour, issued his declaration endorsing the movement's wish to settle Jews in Palestine in order to construct a Jewish national home.

The declaration's purpose was to encourage Jews the world over to support the Allies against the Central Powers. It ran as follows:

> His Majesty's Government view with favour the establishment in Palestine of a national home for the Jewish people, and will use their best endeavours to facilitate the achievement of this object, it being clearly understood that nothing shall be done which may prejudice the civil and religious rights of existing non-Jewish communities in Palestine or the rights and political status enjoyed by Jews in any other country.

The words were carefully chosen. The reference was to 'a national home for the Jewish people' (not '*the* national home', or '*the* National Home'). There was also a deliberate vagueness in the two limitations at the end of the declaration. The words 'nothing shall be done which may prejudice the civil and religious rights of existing non-Jewish communities in Palestine' were to enable Britain to reassure the indigenous Arabic-speaking Muslims and Christians. The other limitation, 'or the rights and political status enjoyed by Jews in any other country', were to allay concerns that the declaration could encourage anti-Semitism and be taken to indicate that Jews did not belong rightfully as citizens of other countries. As the Israeli historian Tom Segev has pointed out, 'The men who sired [the Balfour Declaration] were Christian and Zionist and, in many cases, anti-Semitic. They believed the Jews controlled the world.'[10]

The Balfour Declaration was incorporated into the preamble to the text of the Mandate, which would now provide the framework for administration of the territory west of Jordan.[11] The text itself begins by stating that the administration of the territory of Palestine has been entrusted to Britain 'for the purposes of giving effect to the provisions of Article 22 of the League of Nations', then continues with a statement that the Mandatory would be responsible for putting the Balfour Declaration into effect. This is followed by a recital that 'recognition has hereby been given to the historical connection of the Jewish people with Palestine and to the grounds for reconstituting their national home in that country'.

Then, after granting the Mandatory powers of legislation and administration, it states at the outset of the operative provisions:

> The Mandatory shall be responsible for placing the country under such political, administrative and economic conditions as will secure the establishment of the Jewish national home, as laid down in the preamble, and the development of self-governing institutions, and also for safeguarding the civil and religious rights of all the inhabitants of Palestine, irrespective of race and religion.[12]

This sets the general tone of the rest of the document. It provides later on that English, Arabic and Hebrew are to be the official languages of Palestine, yet there is not a single reference to 'Arabs' or 'Palestinians'. There are provisions which refer to 'the inhabitants', 'the natives' or 'the respective communities', implying that there were other people as well as Jews who lived there and that there should be no discrimination between different categories of inhabitants either as individuals or as communities, but only Jews are mentioned specifically. The establishment of the Jewish national home is thus clearly the overriding intention of the Mandate. 'Whilst ensuring that the rights and position of other sections of the population are not prejudiced', the Administration set up by Britain would 'encourage, in co-operation with the Jewish agency . . . close settlement by Jews on the land, including State lands and waste lands not required for public purposes.'[13]

A specific article is devoted to this Jewish Agency, giving it considerable power although under British control:

> An appropriate Jewish agency shall be recognised as a public body for the purpose of advising and co-operating with the Administration of

Palestine in such economic, social and other matters as may affect
the establishment of the Jewish national home and the interests of
the Jewish population of Palestine, and, subject always to the control
of the Administration to assist and take part in the development of
the country . . .[14]

This national home could only be established by massive Jewish
immigration encouraged and organised by the Zionist movement
and its Jewish Agency. Given the charter in the Mandate to build the
national home, both Zionist leaders and the immigrants who heeded
their call would be all too likely to consider they had political rights
which overrode those of the majority, the native Arabic-speaking
Muslims and Christians. Likewise, it would have been strange indeed
if the Muslims and Christians did not see Zionism as a threat to
the development of their own aspiration for a nation state. Britain,
when all was said and done, had an obligation to ensure 'the wellbeing and development' of the existing inhabitants of Palestine.
Those inhabitants were deemed, as a community, 'to have reached
a stage of development' where their existence as an independent
nation could be 'provisionally recognised subject to the rendering
of administrative advice and assistance by [Britain] until such time
as they are able to stand alone'. This meant nothing less than that
Britain had a duty to prepare them for independence. It constituted
a 'sacred trust of civilisation'.[15]

The British knew full well that the indigenous population was
extremely hostile to the Zionist project, but the men entrusted with
setting up the Mandate felt they had room for manoeuvre since the
concept of a Jewish national home was vague. Sir Ronald Storrs, the
British governor of Jerusalem and Judaea at the start of the Mandate,
arrogantly wrote afterwards that he felt his performance of his duties
had been vindicated by the fact that both Arabs and Jews accused
him of favouring the other. His memoirs show intense frustration,
but this did not crush his belief in his mission. Somehow it would all

come right, and he could be a committed supporter of Zionism and Arab Palestinian rights at the same time. For him, those Zionists who publicly stated that their goal was to create a predominantly Jewish state were just 'a few extremists'.[16]

Even before the Mandate began, two cracks were appearing in the project to establish the national home. The first was the failure of the Zionists to win Arab trust. The second concerned Zionist Jewish identity itself.

In the spring of 1918 while the war was still raging, a Zionist Commission led by Dr Chaim Weizmann travelled to British-occupied Jerusalem. One of the functions arranged in their honour was a dinner hosted by Storrs. The guests included the mayor of Jerusalem (a Muslim), the vice-mayor (an Orthodox Christian), the mufti of the city, and leading clergy of the Eastern Christian communities. At the end of the meal, Storrs explained that the purpose of the dinner was to clear away certain misunderstandings caused by the visit of the Zionist Commission. He then gave the floor to Dr Weizmann, and translated his speech into Arabic. This is how Storrs recounted what Weizmann said and the Mufti's reaction to it:

> Dr Weizmann then pronounced an eloquent exposition of the Zionist creed: Jews had never renounced their rights to Palestine; they were brother Semites, not so much 'coming' as 'returning' to the country: there was room for both to work side by side; let his hearers be aware of treacherous insinuations that Zionists were seeking political power – rather let both progress together until they were ready for a joint autonomy. Zionists were following with the deepest sympathy the struggles of Arabs and Armenians for that freedom which all three could mutually assist each other to regain. He concluded: 'The hand of God now lies heavy upon the peoples of Europe: let us unite in prayer that it may lighten.' To my Arabic rendering of this speech the Mufti replied civilly, thanking Dr Weizmann for allaying apprehensions which, but for his exposition, might have been aroused. He prayed

for unity of aim, which alone could bring prosperity to Palestine, and
he quoted, generalising, a *Hadith*, a tradition of the Prophet: 'Our
rights are your rights and your duties our duties.'[17]

Yet almost exactly three years earlier, Weizmann had been talking to
a different audience: the influential and sympathetic journalist C. P.
Scott, who was the editor of the *Manchester Guardian*. Weizmann said
to him that the Jews would 'take over the country; the whole burden
in organisation falls on them, but for the next ten or fifteen years
they work under [a] temporary British Protectorate'. At the time of
Turkey's entry into the war he had told the same favourably disposed
journalist that a Jewish homeland in Palestine would be 'an Asiatic
Belgium in the hands of the Jews', and that they 'would create a
strong buffer guarding the Suez Canal'.[18]

Once he visited Palestine, Weizmann quickly came to despise
Arabs. They were 'superficially clever and quick witted' but respected
'only power and success' and were 'treacherous by nature'.[19] When
asked at the Paris Peace Conference what the Jewish national home
meant, he replied that the conditions should become such in Palestine
that the country should be as Jewish as America was American, or
England was English. This was a view he reiterated on more than one
occasion. Faris Nimr, a Lebanese Christian journalist in Cairo and
editor of the Arabic liberal daily *Al-Muqattam*, met Weizmann and
his Zionist Commission when it passed through Cairo on its way to
Palestine in early 1918. He was sufficiently impressed by Weizmann's
reassurances, and those of the British officer accompanying him,
that he used his column to encourage understanding of Zionism and
dispel the fears that were building up. When the intractable nature
of the conflict caused by Zionism became apparent in the 1930s, he
regretted what he had done. 'He lied to us,' he said of Weizmann.
'He was not a truthful man.'[20]

The second crack concerned what Zionism meant to Jews.
Although Zionism was a nationalist movement which appealed to

many Jews who were agnostic or atheist – or even Jews who converted to other faiths, such as Jean de Menasce, the son of a pre-eminent Jewish family in Alexandria who became a Catholic and a Dominican friar but seems to have remained a Zionist – it could also appeal to observant Jews. Devout Jews had always gone to Palestine to pass their lives studying the Torah and living its precepts. As Zionism increased in influence, partly through its unholy alliance with imperial Britain, it may have been difficult to know whether support given to a Jewish enterprise in Palestine was motivated by Zionism. To donate to the welfare of Jews in the Holy Land was natural for any Jew.

The first Zionist immigrants – who came predominantly from the Russian Empire and the German-speaking world – also had many cultural differences with the local Jews in Palestine, to say nothing of those in other Arabic-speaking countries. Mordechai Ben-Hillel Hacohen, the first person to address a Zionist congress in Hebrew, considered Sephardic Jews and Arabs to be equally Levantine: they should be kept at a distance and not imitated. Sephardi Jews complained that they were left out of the Zionist decision-making process. The relationship between indigenous Jews and other Arabic speakers worsened once Zionism became a powerful force in Palestine.

At first sight, the official tasks of the Zionist Commission looked innocent enough:

1. To help in establishing friendly relations between the Jews on the one hand, and the Arabs and non-Jewish communities on the other.

2. To form a link between the British authorities and the Jewish population in Palestine.

3. To help with relief work in Palestine and to assist in the repatriation of evacuated persons and refugees, so far as the military situation will allow.

4. To assist in restoring and developing the Jewish colonies, and in reorganising the Jewish population in general.

5. To collect information and report upon the possibilities of future Jewish developments in Palestine in the light of [the Balfour Declaration][21]

The form in which these aims were communicated to Storrs – or at least the form in which he understood them – was for the Zionist Commission 'to act as liaison between the Jews and the Military Administration and to "control" the Jews'.[22] The Commission, which in due course was to develop into the Jewish Agency once the Mandate was granted, was to be the interlocutor between the British and Jews. This meant that the Zionist movement was now given the power to represent all Jews in Palestine, whether they wanted it or not. This troubled Storrs. His observation was that 'the religious Jews of Jerusalem and Hebron and the Sephardim were strongly opposed to political Zionism, holding that God would bring Israel back to Zion in His own good time, and that it was impious to anticipate His decree.' He noticed the repeated signs of Zionist disdain for Sephardic Jews, who were ignored as 'spineless Orientals'.[23]

As a civil servant working for the Egyptian government and then a British political official in Egypt in the years running up to the war, Storrs had become friendly with some of the leading Sephardi Jewish families of Alexandria. He found that this tended to tell against him with the Zionist leaders. For a while he employed a young Egyptian Jew, Ralph Harari, the son of Sir Victor Harari Pasha. Storrs relates:

Not only was Ralph Harari an excellent Finance Officer, but a complete success with Moslem and Christian alike; with all indeed save with an almost ostentatiously-ignoring Zionist Commission. When the Pasha came to visit his son, I was struck by the immediate cordiality of their relations. They were of the same tradition; they spoke (in every sense) the same language . . . For weeks after Harari left I was asked by the Mufti and the Mayor what chance there was of the *Basha*[24] revisiting Jerusalem.[25]

VI

In Ottoman days the Palestinians had made representations to the Sultan, and the members for Jerusalem in the Ottoman parliament had spoken against Zionism. Bitterness against Zionism could be traced back to the 1880s, when Arab peasants had first been evicted from land bought by Zionists so that colonists could be settled there. At first, Palestinians saw a clear distinction between Zionists and Jews – as was noted by the Syrian Congress in Damascus. An assembly which convened in Jaffa in 1919 to demand independence promised equality to the country's Jews but opposed Zionist immigration. One speaker said that the nationalists 'do not at all oppose the Jews. We only oppose Zionism. That is not the same thing. Zionism has no roots at all in Moses' law. It is an invention of Herzl's.'[26] The Arab tradition of hospitality was also recalled by another speaker, who said that it must be extended to Jews provided they did not aspire to separation. Palestine, the meeting resolved, was part of Syria and should be an autonomous part of Faisal's Arab kingdom.

The development of a specifically Palestinian Arab nationalism was boosted by events in 1920. Riots broke out in Jerusalem at the time of the annual Muslim procession in honour of the Prophet Moses, which brought many Palestinian Muslims to the city at approximately the same time as Easter. There was a political element in the procession, since the Muslims wished to show that the city would not be overwhelmed by the Christian pilgrims who came to the city to celebrate their festival. In Turkish times, the authorities had feared trouble and brought out thousands of troops as a precaution, but the British did not. Although, as always in such circumstances, there were disputed accounts of how the disturbances began and which parts of the violence were revenge attacks, many Jews were besieged in their homes and there was much pillage and some cases of rape. This is shown by the casualty figures. When it was over, the tally was five Jews dead and 216 injured, of whom eighteen were critically wounded. Four Arabs had died and twenty-three were injured, of whom one was critical. There had been no clashes like this for hundreds of years, commented a writer in the Hebrew daily Ha'aretz.[27]

The British Court of Inquiry which looked into the disturbances saw the Jewish nationalist movement as giving the Arabs grounds for their fear that the Zionists had a clear plan to expel the Arabs from Palestine.[28] It also noted that the Balfour Declaration was 'undoubtedly the starting point of the whole trouble'. Nevertheless, this did not prevent the Mandate for Palestine being drafted in the way described above, including the insertion of the Balfour Declaration in its preamble.

When further violence broke out a year later it was equally unforeseen by the authorities, but was more intense and claimed more casualties. It was sparked by disturbances following clashes during predominantly Jewish May Day parades in Jaffa, beginning with Arabs attacking marchers who had taken part in a Communist rally and were fleeing after a scuffle with a rival demonstration. Arab rioters invaded Jewish homes and businesses, murdering and looting. For the British High Commissioner, Sir Herbert Samuel, who was himself a Jew and a Zionist, there was an echo of the troubles that were then sweeping Ireland. He temporarily suspended Jewish immigration, a step which the Zionists considered rewarding terrorism. Soon armed Jews were carrying out revenge attacks very similar to those of the Arab rioters, and the disturbances spread. The casualties were much higher than the previous year, including forty-seven Jews and forty-eight Arabs killed.

The ensuing Commission of Inquiry came to the view that the

riots had been started by Arabs but had not been premeditated. It also accepted that the riots had been caused by opposition to Zionism, not hatred of Jews. In response, the *Jewish Chronicle* in London carried a leader column with the title '. . . *In Blunderland*', in which it robustly asserted that the Mandate (the text of which had not yet been promulgated) was 'chiefly a direction to the Mandatory Power so to govern Palestine as to fulfil the promise of the Balfour declaration and to establish in Palestine the Jewish National Home'. It then went on to comment acidly on the Commission's findings, in a disturbing way that can only have betrayed something about the underlying attitudes of some in the Zionist movement:

> Imagine the wild animals in a zoological garden springing out of their cages and killing a number of spectators, and a commission appointed to enquire into the causes of the disaster reporting first and foremost that the animals were discontented with and hostile to the visitors who had come to see them! As if it were not the business of the keepers to keep; to know the habits and the dispositions of the animals, and to be sure that the cages were secure![29]

The riots helped the growth of Tel Aviv as a distinctly Zionist city where Zionists could build their own society instead of living among Arabs, as they had done in Jaffa. Henceforth, this would be the way forward. The Zionist movement had many problems during the 1920s, not least the fact that many Jews who came to Palestine chose to move on elsewhere, having failed to find a means of livelihood. Ideologically, however, it became stronger.

British officials found it absurd that Hebrew was being fostered for all official dealings with the Jewish community, since most Jews could not speak it and it seemed to be the artificial creation of an identity, a determination to show that Jews were neither Arabs nor Europeans. Yet the identity was becoming a reality. Children in the new Hebrew schools, who spoke Yiddish, Polish, Russian or German at home, were using the revived language among themselves and thus guaranteeing its permanence. In these schools their teachers taught the children a Zionist narrative of the history of the country, passionately portraying Palestine as the true homeland of the Jewish people.

The adoption of Hebrew erected yet another barrier between Jewish incomers and the Arabic-speaking majority. A new archetype of what a Jew should be was coming into existence: the tanned, muscular farmer or labourer who relied on his own efforts and was not beholden to either Christian Europe or the despised Levantines who surrounded him. Socialism and Communism, as well as other Western ideas such as the romantic dream of the return to nature, the concept of progress and the theories of Freudian psychology, all played their part in the development of this new identity. It was exemplified by the co-operative farms of the Kibbutz movement. The new archetype was also a warrior, since his destiny should be to conquer the land and subdue it.

Although an Arab Palestinian identity which was also part of a wider Arab national consciousness strengthened itself among Muslims and Christians at the same time, Arab political activity was bogged down in the politics of leading families and notables. Local loyalties to village or town – and above all loyalty to co-religionists – frequently remained much stronger than identification with an Arab or Palestinian nation. Factions tended to be formed around clans, especially rich and influential families such as the Husseinis and Nashashibis of Jerusalem. Both the British and the Zionists played on this in their different ways. The British used networks of patronage and policies of divide and rule, and in this respect were doing much the same as their Turkish predecessors. The Zionists would make payments to foster Arab notables who they believed would be less likely to oppose their cause. Another feature of this period was how many prominent members of the Arab nationalist movement sold land to Zionists, sometimes finding afterwards that they were subject to blackmail because of it.

The British officials became disillusioned, but saw no way out from the pledges they had made in the Balfour Declaration except to implement them stoically. Military figures began to question whether Palestine really was a strategic asset. Yet which way would the Arab countries go, if they were given a genuine choice, as evidence of British unpopularity became irrefutable in Palestine, as well as in nearby Egypt and Iraq? What if the Arabs did establish their own strong state like the new, secular Turkey of Ataturk which appeared in the 1920s and consigned the Ottoman Empire to history? This was a fear that Zionists could play upon. A Jewish colleague told Sydney Moody, an official in the Palestine government who was temporarily seconded to London, that a Jewish Palestine would be like a bone stuck in the throat of an Arab empire.[30]

The next major outbreak of violence was in August 1929. It began in Jerusalem during the build-up to prayers at the al-Aqsa mosque on a Friday but the most serious violence was in Hebron, when Arab rioters, many of whom had come into the town from surrounding villages, attacked the Jewish community. They killed sixty-seven people, including a dozen women and three children under the age of five. The rioters also tortured and mutilated some of their victims, including seven men who were castrated. Yet in Hebron it seems old ideas of community cohesion had not entirely died. This may have been because the majority of the Jews were families who had lived there for 800 years, not Zionist incomers. Two-thirds of the Jewish community took refuge in Muslim homes and survived, although some of those who gave them shelter were themselves attacked and injured. One list from a Zionist source numbers 435 people who were saved in this way.[31] Before the disturbances subsided the violence spread more widely around the country, with members of each community terrorising the other. When it was all over, 133 Jews and 116 Arabs were dead.

Following on from this, an attempt was made by Britain to place a gloss on the Balfour Declaration to the effect that it placed equal obligations on the Mandate towards Arabs and Jews. The attempt was abandoned because of Zionist pressure in London. This frustrated Sir John Chancellor, the British High Commissioner. The continuation of the Zionist project only seemed possible to him because the Jewish colonists were shielded by British bayonets.

Britain did not establish a parliament in Palestine, as it did during the 1920s in Iraq and Jordan and encouraged in Egypt. Democratic elections would have meant the end of the hope of Jewish immigration on a massive scale. The Legislative Council Britain initially proposed for Palestine would have enabled the ten appointed British officials and two elected Jews to outvote the ten elected Muslims and Christians. It was consequently rejected by the Arab leadership. When British officials finally acceded to the principle of a democratically elected Legislative Council for Palestine in 1936, it was vetoed by both Houses of Parliament in London which feared it would frustrate the Zionist project.

Britain had put itself in a position where it discouraged secularism. As was seen in Chapter 3, secularism had made slow but incremental progress in the Ottoman Empire between the first reforms of 1839 and the First World War. The incorporation of the Zionist programme into the British Mandate had been a step in the other direction. The concept of the Jewish national home was intelligible solely in terms of religious affiliation, so the British authorities were actually going back in the direction of the decayed Ottoman *millet* system, the old Islamic framework under which the government dealt with minority groups through either their recognised religious leaders or community notables. This had been finally abolished by the Ottomans in 1917. It seemed incompatible with new ideas of nationhood. Thus, in Egypt, when a suggestion was put forward to safeguard the Coptic minority by reserving a quota of seats for them in Parliament, the Coptic leaders declined it and opted instead for Copts to vote at elections in the same way as other Egyptians.

Another bow made by Britain in the direction of the *millet* system was the creation of the new post of Grand Mufti to provide a leader for Palestine's Sunni Muslim majority. The British authorities selected Hajj Amin al-Husseini for the post in 1921. He was a member of a leading Muslim family of Jerusalem who had been an officer in the Ottoman army but joined the Sharifian cause in 1917, to which he recruited Palestinians. His power over his community was increased because of the British refusal to allow democratic elections for a Legislative Council, which in the other Mandates was a step on the road to independence. Now a religious as well as a nationalist leader, Husseini was in an unenviable position. He had followers among Christians as well as Muslims and always made a point of having Christian members on his staff, but his official task was to represent the Muslims to the Mandate Authorities. These authorities expected him to be able to control his constituency, rather in the way that Storrs understood the job of the Zionist Commission was to 'control the Jews'. He might have reflected on the fate of the Greek Orthodox patriarch who was hanged at the time of the Greek War of Independence because of Ottoman rage at his failure to procure the loyalty of his community. The day would come when Churchill, as Britain's wartime prime minister, would try to arrange al-Husseini's assassination.[32]

As Arab outrage grew, and peaceful means of struggling for Palestinian rights seemed to get nowhere, al-Husseini developed illusions about his importance and moral authority, as well as a taste for intrigue which may have reflected paranoia. There was inflexibility in his nature which showed in his uncompromising view of himself as the leader of the Palestinian people, despite the fact that there were always important Palestinian factions that opposed his leadership. In time, this inflexibility grew into a megalomania which made him see himself as the leader of the entire Muslim world.[33] These were to prove fatal character flaws, as was his unswerving descent into full-blown Nazi-style anti-Semitism.

The country simmered as spasmodic incidents of violence continued. One could say it has never returned to peace since then. Most Arab attacks were on Jewish agricultural settlements, but in 1932 a British official was assassinated for the first time. The nationalist movement repeatedly organised demonstrations against Jewish immigration. As battle lines were drawn, both sides engaged in military and terrorism training. Jewish immigration was partially matched by a population explosion in the Arab villages, which led to an influx of young Arabs into the towns where nationalism and Communism were movements that could easily attract the alienated, and nationalism frequently expressed itself in terms of Islam. Other Arabs came to the towns after they were evicted from the land they worked to make way for Jewish settlers. The Zionists also developed policies to encourage 'Hebrew labour' which were designed to maximise Jewish participation in the workforce at the expense of Arab workers. The flow of Jews from Europe accelerated as the Nazis came to power in Germany. Between 1933 and 1936, the Jewish population increased from 18 per cent to nearly 30 per cent of the total, and continued to grow thereafter.

Events in the wider world seemed to offer hope. In 1923 Britain had made Jordan independent under Abdullah, another son of the Sharif Hussein of Mecca, although the new state remained tied to Britain by a special treaty relationship. The far more significant countries of Egypt and Iraq seemed to be following on the same path. The desert heartlands of the Arabian Peninsula had been united as Saudi Arabia whose founder, Ibn Saud, conquered the Hejaz and its Holy Cities in 1924-6. To the north, the French seemed to have learned some lessons from the Syrian rebellion of 1925. There were parliaments in Syria and Lebanon, and it looked as though they might also be given their independence one day. Most Arab nationalists were wary of Fascist Italy and Hitler's Germany, but they might even be potential new allies against Britain – a thought that also occurred to some in the Zionist movement.

An Arab rebellion broke out in 1936 and lasted until 1939, when it was finally crushed by the British who had been obliged to bring an extra 20,000 troops to Palestine and let the Hagana, a Zionist militia set up to protect the Jewish population, work alongside them as auxiliaries. Over 400 Jews and 150 Britons were killed. The number of Arab dead is unknown, but there is no doubt it was much larger and would need to be counted in the thousands, including those killed in inter-Arab disputes. Some of these were attacks on collaborators, but the disorder provided the opportunity to settle scores and pursue inter-Arab political feuds under cover of the rebellion. Nevertheless, the Palestinians were fighting against the expropriation of their homeland. The increasing poverty of the Palestinian peasantry has also been suggested as a major cause behind the rebellion.[34]

In the early stages of the rebellion, Britain gave thought as to how the mess the Mandate had created could be sorted out. For the first time, partition was raised as a possible solution. This was proposed by the Peel Commission which was set up by the British government to look into the question of Palestine in 1937. In July that year, it recommended that a Jewish state should be established in the Galilee and along the coastal plain for about two-thirds of the way to the Egyptian frontier. This happened to be the best watered area of the country, and the intention was for its Arab population to be removed. Britain would retain an international area around Jerusalem with a corridor to the sea, and the rest of the country would become an Arab state.

The Zionist state thus created would have been approximately the size of Lebanon. The Zionists accepted the principle of partition but not the area allocated to them, and deliberately began intensifying their colonisation of other areas of the country, especially those which were important because of their water resources or strategic location. The Arabs rejected the principle itself, and their rebellion escalated. Germany encouraged them by announcing its opposition to partition. This was the point at which the Mufti adopted a systematic policy of intransigence, and actively aligned himself with the Nazis.[35]

Palestinian representatives and delegates from the existing Arab states met in Syria in September 1937, a sign of the distress events in Palestine were now causing across the wider Arab world. It also showed how battle lines were being drawn for subsequent generations. Britain finally reversed its commitment to establish a Jewish national home in 1939. A White Paper was issued which abandoned the concept of partition. Jewish immigration would be limited to 15,000 a year for five years, to be followed by independence for Palestine as a unitary state after ten years. By now, however, the Arab nationalists in Palestine were militarily exhausted and many of their leaders exiled.

VII

The Euphrates passes some fifty miles east of Aleppo, leaving approximately one-quarter of the territory of the modern state of Syria on its east bank. At one place, the Tigris forms Syria's border 300 miles further to the east. There is no clear-cut geographical divide between Syria and Mesopotamia, 'the Land between the Two Rivers', as Europeans have called it since classical times. The three former Turkish provinces of Baghdad, Basra and Mosul were put under British Mandate and the old Arab name Iraq was applied to them all.

Baghdad and lower Iraq had once been contested between the Ottomans and their rivals, the Shi'ite Safavids of Iran. By late Ottoman times, however, Iran and Turkey no longer posed threats to each other, since they were both preoccupied with dealing with the dangers of European expansion and the challenges of modernisation. Yet links between Iraqi Shi'ites and Iran remained. The Shi'ite shrines of Iraq, especially Kerbala (where the Imam Hussein had been martyred) and Najaf (close to Kufa where the Imam Ali had been martyred), received a constant stream of pilgrims from Iran, some of whom stayed to study theology and jurisprudence. Most Iraqi

Shi'ites had tended to keep a low political profile except with regard to internal matters concerning their own communities and their shrines. They constituted an absolute majority of the population of Iraq as a whole, but had not taken much part in civil life under the Ottomans who, to them, were 'doctrinally repulsive'.[36] By contrast, the two major Sunni communities, Arabs and Kurds, had done so. Until the early nineteenth century, Baghdad and Basra had been ruled by Mamluks, but these two provinces travelled in the opposite direction from Muhammad Ali's Egypt and the Ottomans regained direct control. By the late nineteenth century, some of their young men had received a modern education and were becoming army officers or administrators. A high proportion of the former Ottoman officers who joined the Sharifian Arab Revolt during the First World War had been Sunni Arabs from Iraq, and many of them had served Faisal in Syria.

There were other smaller communities in the three provinces which, when added together, may have constituted about 8 per cent of the population. In the north there were Turkomans, Sunni Muslims who spoke a Turkish language. There were also Christians and Yezidis (a small non-Muslim sect) and a Jewish community which traced itself proudly back to the Babylonian Exile. The Jews were concentrated in the cities and made up nearly a fifth of the population of Baghdad. The non-Arabic-speaking Kurds and Turkomans may have constituted up to a quarter of the population of the Iraqi mandate.

Tribalism was an important feature of the Iraqi countryside among both Arabic and Kurdish speakers. Traditionally, much tribal land had been held in common, but reforms to the law in the 1850s had required land to be registered in the name of an individual, frequently the tribal shaykh. Many shaykhs came to treat such land as their personal property rather than as an estate held on behalf of their followers. As landlords, they began to feel an affinity with central government, which ceased to be merely a body which sent its representatives to extort taxes and became a means for enforcing payment of rent. Urban notables, both old and new, frequently proved adept at negotiating tax exemptions for themselves at the expense of their tenants. Whilst powerful interests emerged with a stake in backing central government, unsettled and resentful elements grew at the same time.

Tribal revolts against the British occupation broke out in the summer of 1920, although the uprisings were probably unconnected and some areas remained quiescent. Britain's response was to re-establish the Ottoman elected municipal councils, and notables from the three provinces were approached to form a government. This was made up of Arab Sunnis for the most part, with a few Shi'ites and Christians and one Jew. When the Iraqi army was established its officer corps consisted of former Ottoman officers who were predominantly Sunni: either Arabs or Arabic-speaking Kurds or Turks. Britain asked Prince Faisal, now driven from Damascus, to become king.

After processes of consultation among the notables, during which both the Shi'ite religious leadership and the Kurds (who saw their hopes for autonomy betrayed) were only allotted a minor role, a constitution was worked out. There were two houses of parliament. The senate consisted of members appointed by the King. The lower house, the chamber of deputies, was elected on an indirect basis. The King would appoint a prime minister to head the government. The King's consent was necessary for the enactment of laws, and he was able to refuse his consent. He could also dissolve parliament at will and govern by decree on matters concerned with security, finance and the implementation of the treaty with Britain while parliament was not sitting. The chamber of deputies, however, had an element of real power: it could dismiss the government by a vote of no confidence.

Britain saw Faisal as a leader who would rally support and cooperate with the imperial power. Under the treaty which Britain now granted, substantial powers concerning financial matters, security and international affairs were retained. The Iraqi government had little freedom of manoeuvre if its interests and those of Britain conflicted. Faisal genuinely wished to make the country into a truly independent state, but was aware of the unpopularity of Britain's position in Iraq. His closeness to Britain inevitably tainted him. Britain would have preferred the constitution to give Faisal greater power, but it was accepted that the diverse groups that made up Iraqi society needed to be given a stake in the political process.

Elections to parliament were dominated by the notables of the cities, although tribal chiefs were also important. The Shi'ites and Kurds were never able to break the stranglehold which the notables achieved on the political process and gain a share of real power, although Kurdish deputies began to use parliament as a vehicle to formulate their demands for autonomy, while urban, more educated Shi'ites gradually became more involved in the political process which was to become increasingly secular over time.

Britain's goodwill was necessary for those who ruled Iraq. Its military support was essential if the Kurds ever succeeded in uniting and breaking away, thus reducing the Sunni proportion to one in four Iraqis or even less and making it difficult for the elite to retain its power. The response of the King and the elite was that of nationalists the world over: to do all that they could to build a strong, centralised state.

A new Anglo-Iraqi treaty was executed in 1930, and independence and membership of the League of Nations came in 1932, only a year before his death. The Iraqi Mandate was thus the only Mandate to be terminated before the Second World War. But this was at the price of provisions in a new treaty under which Britain retained two airbases and the right to use Iraqi territory for imperial communications in time of war. Iraq would also have to rely on Britain for military advisers and equipment. Although Iraq was now officially in charge of its own foreign policy, the reality was that it was still impossible for Iraq to behave in a way that went against a major British interest.

The years after independence were marked by determination to build up the Iraqi state. The small Assyrian Christian community in the north of the country sought autonomy but was brutally crushed when it rebelled. Parliament voted for conscription to expand the armed forces. When there were uprisings among some of the Shi'ite tribes in the Euphrates valley, the army, led by the commander of the southern region, General Bakr Sidqi, who had suppressed the Assyrians, had no difficulty putting them down.

Faisal's son Ghazi was only twenty-one when he succeeded his father in 1933 and lacked his father's political acumen. In 1936, violence entered political life when General Bakr Sidqi, the hammer of all who threatened the integrity of the Iraqi state, staged a coup in favour of his preferred candidate as prime minister. This was the first intervention in political life by an army officer in a modern Arab state. Bakr Sidqi was a Kurd, and Hikmat Sulayman, his nominee as prime minister, a Turkoman. They were what Charles Tripp has called 'Iraq first' nationalists, rather than pan-Arab nationalists like the majority of the officer corps and senior civil servants. Their lukewarm support for Arab nationalist ideals and relative lack of concern about what was happening in Palestine put them out of step with the Sunni Arab establishment and the army.

Bakr Sidqi was assassinated and Hikmat Sulayman overthrown the following year, possibly in retaliation for the cold-blooded murder of Ja'far al-Askari, the minister of defence and creator of the Iraqi army who had been shot when he bravely went to meet Bakr Sidqi's mutineers and tried to forestall the coup by negotiating with them. The elected politicians now had to bow to the wills of influential figures in the army who used patronage to build up their own power bases. This put an additional brake on any reform of the Iraqi system towards greater democracy. With Bakr Sidqi's coup, the army had entered Iraqi politics. With his assassination, its position became firmly entrenched. Perhaps King Faisal foresaw that something like this was likely to happen. Shortly before his death, he had been in despair about the precariousness of the state which had been built on such a divided society.[37]

The members of the elite were jealous of their positions. Landowners, who might be merchants from the cities, officials of the state or rural or tribal shaykhs, pushed legislation through parliament that shifted the burden of land taxation from large estates to small tenant farmers, and generally increased their own powers. More and more destitute peasants gave up the struggle and migrated to Baghdad in the hope of finding some other means of livelihood. There were the first signs of a new politics that would cut through Iraqi society at a different angle. Calls for reforms began. Trade unions became more significant, and in 1935 the Iraqi Communist Party established its first central committee – although most of its members were soon under arrest.

The government's solution to the problems of looming dissent was to attempt to increase its control over society. Military training was introduced into schools, where the influence of Arab nationalism was already strong because of the policy of officials in the ministry of education. Iraq had a dilemma – was Iraqi nationalism to be concerned primarily with Iraq and its unique society, or was its nationalism that of a wider Arab nation of which it formed a part? The officers who had overthrown Bakr Sidqi and Hikmat Sulayman ensured the latter view would prevail.

CHAPTER FIVE

SECULARISM AND ISLAMISM

I

At the outset of the First World War, Britain had promised that Egypt would not be involved in the hostilities against Turkey. Yet grievances were exacerbated by the requisitioning of animals and crops, and perhaps most of all by the conscription of large numbers of peasants to build military railways and other infrastructure. This entailed the conscripts being sent a long way from home, frequently outside the Nile valley which many rural Egyptians found it psychologically difficult to leave. Real hardship was also suffered by poorer Egyptians because of the inflation and shortages which arose as the war progressed, while at the same time the urban proletariat grew.

Contradictory trends were now in motion. On the one hand, the war made Britain realise more than ever the strategic importance of Egypt for its empire, something that was increased by the dissolution of Ottoman Turkey and the uncertainty over what would replace it. On the other hand, Egyptian expectations of real independence were raised because Britain had undertaken to accelerate progress towards self-government, although some British officials wanted to annex Egypt as a colony. Expectations grew when Britain subsequently promised to support independence for the Hejaz and possibly other Arabic-speaking provinces of the Turkish Empire – regions which were in a less advanced state of development.

A group of members of the National Assembly led by Sa'd Zaghloul, an effective administrator who had been minister of justice and minister of education, founded the first successful countrywide mass political movement in modern Egyptian history. Known as the Wafd (Arabic for 'delegation') they demanded the right to send representatives led by Zaghloul to London to negotiate independence. The British representatives in Cairo refused to accord them any recognised status and exiled the leaders.

In response, the country erupted in disturbances still known as the 1919 Revolution. Different groups which might not have been expected to make common cause in the years leading up to the outbreak of war joined together. 'Religion is for God, and the homeland (*watan*) is for all', was one of their slogans.[1] Students from the Azhar and the new government schools demonstrated, as did Muslims and Copts, and for the first time ever women took part. Egyptian troops sent to control the crowd at the Azhar had to be withdrawn because they could not be relied on, while railway and telegraph lines were cut and much property was damaged. Murderous mobs hunted any British soldier or male civilian in their reach.

Zaghloul and his delegation managed to reach the Paris Peace Conference, but found themselves cold-shouldered. Britain had achieved international recognition for its protectorate over Egypt, including from the United States. In demonstrations in Cairo a few months earlier, the British commander of police, Russell Pasha, reported how the marchers had serenaded the American legation and hooted the British one,[2] and a photograph of the event in his memoirs seems to show the demonstrators optimistically waving an American flag outside the British legation. American recognition of the protectorate must have been a moment of disillusionment for Egyptians.

Britain wished to negotiate a treaty granting Egypt full independence in exchange for what it considered to be its own legitimate interests in the country. Yet Egyptian recognition of those rights would detract from full independence, which would thus have been granted by Britain only to be handed back. Furthermore, who could represent Egypt in the negotiations, and what Egyptian negotiator would agree to Britain's demands?

The unstable triangle of power that had developed at the end of the nineteenth century remained in place. Britain was in one corner. In the second was the Sultan who had been placed on the throne of the nominally independent Egypt when the links with Turkey were severed in 1914. The third corner comprised nationalist sentiment which no Egyptian government could now ignore. Britain regarded the Sultan as the legitimate government, and it was his ministers alone who were authorised to grant Britain the concessions it required. The Sultan, on the other hand, could not move without the support of the Wafd which was implacably opposed to Egypt making those concessions.

As attempts at compromise failed, Britain acted unilaterally. In 1922 it issued a declaration which recognised Egypt as an independent state, but reserved four matters as exclusively within its own jurisdiction: the security of the communications of the British Empire in Egypt, the defence of Egypt against all foreign aggression or interference, the protection of foreign interests and minorities, and the Sudan.

Egypt continued to smoulder. The Sultan, who had now become the King, had instinctive autocratic leanings which made him reluctant to become a constitutional figurehead or even to get too close to liberal and nationalist politicians. These politicians, on the other hand, were concerned about the way in which the ruling family had traditionally looked upon Egypt as its private fiefdom: a state of affairs they were determined to end. At the same time, the 1919 Revolution had unleashed fear of the mob, and the King could have reasonable hopes of splitting the nationalist movement so that its more moderate politicians would work with him.

Britain looked favourably on a constitutional framework for government of Egypt, but a sticking point emerged immediately over the Sudan, which an Egyptian constitutional commission refused to allow to be severed from Egypt. The King and the commission could not agree over the extent of the monarch's powers. Eventually, British pressure led the King to accept a draft, but all mention of the Sudan had been deleted from it. Elections were held and the Wafdist nationalists, who had opposed the draft constitution, won a convincing victory.

The following period, from 1924 to 1936, was one of frustration for all parties. The King's main concern, if he could not get rid of the constitution entirely, was to increase his powers under it. For a time, palace-led governments achieved this and even removed the franchise from some voters. The King was at least indifferent to the continuation of the British occupation. In this his feelings were very different from those of the bulk of his people, for whom the ending of Britain's special position in the country had become an overriding issue of identity and honour. Liberal constitutional politicians who could have come to a compromise with Britain did exist, but their hands were tied by the knowledge that the Wafd controlled parliament and would continue to win elections. For its part, Britain hoped to find a legitimate Egyptian government which would make the concessions it required, while the Wafdists concentrated their efforts on trying to get Britain to give way to its demands.

Once they were a majority in parliament, the Wafdists found themselves unable to deliver the full independence they had insisted on. The Wafd continued to press for the constitution to be made more democratic and for the powers retained by the King to be reduced. Yet until his death in 1927, Zaghloul considered the handful of members of parliament who opposed the Wafd virtually traitors to the national cause, and had no scruples about using legislation restricting the freedom of the press against them.

Eventually, a new development concentrated British and Egyptian minds alike. Mussolini's Italy was the last European power to try to extend its colonial empire by painting the world map with its national colours. Although Italy had seized Libya from Turkey in 1911, it had failed to subjugate the territory. In the early 1930s, Mussolini was finally achieving this. Further away, but crucial to Egypt because of its significance in terms of control of the waters of the Nile and the entrance to the Red Sea, Italy invaded Ethiopia in 1935 to create an East African empire. Egypt risked being encircled by a state which had created a new national myth based on restoring the Roman Empire and turning the Mediterranean into an Italian lake.

Although it stuck in the throats of nationalists, a treaty was negotiated in 1936 which conceded British requirements for security and imperial communications. However, Britain gave way on the privileged position for the foreign minorities. The occupation was ended in theory although not in practice, and was replaced by a treaty of alliance which allowed Britain to station 10,000 men in the Canal Zone. The Egyptian army also finally came under Egyptian control, although it still had to look to Britain for its weapons and training.

The 1920s and 1930s saw changes in Egypt which, as in other countries, cut across traditional divisions. Egyptian investors set up Banque Misr, a bank to encourage the enterprise of native Egyptians and produce an indigenous urban capitalism. The cities grew and an urban proletariat developed. New ideas gained ground. Socialism spread in some circles, whilst a fresh tinge was added to Egyptian nationalism. The Arabic-speaking mandated territories which had once been Ottoman provinces were now struggling towards independence. A new thought began to find expression: Egypt was part of a wider Arab community, of which it should be the natural leader. For the first time, Arab nationalism began to merge into Egyptian nationalism, aided also by fellow feeling among Muslims. Egypt developed a commanding lead in the new media of the gramophone, radio and cinema which, together with the press and modern methods of travel, began to create new links between Arab countries.

As the years between the two World Wars slipped away, the record of the politicians in parliament did not seem impressive. The Wafd was heavily influenced by large landowners, while the new industrialists dominated some of the smaller parties. The political parties were not obvious vehicles for social reform, and their leaders were frequently more concerned with the acquisition of power than the implementation of parliamentary democracy. The moral leadership of the nation which the Wafd had acquired in the years after the First World War gradually seeped away. One of the consequences was a gravitation towards the extremes. Clashes took place between the uniformed youth wings of political movements. There were echoes of the Fascist agitation then taking place in some European countries. Much of it was also aimed against the powerful foreign communities who lived apart and made little effort to speak Arabic.

Young Egypt (*misr al-fatat*), for instance, which became a political party in 1938, aimed to appeal to the masses by restoring pride in their heritage. It dreamed of an Egyptian Empire which would include the Sudan and be allied to the other Arab states, and saw Egypt as exporting Islam and its culture throughout Arab countries and beyond to enlighten the world. Its programmes included mass education, nationalisation of foreign businesses, an Egyptian monopoly on trade inside the country and enhancement of agriculture and industry by initiatives of the state. It dreamed of athletic fields for rallies throughout the country, and a gigantic one in Cairo where there would be a national mass rally every year. Cairo would be rebuilt on Pharaonic lines, and only art which propagated a sense of the greatness of the Pharaonic and Arab past should be encouraged. It also had a moral programme which was to be inculcated through military service and education. It urged its followers to attack the drinking of alcohol, prostitution and corruption, and to discourage speaking in languages other than Arabic, buying from foreigners and wearing clothes that had not been made in Egypt by Egyptians.

There was also a grievance that more and more people felt strongly about. Events in Palestine, especially after the outbreak of the Arab Revolt in 1936, increasingly impinged on the national consciousness. Idealistic young people were likely to see the cause of the Palestinian rebels in much the same way as their counterparts in Britain, France or America saw the Republican cause in the Spanish Civil War which happened to be raging at the same time: a struggle for justice that was as forlorn as it was inspirational, as lightly armed peasants fought the might of a sophisticated army.

II

These years saw the onward march of secularism in Arab countries. Nationalism was the idea of the day. The big question seemed to be whether the identity which would triumph would be that of nationalisms based on the territorial units into which the Arabic-speaking world was now divided, or a wider pan-Arabism based on the twin concepts of the Arab people and their putative ancestral homeland. The fragile parliaments that were appearing in Egypt and all the mandated territories except Palestine were dominated by nationalists and those who sought to retain or extend their power such as landlords, tribal leaders and urban notables. It seemed an axiom of the age that religion and politics should be separated in order to achieve a healthy life for the nation. For many educated Muslims this did not pose a problem.

The rulers of Arabic-speaking countries aspired to be part of the Western system of sovereign states. The strategic goal of Muhammad Ali and his successors had been to make Egypt an independent state under their own control. Likewise, Western-style statehood was the aim of the politicians who aspired to lead the mandated territories to independence. Even Ibn Saud, the creator of Saudi Arabia, progressed from tribal shaykh to Ottoman governor (*wali*), before becoming an independent sultan and then adopting the title of 'king' (*malik*) on the European (and Egyptian) model – a title retained by his descendants to this day.

This did not mean that there was any doubt about the importance of Islam as a religion to be lived or a light from which to seek guidance in a perplexing world. The role of Islam was too central to Arab culture and identity to be displaced. Religion remained strong at a popular level, and religious rhetoric was put to the service of nationalism. Wherever there was a struggle for independence, it was only natural that the conflict between Muhammad's polity and pagan Mecca, the great Arab conquests of the seventh century and the defeat of the Crusaders should inspire soldiers and resistance movements. As we have seen, the Muslim epithet *mujahid* was applied to fighters for Syrian independence, while the term 'martyr' or 'witness', *shaheed*, was now used for a soldier who fell in battle for his country or in a nationalist uprising. Such words came to be used to refer to fighters who were not Muslim, as well as Muslims themselves.

Religion and nationalism thus frequently commingled with each other and with the ideal of the modern state, and there was nothing inconsistent in the way that religious fervour was summoned as an aid to nationalism – as it often has been in the West. Indeed, Muslim volunteers inspired by the ideal of jihad would still come from other countries to assist in efforts to repel an infidel invader. Precedents for this dated back to the wars on the Byzantine marches in the tenth century, if not earlier. During Napoleon's invasion of Egypt, volunteers from Arabia had crossed the Red Sea to fight the French.[3] This continued. In the 1930s fighters inspired by jihad made their way to Palestine to fight for their co-religionists.

Despite this, pan-Islamism played a tiny role compared with nationalism during the First World War. The Senussi uprising against the Italians in Libya and the British in the western deserts of Egypt was virtually the limit of the response to the Sultan-Caliph's call for a jihad, and this was in any case essentially no more than a local attempt to throw off the colonial yoke. When Turkey was defeated, some Muslim leaders, particularly in British India, feared the Allies would abolish the caliphate. A vigorous campaign to protect it from the Christian powers was getting under way, but then Turkey itself abolished the institution in 1924 after the last Sultan-Caliph cooperated with the Allies against Ataturk's nationalist uprising.

Over the following years, there was some discussion of the ideal of the caliphate and how to preserve the institution, but the shock of the abolition faded. Thinkers who favoured re-establishing it realised the time was not right, since scholars from different countries tended to back the election of their own ruler and consensus could not have been reached. It was soon found that the abolition made little difference, and the effect of the Ottoman propaganda which had recreated the institution in the eighteenth century, and which Abdul Hamid II had exploited for political ends, faded.

III

Nevertheless, many people believed Islam should have a major role in public life and be the inspiration for the new emerging states. The search to find an authentic Muslim response to modernity continued. Its best known exponent in the Arab world was the Syrian[4]-born Rashid Rida (1865–1935), a pupil of the great Egyptian reformer Muhammad Abduh.

He urged Muslims to find in Islam the principles of unity and the focus for their loyalty. They should rediscover a dynamism in their own tradition similar to that of the Europeans, and apply it to the service of their religion. Such effort, he believed, was the essence of jihad, and Muslims had a positive duty to acquire the expertise of the modern world. He reiterated Muhammad Abduh's distinction between the unchanging rules for worship and the possibility of flexibility in teachings on social behaviour, and devoted much effort to considering mechanisms that would enable the principles of Islam to be used to legislate for the needs of society. The end result must be that a Muslim nation acquires for itself 'a system of just laws appropriate to the situation in which its past history has placed it'.[5]

Return to the Qur'an was the key, since it was the Qur'an that had created Islam and its civilisation. The essentials of Islam, those precepts which were clearly spelled out in revelation, were unchanging. It was thus usually best to be guided by the practice of the first Muslims, but the distinctions between what was essential and what was not, and what was clearly laid down and what was ambiguous, meant that there were large areas where rethinking was both possible and necessary. Human reason guided by the general principles of Islam should be used to achieve this. He took up the idea of a new breed of Muslim intellectuals who would be firmly rooted in their Islam but at the same time understand modern civilisation. The Islamic state they produced would be just. In his view, this would be better for Christians and Jews than a secular state. He saw secular states as based on an essentially amoral sense of solidarity which allowed space for hatred between different communities.

Rida became increasingly conservative as he grew older. He condemned the abolition of Sharia penalties such as cutting off the hands of thieves and stoning adulterers and prostitutes,[6] if this was done solely on the grounds that such penalties were distasteful. He was also uneasy about Muhammad Abduh's ruling that there were circumstances in which interest payments might be permissible, and chipped away at what Abduh had allowed.[7] Then, towards the end of his life he praised Wahhabism and became a passionate supporter of the new Saudi Kingdom, delighted that it would fight heresies on behalf of Islam. Rida's endorsement of Wahhabism was a major factor in the spread of its influence beyond the kingdom's borders. It was also one of the reasons why he has been described as advocating return to a medieval, sectarian past.[8]

Wahhabism is named after Muhammad Ibn Abdul Wahhab, a religious scholar born in Nejd in central Arabia in 1702/3. The nineteenth century reformer Jamal-al-Din al-Afghani had said that Islam needed its Martin Luther. It has since become a kind of cliché to suggest that Islam has to go through a Reformation in order to catch up with the modern world, even though the persecutions and religious wars of the Reformation might suggest this was not an altogether ideal model to emulate. However that may be, Ibn Abdul Wahhab is reminiscent of some of the most zealous Protestant reformers. Like them, he could be very divisive of communities, whilst his teachings provided a focus unifying his followers.[9] He attacked unscriptural practices such as relics of nature worship, and was obsessed with the danger of polytheism in the veneration of saints – particularly in visits by devotees to the tombs of holy men and women for prayers and celebrations. He also maintained that all believers should engage directly with the Qur'an and *hadith*, discerning the true import of the revelation for themselves rather than approaching the scriptures through the filter of religious scholarship or relying on the example of the Prophet's companions and followers. Indeed, slavishly following the teachings of a scholar could in itself amount to a form of idolatry. Natana Delong-Bas has recently shown that he was very much concerned with the intentions behind actions as well as the context in which particular verses of scripture were revealed, and that he was not the literalist bigot which many people see him as today. Yet he advocated the most scrupulous – and often the most inflexible – interpretation of Islam. It may well be under his influence that *ijtihad*, which is envisaged by modernist reformers as a tool to adapt Islam to the environment of today's world, is in practice often used to develop ever more restrictive interpretations of Sharia.

Take his prohibition on statues. He accepted that the maker of a statue might not intend to worship it as an idol, but believed he should refrain from erecting it because there was always the danger that weaker minds might do so. Islam is a communal matter, not merely a private belief, and Muslims should therefore assist each other by showing solidarity and correcting each other in the practice of their faith. But when it came to statues, did Ibn Abdul Wahhab really know what he was preaching about? He would not have encountered statues of rulers or eminent personages in eighteenth-century Arabia, but in 1872 the Khedive Ismail unveiled a massive equestrian statue of his father, Ibrahim Pasha, in Cairo. Statues of many political and other eminent figures followed. By the late twentieth century, Arab dictators would be erecting statues of themselves as a propaganda exercise, whilst statues of glorious figures from the past such as Saladin and Ibn Khaldun adorned capital cities and reinforced national narratives. Yet it is absurd to think of anyone falling down before one of these statues and worshipping it as a god.

Ibn Abdul Wahhab taught that Muslims who did not share his strict interpretations of the affirmation of the oneness of God (*tawheed*) and Sharia should be engaged with gently by attempts at persuasion. But if, after receiving instruction, they persistently failed to accept his teaching and behave correctly in accordance with it, the community should take up arms against them. The purpose was to bring them back into the fold, not to kill them, and the action should not be considered a jihad. This was also his general position with regard to Shi'ites.[10] Only adult males who fought against Islam on the battlefield and were polytheists (i.e. not Muslims or other People of the Book) who refused to convert should be executed.[11]

The Al Saud family, backed by zealous Wahhabis who consider it their task to purify Islam, have dominated central Arabia ever since the mid-eighteenth century. The endorsement by leading Wahhabi scholars has always been essential to the legitimacy of the Saudi monarchy and remains so to this day, something that has given them a stranglehold over the way in which the kingdom's citizens live their lives. In the first decade of the nineteenth century, the Saudis took the Hejaz for the first time and struck deep into Iraq, even sacking the Shi'ite shrine to the Imam Hussein at Kerbala in

1802. The Ottomans requested Muhammad Ali to send an Egyptian army to recover Mecca and Medina and crush them. Muhammad Ali did this successfully, but the Saudi entity soon reconstituted itself. After another period of eclipse, the charismatic Abdul Aziz Ibn Saud disposed of his local rivals in the first two decades of the twentieth century. He then conquered the Hejaz and the Holy Cities in 1924-5. His new Kingdom of Saudi Arabia was formally proclaimed in 1932.

The interpretation of Islam enforced in Ibn Saud's dominions shocked many Muslims, particularly when it was implemented in the Holy Cities. The veneration of saints and celebration of their festivals was customary throughout the Muslim world. Now Ibn Saud's Wahhabi preachers razed not just the shrines of saints, but the tombs of members of the Prophet's family which had also been the focus of pilgrimage. They even had to be restrained from demolishing the tomb of the Prophet himself. The strictest interpretations of Sharia teaching on women were implemented, and they were not allowed to venture out of the house unless accompanied by a *mahram*, a close male relative or guardian. This interpretation is the origin of the prohibition on women driving cars in Saudi Arabia today.

Rida's adoption of Wahhabism would also seem to be connected with a very disturbing feature of his later thought. Until 1914 Rida had advocated coming to an arrangement with Zionism which could be mutually beneficial to both Arabs and Jews. In 1898, in the context of the Dreyfus affair and against the background of the emergence of European-inspired anti-Semitic literature in Arabic, he attacked European anti-Semitism. He even saw the 'resurrection of the Jewish *umma*' as an example for the Arabs to copy.[12] Provided the Zionists did not try to establish their own state in Palestine, he believed the Arabs would be able to benefit from their resources and expertise. However, the Zionists would have to do this in cooperation with the Arabs, not by conspiring with an imperial power:

> If the Jews wish to settle in large numbers in the Arab countries
> (Palestine and other countries as well) and live there in freedom
> and security, they would do better, in their own interests, to come
> to an understanding about means and ends with the Arab leaders
> themselves; I think that that is possible . . .[13]

After the war, he met Zionist leaders in Egypt, including Chaim
Weizmann, to discuss his ideas, but they preferred to follow another,
more certain way to achieve their objective: cooperation with imperial
Britain. For Rida, this put them on the other side of the great divide,
and like many other Arabs he came to see Zionism as a British tool
to split and dominate the Arab world. From the late 1920s onwards,
he mined the most hostile traditions to Jews in Islam and combined
such material with the conspiracy theories of European anti-Semitism
to attack the Zionist project and Jews in general.

Thus, he focused on the *hadith* 'The Jews will fight you and you will
be led to dominate them until the rock cries out: "O Muslim! There
is a Jew hiding behind me, kill him!"' He claimed that the Torah
exhorted Jews to exterminate people that they conquered, and that
the Jews rebelled against God by killing the prophets he sent them
after Moses. They invented Freemasonry and the Western banking
system, and in recent years had created capitalism in Western Europe
and Communism in Eastern Europe with which to plot against the
European nations. He also saw international Jewry as contributing
to Germany's defeat in First World War in exchange for Britain's
promise to grant them Palestine.[14]

From this final period in his life, we can see the origins of the anti-
Semitism which has infected some parts of the Arab and Muslim
struggle against Zionism and is now reflected, for instance, in the
Hamas charter and the propagation of Holocaust denial in sections
of the Arabic media.

IV

By the 1920s, there was room for a movement dedicated to building a political and social programme as a windbreak against the secular gale. Hassan al-Banna, a charismatic Egyptian teacher who had formidable organisation skills, founded the Muslim Brotherhood in 1928. His writings contain the anger of someone who perceives the West as having taken over his country and excluded him from its future, unless he was prepared to change himself into something that he did not want to be:

> [The Europeans] brought their half-naked women into these regions, their liquors, their theatres, their dance halls, their entertainments, their stories, their newspapers, their romances, their fantasies, their frivolous pastimes and their insolent jokes. Here they countenanced crimes they would not tolerate in their own countries, and decked out this boisterous frivolous world, reeking with sin and redolent with vice, to the eyes of the simple-minded deluded Muslims of wealth and influence, and to those of rank and power. They were not satisfied until they had founded schools and scientific and cultural institutions in the very heart of the Islamic realm, which cast doubt and heresy into the souls of its sons and taught them how to demean themselves, disparage their religion and their fatherland, divest themselves of their traditions and beliefs, and to regard as sacred anything Western, in the belief that only what came from the Europeans could serve as the supreme model to be emulated in this life.[15]

His education at a government school was secular, but he had not been taught French or English. This, and his lack of family 'connections', disadvantaged him and many similar entrants into the newly urbanised middle classes, setting a glass ceiling between them and the elite. When they arrived in Cairo, these young men from provincial Egypt could feel as though they were trespassing in a foreign country. One can imagine them in stiff and unfamiliar Western clothes, making their way cautiously from the main Cairo railway station through the European city. They might have passed down Clot Bey Street where, until the area was cleaned up in 1924, they would have been appalled by the prostitutes who had boarded ship in Marseilles to ply their licensed trade in the land of the Pharoahs. They would have stared in awe as they crossed the central commercial district with the well-polished marble porticoes of banks, departments stores and hotels, all built in a loud European style. The sounds coming from the windows would be as likely to be the strange vowels and stresses of French, Greek or Italian as the comforting ones of Egyptian Arabic. Finally, they might have come to Midan Ismailiah, the large square in front of the Egyptian Museum – known today as Tahrir Square and world famous since January 2011 – and gazed sullenly at the British soldiers leaning out of the windows of the Kasr al Nil barracks and whistling offensively at Egyptian girls.

Prostitution and the consumption of alcohol had been far from unknown in Egypt before the advent of Western influence. Indeed, the European prostitutes in Clot Bey faced competition from the Egyptian, Nubian and Sudanese girls of the nearby al-Wasa'a, where the huge, fat Nubian transvestite Ibrahim al-Gharbi presided as the chief pimp. But al-Banna succeeded in combining a clarion call to moral revival and the restoration of Sharia with nationalist fervour and resentment of alien domination. At first, the Brotherhood recruited chiefly among young men like himself then quickly developed into a mass movement and became a natural home for the xenophobic. It saw itself as providing guidance from a Muslim perspective: enjoining the good and prohibiting the wrong. It engaged in educational work and then, over time, provided medical and other services for which there was a desperate need.

Hassan al-Banna did not have the credentials of an Azharite scholar like Rifa'a al-Tahtawi, Muhammad Abduh or Rashid Rida. He was the first major Islamist political leader to emerge in a modern Arab, urban environment, although Arab identity and Egyptian patriotism were also important elements of his appeal. He spoke positively about the Pharaonic heritage, and his programme of activism and moral improvement may have been unconsciously influenced by Western ideas such as those of Samuel Smiles, whose work *Self-Help* had been translated into Arabic in the late nineteenth century and was widely read. Nevertheless, his world view 'left no room for subtlety: it was either Islam or perdition, moral integrity or moral dissolution, faith-based power or collective humiliation'.[16] His followers soon took to calling him their shaykh, and endowed him with a religious authority to which, strictly speaking, he was not entitled. The movement was a sign of what has been called 'the democratization of Shari'ah reasoning'.[17] With the spread of literacy, books and newspapers, people could form their own view on religious practice.

Al-Banna seems to have kept a certain distance from Rashid Rida.[18] As a young man, he visited the tombs of shaykhs and was not hostile to some of the Sufi practices of which Rida would have disapproved. Sufism had become a permanent and important part of popular devotion in Egypt and many other predominantly Muslim countries. At a popular level, it was characterised by music, dancing and other practices that had no foundation in scripture and often went against a strict interpretation of Sharia – or, sometimes, against any possible interpretation of Sharia at all. The Sufi brotherhoods were deeply entrenched in Egyptian society, and it is unsurprising that Hassan al-Banna was initiated into a branch of the Shadhiliyya, one of the most influential, when he was still in his teens. But Sufism and Wahhabism are as incompatible as fire and water, and by the late 1940s a discernible Wahhabi influence would creep into the Brotherhood, leading to condemnations of Sufism.

Two features characterised the Brotherhood from its inception to this day: its culture of secrecy and the ambiguity of many of its positions. Secrecy was necessary since the organisation soon attracted the attention of the security services, but it also provided an excuse for vagueness about what it really taught. It was pragmatic, but this just increased the uncertainty about what its true goals were. As it had a rigid hierarchy, including a supreme guide (initially al-Banna himself) to whom its members were expected to show obedience, those who disagreed with its teachings had little choice but to knuckle under or leave. In the early stages, it attracted plenty of religious scholars, but many of them drifted away or were expelled.

'The Qur'an is our constitution' and 'Islam is the solution' were (and are) two of its slogans. They are designed to appeal to all Muslims at an instinctive level, but are not policies. Where did the Brotherhood stand, say, on the use of violence to achieve its goals, or on the status of non-Muslim minorities? On the latter question, it tended to say different things to different audiences. For the Brotherhood, Islam was the core of Egyptian national identity and to renounce Islam was to betray the Egyptian nation. But it was never quite clear where Copts, for instance, fitted into this scheme of things although al-Banna reassured them that they were his fellow countrymen and had nothing to fear.

The Brotherhood's educational activities included forming scout troops which might (or might not) one day be developed into paramilitary organisations. It also spawned a 'special apparatus' which carried out sabotage and other activities aimed at ending the British occupation, but denied that this and the youth movements which could be the nucleus for an armed militia were under its control. Its emotional appeal enabled it to take on the appearance of a nationalist mass party which claimed to represent the nation. It infiltrated the officer corps and spread its activities to other countries, especially the Mandated territories of Greater Syria. By the end of the Second World War, it would have many features similar to a revolutionary movement and be a force in Egyptian politics which no one could ignore.

CHAPTER SIX

THE WEST SEEMS TO RETREAT

I

The Second World War found the Arab world an intermediate place, somewhere on the way to somewhere else both literally and metaphorically. It was important strategically because of the Suez Canal, the loss of which would have been close to a hammer blow knocking Britain out of the war. It was now Germany and Italy that had an interest in encouraging and supporting uprisings in Arab countries, almost all of which (with the notable exception of Italian-held Libya) were still under British and French control. If there had been another 'Arab Revolt' during the Second World War it would have been aimed at liberating the area from Britain and France. The Axis made use of the still relatively new medium of radio to reach the remotest parts of the Arabic-speaking world. Glubb Pasha, the British general who commanded the Jordanian Arab Legion, was disturbed to find illiterate tribesmen in central Arabia learning about events in Palestine from Axis broadcasts.

Arab nationalists were suspicious of Germany just as they had been hesitant about Britain in the First World War, but saw no reason why they should not accept Axis help when it was expedient to do so. The struggle in Europe was not their struggle. From their perspective the war was essentially another round of that rivalry between the Western powers which had circled like vultures over the Ottoman Empire and gobbled up most of the region. Khalil al Sakakini was a reflective and moderate Palestinian nationalist who had once sheltered a Zionist fugitive from Turkish police in the last hours of Ottoman rule in Jerusalem. Yet he could write after the fall of Tobruk in 1942, 'Not only the sons of Palestine were happy when Tobruk fell to the Germans, but the whole Arab World, in Egypt and Palestine and Iraq and Syria and Lebanon. Not because they like the Germans, but because they don't like the British . . .'[1]

British policy in Palestine remained that set out in the 1939 White Paper. Jewish immigration was to be limited to 15,000 a year until 1944 and democratic elections would take place five years later. These would lead to an independent Palestine. If they had been carried through, the policies in the White Paper would have meant the end of the project for a specifically Jewish state. The Zionists were determined to change this. Their leader, David Ben Gurion famously stated that the Zionists should fight Nazism as though there were no White Paper, while at the same time struggling for the reversal of the White Paper as though there were no war. Zionists joined the British colours to fight Germany. Because of the extreme anti-Semitism integral to Nazi ideology, this was only natural. However, it was yet another divide separating the Zionists from the Arab world. There was an ironic parallel between the United States and the Arab world in their semi-detachment from the fighting in Europe during the early years of the war. But the Arab world was powerless, disunited and largely occupied, so there could be no equivalent of Pearl Harbor to force it to take sides and get involved.

Britain's main problems in the Arab world during the war occurred in Iraq and Egypt. In Iraq Nuri Said, who was prime minister at the start of the conflict, would have liked to join the fight against Germany by supplying the British war effort with two Iraqi divisions. Yet, as General Hussein Fawzi said to him,

Supposing the two divisions were to pass through Aleppo and an Aleppan were to ask an Iraqi soldier, 'O brother, where are you going?' and the Iraqi were to answer, 'To the Balkans to fight the Germans', what do you expect from the Aleppan except to say, 'Allah, Allah, O brother, what about Syria and Palestine?'[2]

As initial Axis successes continued, nationalist politicians were reluctant to antagonise the powers that might be about to defeat Britain. The exiled leader of the Palestine rebellion, the Mufti of Jerusalem, was given shelter in Baghdad and allowed to raise support for the Palestine issue and the pan-Arab cause. Nuri Said tried to persuade him to back the 1939 White Paper: something no Iraqi politician could support in public unless the Mufti had first approved it, but the Mufti's position was that the White Paper was inadequate since it did not give a commitment to immediate independence. Although that position may not have been practical wartime politics, his concern that Britain would abandon the White Paper was to be vindicated.

In April 1941, the pro-British politicians in Baghdad fled and a new government with a militantly nationalist flavour was installed under Rashid Ali Kailani. In response to Britain's determination to remove him, he sought help from the Axis powers and the Soviet Union, but little arrived from the former and the latter made no response. Within two months, the British had retaken Iraq. Nuri Said and the other pro-British politicians were back and in charge, while Kailani and the Mufti had fled.

When Italy invaded Egypt in the summer of 1940, some Egyptian ministers wanted to declare war, but the government accepted that Italy had only invaded in order to attack the British presence. Egypt had a new young king, Farouq, who was popular at the start of his reign. Unlike the majority of his people, he felt no instinctive hostility to the British occupation and appreciated the protection it gave him, although he resented British high-handedness. By the same token, however, he might not have found an Italian or German occupation worse. His policy was to maintain Egypt's neutrality. Both he and many leading politicians were suspected of pro-Axis leanings by Britain.

On 4 February 1942, the British Embassy effectively staged a coup. Rommel's Afrika Corps were pushing the British back in the western desert, and crowds were demonstrating in the streets of Cairo defiantly shouting, 'Forward Rommel! Long live Rommel!' It was feared that Farouq was hedging his bets with the Axis. British troops surrounded his palace and forced him to appoint the leader of the Wafd party, Nahas Pasha, as prime minister. Britain wanted a government that could rule Egypt effectively while being politically reliable. It did not matter that Nahas had a certain reputation for corruption.

If the coup is excused because Britain was acting under the duress of wartime conditions, it could be replied that it was the British presence that brought the two World Wars to Egypt. Mussolini might still have invaded Egypt if it had not been held by Britain, in the same way as he invaded Greece. But a truly independent Egypt would have defended itself and called for assistance from friendly powers – just as Greece did. As it was, Egypt's army was not equipped to repel a European invader and the Egyptian government did not see why it should fight on Britain's behalf. After the 1936 treaty, Britain still retained an important role in the Egyptian armed forces and had no desire to see them become too strong. An element of the inadequacy they were to demonstrate in the Palestine campaign of 1948-9 also lies at Britain's door.

The British action reflected all that was wrong in the British–Egyptian relationship. Many of Britain's top brass in the region thought the action ill-advised. Russell Pasha, the expatriate in command of the Egyptian police, had not been informed in advance of what the Embassy intended to do. He felt that the action destroyed all the hard work that people in his position had put into building up Egyptian trust in Britain.[3] The events were to destroy Farouq's prestige and compromise the Wafd in the eyes of Egyptians. It also brought closer the day when British control of Egypt would end.

Britain still had important friends in the region. Nuri Said in Iraq and King Abdullah I of Jordan were staunch supporters. Yet the monarchies in Iraq and Jordan would need to prove their continuing enthusiasm for Arab nationalist aspirations if they were to survive. The stakes were raised when France conceded independence to Syria and Lebanon in 1943. Three years later, the French were still reluctant to acknowledge that their Levantine adventure had ended but had no option but to pull their forces out. They left with extremely bad grace, even shelling Damascus in a fit of pique, but without shackling the two states with special treaty relationships. Politicians in other Arab countries would now be expected to achieve the same.

Egypt claimed the position of natural leader of the Arab world. Its population may have almost equalled that of all the Arabic-speaking countries to the east. It had an elite that saw itself as the bringer of modernity and progress to Egypt's Arab brothers. Egyptian professors, doctors, engineers and lawyers proudly travelled to other Arab states to set up new institutions and educate the local professions. Cairo had impeccable credentials to be the centre of the Arab world, being its largest city and a major seat of Muslim scholarship for nearly a thousand years. Egypt also had a strong, centralised state and had existed as a single political unit ever since the Pharoahs united the kingdoms of Upper and Lower Egypt.

Its main rival was Iraq. Baghdad could claim to surpass Cairo in terms of its significance in the history of Islam and the glory days of Arabic civilisation, but only a few traces of the golden city of the Abbasids remained. It was a backwater compared with either Cairo or Alexandria. Behind Egypt in terms of sophistication, it also had a much smaller population. Yet it had one advantage: there was still a feeling among many that the Ottoman provinces that now made up the separate entities of Syria, Palestine, Lebanon and Jordan should never have been split up, and that these should have been in confederation with Iraq, or even tied more closely. Syria had once, albeit briefly, been ruled by Faisal who later became king of Iraq, and there was no natural frontier between the two countries.

Jordan had been part of Faisal's short-lived kingdom of Syria. King Abdullah of Jordan had the best army in the Arab world under General Glubb, its capable and experienced British commander. If the Hashemites could unite the provinces which Turkey lost in 1918, they could form a kingdom that would be Egypt's equal. Their credentials to provide the Arab world with a king were infinitely better than those of Egypt's Farouq, for whom Arabic was a second or third language and whom many Egyptians considered to be a Turk. By contrast, the Hashemites were not just Arab but descendants of the Prophet.

Yet uniting these areas under a Hashemite monarch or confederation of Hashemite kingdoms would be difficult. Although Britain looked favourably on some sort of role for Jordan in Palestine when the Mandate terminated, this did not apply to any Jordanian designs on Syria which were anathema to the other Arab states. Iraq also hoped for a union with Syria and did not welcome King Abdullah's ambitions. Saudi Arabia was still a minor player. It had only been united as a single country for some twenty years, and the vast distances between its major provinces and almost total lack of modern infrastructure meant that many observers thought the kingdom would not outlast the death of Ibn Saud, the man who had established it by conquest. The Hashemites resented the loss of Mecca and Medina. This meant that his relationship with the royal families of Jordan and Iraq remained uneasy, and that Saudi Arabia became a natural ally of Egypt.

A League of Arab States was set up in the last months of the war with British encouragement. This consisted of those states judged to be independent: Egypt, Iraq, Saudi Arabia, Syria, Jordan, Lebanon and Yemen. Representatives were also invited from Palestine, and all other Arab countries could join when they achieved independence. The establishment of the League implied a ratification of the political units and boundaries that had been set up when the Mandate system was created. Its constitution was no more than an agreement for the Arab states to cooperate, not a charter for their unification.

II

Such was the state of the Arab world, or at least of those Arab countries that were independent, in the immediate aftermath of the Second World War. Disunited and conspiring against each other, even while they dreamed of uniting their peoples, the Arab governments were to prove unable to deal effectively with the first major challenge that faced them: the end of the Palestine Mandate and the creation of Israel. They saw their cause as a moral one and, as will shortly be seen, the historical record shows that they had every right to do so. That said, the ways in which they acted in ostensible furtherance of this moral cause were self-serving and short-sighted. It has been the Palestine conflict, more than any other single factor, that has led to widespread alienation from the West in the Arab world and among many non-Arab Muslims. To understand why this is so, we need to enter more fully into the end of the Palestine Mandate than we do with regard to the other Mandates. But whatever blame can be placed at the doors of myopic Arab governments – and at the doors of the Arab populations that pushed some rulers into courses of action that wiser ones would have resisted – one important fact must be stressed. The challenge Arab rulers faced was not one they had brought upon themselves. The prime culprits were actors who were not Arab.

The issue of Palestine dominated the years immediately following the end of the Second World War. The Holocaust gave Zionists a burning anger which was harnessed to their cause, as was the greatly increased sympathy for their project around the world, particularly in America. Sadly, this sympathy with Zionism fitted all too neatly with reluctance in America and many other countries to admit sizeable numbers of Jewish refugees. Some Holocaust survivors who were not initially Zionist saw a new life in Palestine as preferable to returning to a shattered home among neighbours who might sometimes have turned against them, or failed to lift a finger on their behalf. Zionists fought against the desire of refugees who wished to choose homes elsewhere. In these circumstances, it is perhaps remarkable that a mere 300,000 Jews emigrated to Palestine in this period, only some 10 per cent of the Jews in the whole of Europe.

The Mufti of Jerusalem was *persona non grata* to the British authorities and was barred from returning to Palestine while the Mandate lasted. After fleeing Iraq in 1941, he reached Berlin where he tried to win a German commitment to Arab independence. He did whatever he could to dissuade Germany and its allies from allowing their Jewish populations to emigrate. In the latter years of the war, he urged that Jews should instead be sent to Poland although he was aware of the Nazi genocide. There seems little doubt that his actions added to the numbers killed in the Holocaust, and his prominence as the best known Palestinian leader did his people no favour with Western or Jewish public opinion.

In October 1945, Zionist terrorism and sabotage erupted to force Britain to abandon its commitment to independence for Palestine as a unitary state. Bevin, the British colonial secretary, saw the double-bind that had arisen. The Arabs demanded an end to Jewish immigration. Whilst he rejected this, he could also write 'steps must be taken to prevent a real flooding of the country by Jewish immigrants'. He knew that if a Jewish state was established, it would not accept partition lines as final and the time would come when it would seek to expand them. Yet he wrote prophetically at the same time, 'if Jewish irredentism is likely to develop after an interval, Arab irredentism is certain from the outset. Thus the existence of a Jewish state might prove a constant factor of unrest in the Middle East.'[4]

Policing Palestine now required the presence of a massive British army of conscript soldiers who hated their work of keeping the two communities apart and enduring insults and worse from both. Among their disagreeable tasks was herding illegal Jewish immigrants, many of them sickly and still malnourished victims of Nazi concentration camps, onto ships to return them to Europe. At the same time, the army and civilian administration took casualties from the Hagana and other Zionist groups. British morale plummeted. Palestine was an expensive commitment which Britain could no longer afford, as well as a diplomatic nightmare. In February 1947, Britain decided to terminate its Mandate and place the question of Palestine in the hands of the United Nations.

The Zionists pressed for partition. A resolution advocating this passed through the General Assembly of the United Nations on 29 November 1947 when, in a rare display of common ground, the USA and the USSR were part of the majority that voted the proposal through. The partition resolution provided for 'Arab' and 'Jewish' states which would be economically and politically entwined, as well as a separate international zone for Jerusalem and Bethlehem. The Arab League refused to accept the resolution, and demanded a unitary state in which the Jews would have specific minority rights.

The map of the two proposed entities has been described as looking like a pair of fighting serpents.[5] The Jewish population amounted to a maximum of 33 per cent of the inhabitants of the Mandate, assuming that recently arrived immigrants who did not yet fulfil the conditions for Palestinian citizenship were included.[6] Nevertheless, the Jewish state was awarded 57 per cent of the territory's landmass and 84 per cent of its agricultural land, the clear majority of that 84 per cent being under private Arab ownership. At least 40 per cent of the inhabitants of the proposed Jewish state would be Arab Muslims and Christians, and it is possible that they constituted a majority since the official figures did not include the Bedouin population.[7] Partition envisaged that the Jewish and Arab states would be Siamese twins, permanently joined at the hip and sharing most of their vital organs. It did not provide a workable solution and made war inevitable. It has recently been described with some force as 'impracticable, most probably illegal, contrary to the League of Nations Covenant, the Mandate and the UN Charter, manifestly unjust to the Arabs, and ultimately unenforceable'.[8]

The Jewish state could not come into existence except by using force of arms to establish control over the areas allocated for it; nor could it be viable unless it went to war to seize substantial territories the plan had allocated for the Arab state. The ensuing war was, as Benny Morris has succinctly put it, 'the almost inevitable result of more than half a century of Arab-Jewish friction and conflict that began with the arrival . . . of the first Jewish immigrants from Eastern Europe in the early1880s'.[9]

Thus, the partition plan was not a legal root of title which brought Israel into existence and gave it the territory the plan had allocated to the Jewish state. What happened, when seen through the lens of international law, was as follows. Britain renounced the Palestine Mandate. A kind of vacuum was created in the territory of the Mandate on its termination, although residual sovereignty belonged to the people (both Arab and Jewish) of Palestine as a whole. The UN resolution was a recommendation to partition the territory, but no more than that. As Gerald Fitzmaurice, one of the most distinguished international lawyers of his generation, who at that time was a senior legal adviser in the British Foreign Office, noted in a legal brief he wrote for the British delegation at the UN:

> If the Jews claim to set up a state in the boundaries of the Jewish areas as defined by the United Nations Resolution of November 29th and the Arabs claim to set up a state covering the whole of Palestine, there would be nothing legally to choose between these claims.[10]

The Jewish state was the only one that was proclaimed. Yet its establishment did not follow the procedures envisaged in the partition plan. These had included the setting up of a Commission to which the administration of Palestine would be progressively turned over by Britain as the outgoing Mandatory. The Commission would provide the 'general direction' under which the activities of 'both Arab and Jewish Provisional Councils of Government' would be carried out.

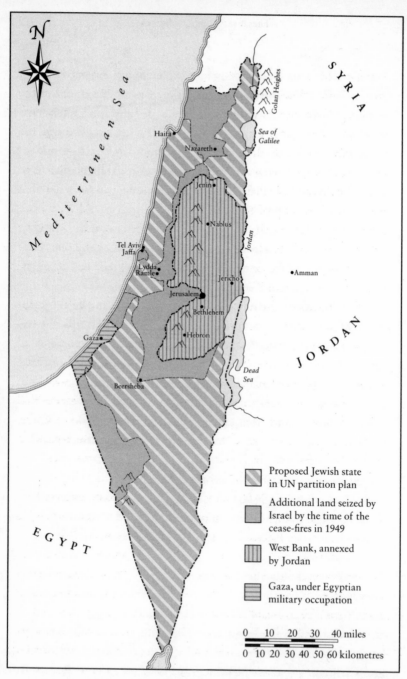

THE PARTITION OF PALESTINE AND THE 1949 ARMISTICE LINES

Furthermore, the Commission's responsibilities included that it should 'proceed to carry out measures for the establishment of the frontiers of the Arab and Jewish States and the City of Jerusalem'. This would be done 'in accordance with the general lines of the recommendations of the General Assembly on the partition of Palestine' but modifying the boundaries set out in the plan so as to avoid the division of village areas 'unless pressing reasons make that necessary'. Yet none of this was to happen, and would have been impossible in the anarchy that the decision to terminate the Mandate brought to Palestine. The only way Israel could come into existence was by the use of force exercised against the will of the majority of the existing population of Palestine.

After they heard the news of the partition resolution, Palestinian irregulars attempted to besiege Zionist settlements and disrupt communications, essentially trying to rekindle the rebellion of the 1930s. They concentrated their attacks on the road between Tel Aviv and Jerusalem, although most of the violence was local to the immediate area in which they lived. The Palestinians had one competent and charismatic military leader, Abd al-Qadir al-Husseini, who succeeded in temporarily closing the Jerusalem road to Zionist traffic, but the Palestinian forces were untrained and rarely coordinated their actions among themselves.

In the spring of 1948 as the end of the Mandate approached, the Hagana and other Zionist militias went on a systematic offensive against which the Palestinian irregulars and volunteers from other Arab countries stood no chance. The Zionist strategy was to secure the territory allocated to the Jewish state, all Zionist settlements elsewhere in the country, and the communication routes needed to reach them. This meant clearing the country – areas allocated to the Arab as well as the Jewish state – of potentially hostile elements by emptying many urban areas and villages of their Arab Muslim and Christian population. Even when that population fled of its own accord, the reason was fear of the war that was now inevitable.

Rather like evacuees from British cities during the Second World War, they expected to be back as soon as it was safe, but Ben Gurion told the cabinet of the new state of Israel that June that the return home of refugees expelled before the proclamation of the state must be 'prevented at all costs'.[11] By the time the fighting finally ended, with separate cease-fires concluded between Israel and each of its neighbours in 1949, some 750,000 Palestinians had been turned into refugees.

If cities like Haifa and Jaffa and the villages in the Jerusalem corridor had not been emptied of the vast majority of their Arab inhabitants, the Jewish state could never have hoped to survive. The indigenous Palestinian resistance collapsed as a result of the Hagana operations, although the death of Abd al-Qadir al-Husseini in battle was also a factor.

Initially, the Arab League had only resolved to arm and finance the Palestinians but this policy changed under the impact of the collapse and the flight of the population. As late as 26 April, the Egyptian foreign minister said his country would not send regular forces.[12] Yet as fear of the Zionist militias spread among Palestinian Arabs and news of Zionist atrocities, both true and imagined, reached Arab capitals, there was a massive surge in public anger. Rulers and governments feared they would be overthrown if they did not react. The Zionist actions during the run-up to the end of the Mandate were also such as to give the Arab states ample justification for an intervention that one would now describe as humanitarian. Yet, although the Arab states sent expeditionary forces which had been assembled at the last minute, their war aims were mixed and often incompatible.

In the last days of the Mandate, the Zionists had tried to ensure Jordan's neutrality. At one stage they reached an understanding with King Abdullah that he would send his army into Palestine to occupy these areas allocated to the Palestinians – which he would add to his kingdom – but not to fight the Zionist state. Both he and the Zionists saw the Mufti and the Palestinian nationalist movement as their main enemy, and thus had common ground. Yet the discussions were tentative and lacked detail, and whatever may have been agreed in principle broke down as facts changed on the ground. The discussions had not resolved what would happen to Jerusalem and the surrounding area, which the partition plan intended to be an international zone.

The Mandate terminated on 14 May and Ben Gurion read out the proclamation of Israel's independence as a sovereign state in Tel Aviv, taking care not to say anything that might limit the territorial extent of the new state. The Israelis liked to think of the entire area of the Mandate as historic Jewish land which they were reclaiming. They considered Arab armies which entered Palestine as 'invading the land of Israel'. At various times, Ben Gurion spoke of conquering the territory up to the Litani River in south Lebanon,[13] and of continuing the war until Shechem (Nablus) had been conquered.[14] He also expressed the hope that when the central Galilee (allotted to the Arab state in the partition plan) fell to Israel, it would be 'empty of Arabs'.[15] When the time came, his soldiers ensured that much of it would indeed be empty, as they did in many other areas. The first decisions to establish new Jewish settlements on land allocated for the Arab state were taken as early as July 1948, which was also the month in which the first Jewish settlers moved into captured Jaffa.

The Israeli advances in Jerusalem and operations to secure access to it through territory allotted to the Palestinians forced the Jordanian Arab Legion into battle. The Legion was too late to stop the Israeli army and Zionist militias seizing the mixed and Arab areas of west Jerusalem, but arrived in the nick of time to halt their advance into the eastern parts of the city. In doing so, and using the city wall as its line of defence, it besieged and took the Jewish Quarter in the Old City, one of the few Jewish areas during the entire conflict that fell into Arab hands. Glubb's small army was the only one the Israelis respected and feared. By the end of hostilities it had secured for Jordan what is now known as the West Bank, including East Jerusalem.

The Legion never attacked areas allocated for the Jewish state and remained in the defensible hill country of Judaea and Samaria. It was too small to make a serious attempt to protect areas on the coastal plain such as the towns of Ramle and Lydda from the Israelis, who ruthlessly expelled the inhabitants. In negotiating the cease-fire at the end of hostilities, the Israelis used the threat of force to occupy some additional areas which had been held by the Iraqi expeditionary force to the north. Jordan had no choice but to accept.

Wise counsels in Egypt had argued against entering the war. Volunteers from the Muslim Brotherhood set off to help the Palestinians, but the army was not in a state to fight in such a conflict, even though the common Egyptian view was that the Zionists were essentially armed gangs terrorising the indigenous population. Israel was not even seen as an entity on which Egypt could declare war.[16] However, when it became clear that Egypt had found itself in a war with a sovereign state which was winning that war, the Egyptian government was pragmatic. During a truce, Egypt put out peace feelers to Israel,[17] offering Israel *de facto* recognition in exchange for Egypt annexing areas in the Negev desert which it was then occupying. Ben Gurion, the Israeli prime minister, would have none of this, since he wanted the Negev for Israel. The area had been allocated to the Jewish state in the partition plan, although its Arab inhabitants far outnumbered its Jewish ones and Israel had already seized substantial other areas which were intended for the Arab state. He broke the truce to go on the offensive. When the fighting finally stopped Israel was in occupation of all the Negev and an area of Egyptian territory in the Sinai Peninsula. It withdrew to the international border under American and British pressure. The armistice allowed it to retain the Negev but left the Gaza Strip in Egyptian hands. Egypt continued to insist on major Israeli territorial concessions in the Negev and the repatriation of the Palestinian refugees in exchange for a non-aggression pact,[18] but this was not forthcoming.

The tiny Syrian expeditionary force never pushed far into the territory of the former Mandate. In the course of the armistice negotiations, the government of Husni Zai'm offered a full peace treaty to Israel under which it would resettle 300,000 Palestinian refugees – getting on for half the total, and three times as many as those who had fled to Syria during the fighting. Whether Zai'm could have persuaded his own country to sign up to this offer is doubtful, such was the anger against the Zionists. Yet we will never know what would have happened since Ben Gurion rejected it. Instead, the armistice agreement saw the Syrians pull back from a few positions they had established in the territory of the former Mandate which would be left demilitarised but under their civil control. Three weeks after the agreement was signed, Zai'm was overthrown in a bloody coup. Formerly the chief of staff, he had himself seized power only a few months earlier. The role of the army as a major factor in the politics of Arab states was spreading beyond Iraq.

The Israelis were initially short of weapons and military equipment, but were far better equipped than the Palestinian Arabs and other Arab irregular forces. When the Arab states intervened after the state of Israel was proclaimed, the balance in *materiel* swung initially in favour of the Arab armies. However, this quickly changed. The Zionists had the contacts in Europe to circumvent the international arms embargo which the UN imposed on all belligerents, and had already agreed their first arms contract with Czech suppliers in January 1948.[19] The Arab states had no such possibility. For the most part they were tied to Britain as their sole supplier, but Britain scrupulously observed the embargo.

At every stage in the conflict, the Arab forces when added together were inferior in numbers. The Israelis also had the benefit of interior lines and were able to pick one Arab army off after the other. In retrospect, the overall outcome of the conflict was never in doubt. But for fear of diplomatic pressure or even British military intervention, as well as a reluctance to destroy their relationship with King Abdullah, the Israelis could have overrun the entire West Bank in the final stages of the conflict. Six thousand Israelis died in the fighting, almost 1 per cent of the Jewish population of the new state. Arab casualties are not known, but it is safe to assume they were considerably greater.

Victor Kattan, an Anglo-Palestinian scholar, has recently drawn attention to the reluctance in many English-language international law textbooks to examine properly the legality (or otherwise) of the establishment of Israel.[20] This is perplexing, since the establishment of that state is a most interesting and unusual case for the academic international lawyer. One senses a taboo which has caused many distinguished and extremely learned professors to gloss over the issue rather than address it. Kattan shows that they have sometimes been actively encouraged to do so. To exist in international law, Israel – like any other new state – had to fulfil the four requirements set out in the definition of a sovereign state in the 1933 Montevideo Convention: it had to have a population, a government, a defined territory (even if the extent of the whole of that territory is unclear) and the capacity to enter into relations with other states. Historians can argue over the precise point at which Israel fulfilled all four requirements, but the initial Egyptian position in May 1948 that Israel was not an entity on which it could declare war was perfectly reasonable at that time. Despite that, no one can seriously dispute today that Israel has long since fulfilled the four requirements, although it came into being with obligations towards those Muslim and Christian Palestinians who were adversely affected by its creation.

The extent of Israel's sovereign territory also poses a problem. By the time of the partition resolution the acquisition of territory by war had become illegal under international law. Although, as has been mentioned, Ben Gurion took care not to limit the territory of the new state when he proclaimed its independence, the Zionist representatives in America gave the impression that Israel did not seek to acquire land allocated by the partition plan to the proposed Arab state.[21] It may well be because of this that it was not until 1964 that the USA recognised Israeli sovereignty over the territory conquered up to the 1949 armistice lines.[22] Israel's title to that territory is no longer seriously disputed, but those armistice lines still provide an invisible legal barrier on the ground to Israel's unilateral expansion beyond them, whatever facts it may create on the ground.

Edward Said suggested that the Palestinian and Israeli narratives of history should be taught in counterpoint with each other. This is so, subject to the obvious caveat that it is important to avoid the moral equivocation of saying that the narrative one side would like to present is as valid as whatever the other might have to say. Yet what happened between 1947 and 1949 traumatised both Palestinians and Israelis, leaving scars on each side that have not healed to this day. The deepest of these scars is the difficulty of trusting the other side. As was seen in Chapter 4, the initial wounds had already been created in earlier decades. More recent events would inflame them yet further. Israel perceived itself from the outset as a nation with a moral purpose, and proudly calls the armed conflict which led to its birth its 'War of Independence'. This would be enthusiastically endorsed by many in the West but greeted with incredulity and disgust by Arabs, whose lived experience of the Jewish state was as a cold, calculating and merciless predator.

In brutal and succinct contrast to the Israeli name for the conflict, Palestinians call what happened simply the Nakba, 'the disaster' or 'the calamity'. It has had an impact out of all proportion to the relatively small population and area of land involved. It is a stain which haunts the West's unconscious like the 'damned spot' which the sleep-walking Lady Macbeth could not wash out. For Arabs, the Palestinian cause has become a symbolic struggle against oppression in which the West has used its power in order to deny justice, or at least wilfully to acquiesce in its denial.

This book is about the history of the Arabs, not of Israel, and therefore only deals with the consequences of the Zionist project and the creation of Israel to the extent that they had an impact on

Arabs. Nevertheless, to understand that impact it is also necessary to be aware of Israeli trauma, since it caused a fear and demonisation of Arabs that already had roots in attitudes like those contained in the editorial in the *Jewish Chronicle* in December 1921 which was quoted in Chapter 4. The facts of the Holocaust need no repetition here. The essence of the trauma among the Jews of Palestine, who were overwhelmingly of European origin in 1947–9, was a fear of annihilation in the war which their decision to push for partition made inevitable. The conflict was hard fought, yet at the start many Israelis were terrified that it would be much worse. They did not know how quickly Palestinian resistance would collapse, how small and badly prepared the Arab armies that entered Palestine would be, how those armies would be starved of supplies as the fighting progressed, or how there was an almost complete lack of coordination between them. The myth of the Israeli David against the Arab Goliath still endures in Israel and the West. As Avi Shlaim has written, 'it is precisely because this version corresponds so closely to the personal experience and perceptions of the Israelis who lived through the 1948 war that it has proved so resistant to revision and change.'[23]

Much of the flexibility which individual Arab leaders initially showed towards Israel in the aftermath of its 'war of independence' has only become known to historians as a result of the opening up of the Israeli government archives for the period. Those of the Arab states remain closed, but the reality was that the new state of Israel did not need peace. It felt militarily secure, and its leaders were to dream on many occasions over the following decades of seizing more Arab land when the opportunity presented itself. Ben Gurion believed the passage of time would strengthen its position on three crucial points. These were the consolidation of its hold over those areas which it had seized during the fighting but which had been allotted to the proposed Arab state; acceptance by the international community that the areas of Jerusalem it controlled, and which constituted the greater part of its urban area although they did not include the Old City with its sacred sites, should be recognised as its territory and capital city; and, thirdly, the end of any realistic prospect of return by Arab refugees to their homes. To this day, the international community does not accept Israel has *de jure* sovereignty over the areas of Jerusalem it took in 1948, while the position of the Palestinian refugees remains unresolved.

In the years after the creation of Israel, there was much infiltration by Palestinian refugees back across the armistice lines. Quite apart from those who tried to return to their homes, starving refugees crossed the lines in search of food, to plough their old lands, or to steal from the usurping settlers. Many Palestinian villages on the Jordanian side of the armistice line had fields that were now on the Israeli side, and it was natural for villagers to return to harvest their crops. Roughly one in every five villages on the West Bank lost some of their land – sometimes virtually all of it – to Israel.[24] As time passed, the number of those going back who did so purely for reasons of revenge would grow.

In 1949 it was already clear that the status of the Palestinian refugees was not going to be resolved in the short term. The UN Relief and Works Agency for Palestinian Refugees (UNRWA) was established on a temporary basis, with a mandate that has been periodically renewed. It maintains the refugee camps in Jordan, Lebanon, Syria and in the West Bank and Gaza, and provides education and support. Its work has not, however, included trying to find long-term solutions to the refugees' plight. Mediation attempts to resolve their status have failed.

The refugees in the West Bank and the Egyptian occupied Gaza Strip were to come under Israeli occupation in 1967 and have remained so ever since. Israel admits no legal or moral duty towards them (or other Palestinian refugees), but they have clung tenaciously to the dream of returning to their homes which has become ever more unrealistic as the decades have passed. Those in Jordan have full Jordanian citizenship but Jordan, with its slender economic resources, has quite simply been overwhelmed. The refugees and their descendants now constitute a majority of the population of the kingdom but there is suspicion of Palestinians among the kingdom's elite, and they are often excluded from important positions. Those who fled to Syria and Lebanon have not been granted citizenship, but have been allowed to engage in certain economic activities by their hosts. The refugees in Syria are less integrated than those in Jordan, but have more opportunities than those in Lebanon, and have the same rights and duties (including serving in the military) as citizens of the country. Today the refugee camps have become part of the urban sprawl of the cities outside which they were originally tent encampments. Some of the camps in Lebanon have become a by-word for squalor. On the other hand, the main Palestinian camp in Damascus is now a relatively prosperous area of the city and certainly not one of its slums.

After the establishment of Israel, many Zionists wished to expand its territory yet further. Ben Gurion, however, was mindful of the risk of taking over more territory whose Arab inhabitants might remain on the ground, as had occurred in some areas Israel took from the West Bank as the price for agreeing to a cease-fire with Jordan. King Abdullah was assassinated by a Palestinian in 1951. His monarchy survived, but the assassination ended secret negotiations he had been carrying out with Israel, and led Ben Gurion to dream of seizing the West Bank or Sinai, the latter having the advantage that it did not have a substantial indigenous population. But he made no move. For the time being, building up the Jewish population of the state was more important than increasing its territory.

III

The tragedy of Palestine in the late 1940s put the Jewish populations of Arab countries in a very exposed position. Ever since the coming of Islam in the seventh century there had been an uneasy multiculturalism. Muslims, Christians and Jews rubbed along together but, at a crucial level, felt very much apart and this became increasingly so as time passed. They often lived in self-contained worlds which hardly interacted, although it should never be overlooked that the authorities were Muslim and had at their disposal a coercive power which the leaderships of the other two groups generally lacked.

This state of affairs showed itself in mutual disdain, a snapshot of which can be seen in the poem *The Jewish Wine Seller* by Abu Nuwas, the Abbasid hedonist and literary genius. It tells the story of how the poet and his not very devout Muslim chums arrive at a tavern. The owner scowls at them because he does not like Muslims. They assume he is Christian, but he considers this an insult. Abu Nuwas realises he is

> a Jew who appears to love you
> Yet secretly harbours betrayal[25]

This bigotry does not prevent Abu Nuwas and the Jew establishing mutual respect and even affection. When asked his name, the Jew says it is Samuel but adds, with a touch of sarcasm, that he is known as Abu Amr. This is an Arab name, but it

> has done me no honour
> Nor filled me with pride, or given me high rank,
> But the name is light and has few letters,
> And is not burdensome like others.

When they ask him for wine, the Jew turns his back again 'as if to shun us', then relents with a spot of banter:

> . . . By God! Had you alighted on someone other than me,
> We would have rebuked you; I will excuse you now and be Generous!

The wine is good. Abu Nuwas and his friends had planned to drink for three days, deliberately inebriating themselves so that they would not be disturbed by the Muslim call to prayer, but they have such a good time that they stay for a month.

Muslims have always perceived Jews, like Christians and Muslims themselves, as a purely religious grouping, not as a race: a striking contrast with the traditional perception of many Westerners – including many Western Jews. Moreover, there does not exist in Islam a strand which demonised Jews across the centuries as enemies of the dominant religion in the way that often occurred among Christians in the West. As Bernard Lewis puts it, 'unambiguously negative attitudes' always existed towards Jews, but '[In Islam] there is little sign of any deep-rooted emotional hostility directed against Jews – or for that matter any other group – such as the anti-Semitism of the Christian world.'[26]

The story of the Arabic-speaking Jews as the twentieth century progressed is deeply controversial as a result of the dispute over Palestine. Some Zionists stress persecutions of Arab Jews and calumny and discrimination against them in an attempt to argue that Arab Muslims and Christians always viewed Jews with hatred and disdain in a way that approximates to Western anti-Semitism. Against this, there is a utopian vision painted by some Arab nationalists in which Muslims, Christians and Jews all coexisted happily and peacefully together throughout Islamic history.

Advocates of the latter view point out that, although Sharia imposed extra taxes and certain disabilities on Jews, these were no different from the taxes and disabilities imposed on Christians. They present this as part of a bargain under which members of both faiths received protection and exemption from military duties. Although this utopian vision cannot be sustained – because of the lack of equality before the law and the measures in Sharia which reminded Christians and Jews of their inferiority to Muslims – it is equally wrong to read today's problems between Arabs and Jews back into the distant past, which the Zionist interpretation would have us do.

The strife which Zionism brought to Palestine increasingly spilled over into other Arab countries. Ella Shohat, an Israeli academic of Iraqi Jewish origin, relates her parents' recollections of the chilling fear of mob violence:

> The fears, anxiety and even trauma provoked by chants of '*idhbah al-yahud*', ('slaughter the Jews') are still a burning memory for my parents' generation, who lived the anti-Zionist struggle not as Zionist occupiers in Palestine but as Iraqi Jews in Iraq and Egyptian Jews in Egypt. And while those chants can be seen as directed at 'the Zionists', one cannot overlook the way they marked the psyche of Jews in Egypt, Iraq and Syria.[27]

Zionism considered itself to have a universal claim to loyalty from all Jews. This infected Arab nationalism with tragic consequences. Although many Arabic-speaking Christians increasingly thought of themselves as Arabs and became enthusiastic Arab nationalists, far fewer (if any) Arabic-speaking Jews seem to have done the same. Ya'qoub Sanu', the early Egyptian nationalist who was a Jew, had no successors, although there were important Jewish figures in Communist parties in Egypt, Iraq and elsewhere. What Shohat calls 'the Arab-versus-Jew binarism' led to tragedy for the Jewish communities almost everywhere in Arab countries as anger over events in Palestine mounted.

Murderous riots took place in Cairo, Aleppo and Aden when the partition plan was announced. The worst of these was in Aden, where eighty-two Jews were killed. Thenceforth, there was the risk that any event in Palestine might spark further disturbances. Soon many Jewish communities in Arab countries were reduced to a shadow of what they had so recently been.

Thus, the ancient Iraqi Jewish community which could proudly trace itself back to the Babylonian Exile numbered approximately

117,000 at the time of the partition of Palestine. It had survived the *Farhud*, the anti-Jewish riots in Baghdad in which 200 Jews were killed when law and order broke down as British-led forces drove the Rashid Ali Kailani government into exile in 1941. Now it became the scapegoat for Arab reverses in Palestine. Jews were prohibited from serving in certain government posts, and martial law was used to harass and intimidate them. In September 1948, while the war in Palestine was still in progress, a prominent Jewish businessman, Shafiq Adas, was publicly hanged on charges of selling scrap metal to Israel. Whether the charges were true or not, what was perhaps most significant was that he was charged but his Muslim business partners were not. The event sent shockwaves through the Jewish community while making many non-Jews believe that Jews could not be trusted. The screws were tightened, many arrests were made and for all practical purposes Jews were barred from government jobs and entry to the professions, while restrictions began on Jews carrying on business. In 1950, a law was passed giving Jews who wished to go to Israel the right to leave the country over a twelve-month period on condition that they forfeited their Iraqi nationality and their property. After a very slow start, the number of applicants to leave under the law turned into a flood when a bombing campaign began against Jewish targets.[28]

By the end of 1951, the Iraqi community had been reduced to around 5,000 and the rest had departed for Israel or other countries. By that time, too, the overwhelming majority of the large Yemeni and Libyan communities had also gone to Israel and perhaps a third of the Egyptian community had left Egypt, although thereafter the situation of Jews in that country looked for a while as though it might be stabilising. Lebanon seemed a safe haven for Arab Jews, and its small community continued to grow in the 1950s, although Jews were frequently prevented from leaving Syria, for fear that they might be going to join 'the Enemy'. In Algeria, the position was complicated by the fact that Jews had been offered full French citizenship in the

1870s – something that was not granted to the majority Muslim population – with the result that the Jewish community tended to self-identify with the French and left with them at independence in the early 1960s. In Morocco and Tunisia, Jewish emigration was a gradual process and was spread over the 1950s and 1960s. In these two countries, Jewish emigration was not total, and small communities several thousand strong remain to this day.

IV

Egypt's defeat in Palestine was a major factor in the overthrow of King Farouq, particularly as the last-minute decision to commit troops had been his in person. The bitterness of defeated soldiers returning home, tales of incompetence at the highest level and rumours of corruption in government contracts that had led to the army being supplied with unusable equipment, all played their part. The war had also pushed the Egyptian government into deficit and triggered a financial crisis because wealthy members of parliament were reluctant to vote through tax increases. But there were other factors, too. The urban proletariat had grown during the Second World War. Many of them now faced unemployment. The security situation in the country was deteriorating. The Muslim Brotherhood's 'Special Apparatus' was implicated in the assassination of Egyptian prime minister Nokrashi Pasha in December 1948. The assassin justified his action by an opinion from a religious scholar that Nokrashi had left the community of believers because of the policies he promoted.[29] Probably in retaliation for this, Hassan al-Banna was himself assassinated the following year.

Egypt was still an important strategic asset to Britain. Negotiations for a treaty which would have led to the evacuation of the British army from Egypt in return for a right to return to bases to secure the Canal Zone in wartime foundered on the problem of Sudan, which Egypt saw as rightfully Egyptian sovereign territory. It turned out to be the British problem that finally triggered the end of the old order. Britain, even under a Labour government which had given independence to India and withdrawn from Palestine, stood firm on the rights the treaty gave it. In a defiant populist gesture designed to mobilise public opinion behind it, the Egyptian government repudiated the 1936 treaty and the 1899 agreement establishing the Anglo-Egyptian condominium over the Sudan.

An impasse followed. Nationalist activists, especially those from the Muslim Brotherhood,[30] began to launch hit and run attacks on British installations in the Canal Zone against a background of strikes and boycotts aimed at British personnel and supplies. Britain's only possible response, if it wished to maintain its presence, was to cordon off the Canal Zone. This severed Egyptian communications with the Sinai Peninsula. Attacks on British soldiers and other personnel showed signs of developing into guerrilla warfare.

The Egyptian government now faced a fire which it had fuelled but which it was unable and reluctant to control. While demonstrations in Cairo blamed the king and the government for their inability to resolve the situation in Egypt's favour, a nationalist newspaper published an advertisement offering a reward of a thousand Egyptian pounds to any Egyptian who killed the general commanding British troops in the Canal Zone.

On 25 January 1952, British troops surrounded the police in their barracks in Ismailia in the Canal Zone and demanded the surrender of their weapons. The Egyptian ministry of the interior ordered the police not to comply. Tanks and artillery were used by the British forces, and by the time the fighting ended forty Egyptians had been killed and seventy injured. Cairo erupted in rioting the next day, with wide-scale fire-bombing of British, foreign and Jewish property, and the army was needed to restore order. Over the next six months, the country lurched from one crisis to the next until on 23 July a group of army officers took power. Egypt was set on a new path, but it would be some time before the direction of that path would become clear.

V

The 'Free Officers' who took over the reins of government belonged to a generation which was angry because the 1936 treaty had only given the illusion of independence from Britain. They tended to come from the newly educated middle classes which had grown up feeling, with considerable justice, that the privileged position of foreigners in the country excluded them from many opportunities.

One of the officers, Colonel Nasser, increasingly came to the fore as the leader although he only gained complete control in October 1954. He had many positive qualities. He was intelligent, passionate, hard-working, brave and incorruptible, and was the first true son of the Nile to rule the country since the days of the Pharoahs. He was known to be an observant Muslim, even if he did not wear his Islam on his sleeve. Unfortunately, he also had a penchant for dangerous brinkmanship and self-deception, and relied on incompetent subordinates. His experience of the world beyond Egypt was limited, despite his voracious reading. This sometimes increased his alienation from the West and its policies, as when he learned from Chaim Weizmann's memoirs that Weizmann believed that Zionism could only succeed if it colluded with an imperial power. His strong sense that his task was to right the wrongs which colonialism had done to the Egyptians, the Arabs and the Third World in general led him to rhetoric which made him appear less open to compromise than he was in reality. When confronted with a problem, his popularity was such, during the period 1956–67, that he could generally appeal over the heads of critics to the Egyptian masses.

He came to believe he embodied the will of the Egyptian people as well as that of the wider Arab nation, which entitled him to attack all who stood in his way as traitors to the Arab national cause and agents of imperialism. This ultimately placed him in a prison of his own making, since he had to be seen to fulfil the expectations he had aroused. He steadily gathered the reins of power in his hands and increased repression of opponents, thus making the regime a police state. The efficiency of national institutions suffered, including that of the armed forces.

Beyond ending the British occupation, the main concern of the Free Officers was to restore stability. No blood was shed. Farouq was allowed to sail away to Europe on the same yacht on which his ancestor, the Khedive Ismail, had gone into exile. Many of the civilian politicians assumed at first that the existing system would be cleaned up and survive more or less intact. They were wrong. The constitution was suspended because of the need for strong government, but the suspension became permanent as the new regime gradually adopted a revolutionary ideology. As Nasser put it about a decade later:

> Some have proposed we form two parties and a parliamentary system like the West with a governing party and an opposition. I perhaps thought of this myself in 1956 – but I saw that there existed a social and a political revolution and that the parties and the democracy they spoke of were only the expression of the dictatorship of capital.[31]

He said there had only been pashas and beys, but no workers, elected to the Egyptian parliament, and believed the squabbling and faction-alism of the political parties had held the country back.

Nasser wished Egypt and the Arabs to adopt a positive neutrality in the Cold War, and became a leader of the Non-Aligned bloc along with India's Nehru and Yugoslavia's Tito. He played a game with the Americans and Russians, always endeavouring to enlist their support while resisting any political strings. In this he was ultimately unsuccessful. Despite his strong anti-Communism, he found himself increasingly drawn into reliance on the Soviets, although it was a myth that he ever came close to becoming an Eastern bloc satellite.

In the early years of his rule Nasser succeeded in carrying through land reforms which broke the political power of the old landowning class. He was also strong enough to negotiate a treaty under which Britain evacuated the Canal Zone in return for the right to use bases there in time of war. At the same time, he cured a running sore in Egyptian politics by allowing Sudan to go its separate way and become an independent state.

Yet Nasser's desire to defend Egypt's strategic interests brought him into conflict with the West. He required finance to build the high dam at Aswan, which the Free Officers saw as the key to the modernisation of Egypt, and needed to re-equip the Egyptian army, not least because of the threat which Israel now posed. The high dam was one of the largest dam projects in the world. Not only would it increase the area under cultivation, allow for more than one crop a year on the same land and generate large quantities of electricity, but would free Egypt for ever from the periodic risk of famine caused by the failure of the Nile's annual flood, which was one of Egypt's greatest fears.

America was sympathetic about the dam but unwilling to supply the weaponry Nasser wanted. He therefore turned to the Communist bloc for arms, whereupon America withdrew its offer of financial assistance. He then took a huge gamble and raised the money by nationalising the Suez Canal. The crisis that followed gave him his greatest triumph.

Britain and France were major shareholders in the Suez Canal Company that operated the concession, and thus stood to lose from the nationalisation. The Canal was the artery through which oil from the Gulf supplied Western Europe. The risk of political interference with traffic passing through it was thus a legitimate concern for the two countries and the international community. But they had wider and more emotional objectives in opposing the Egyptian move.

France was fighting to hold on to Algeria against the nationalist uprising that eventually led to independence in 1962, and was furious with Nasser for his assistance to the rebels. The French government acted as matchmaker to build a coalition against him with Britain and Israel. In Britain, there were many people in the governing Conservative party who were not yet prepared for the loss of empire. The prime minister, Sir Anthony Eden, saw Nasser as a Fascist dictator like Hitler or Mussolini transplanted to a later generation and a different continent. He believed passionately that such a person should not be allowed to control the Canal. Once British and French forces landed, he thought Nasser's regime would collapse and another figure found to rule Egypt. In this, he can only be described as delusional, although Nasser had no democratic credentials. Eden's actions were a desperate gut reaction to Britain's decline as a world power.

Before the crisis began, Israel had been worried by Egypt's partial success at updating its military equipment as well as the British withdrawal from the Canal Zone. It was also concerned that American and British diplomacy had sought to enlist Egypt and Iraq as Arab members of an anti-Communist security pact, since Israel was reluctant to see closeness develop between the Arab states and the West. Nevertheless, Israel was not a priority for Nasser. In the first years of his rule, he believed that peace with Israel would come eventually,[32] and there had even been secret talks between the new Egyptian regime and Israel after the 1952 revolution. However, on 28 February 1955, Israel launched a raid on the Egyptian military headquarters on the outskirts of Gaza city, killing thirty-seven Egyptian soldiers. Although there had been guerrilla infiltration into Israel from Gaza, the border was generally quiet at the time and Egypt had consistently been making efforts to keep it so.

Israel's raid was by far the worst incident that had occurred on the border since the cease-fire in 1949, and it led Nasser to break off the secret dialogue. Israel's action seems to have been motivated at least in part by the need of Ben Gurion, who had just returned as defence minister, to impress the Israeli public with his toughness and show Nasser as weak in front of his own people and other Arabs. Gazans rioted against Egyptian and UN institutions in frustration, demanding arms to defend themselves. Nasser had to be seen to respond. Shortly afterwards Egyptian officers began training Gazans in sabotage, and a low-intensity guerrilla war started.

Ben Gurion was afraid Nasser would lead the Egyptians to modernity, as Ataturk had done with the Turks, and unite the Arab countries after the manner of Saladin, who had once ruled from the imposing citadel he built in Cairo and which was still the headquarters of the Egyptian military. He also came to believe that Nasser intended to destroy the Jewish state. When Ben Gurion returned to the premiership in 1955, he began to look for ways to engineer a war which would topple Nasser before Egypt became too strong. There was thus a commonality of interest between Israel and the two senescent colonial powers. A devious scheme was hatched: Israel would attack Egypt in the Gaza Strip and Sinai. On the excuse of intervening to end the fighting and keep the Canal safe, Britain and France would jointly occupy the Canal Zone.

The Israeli attack took Egypt by surprise, but when Britain and France issued their ultimatum there were still Egyptian forces resisting the Israeli advance in Sinai. The Anglo-French landings in Port Said could not, therefore, even be interpreted as a good faith attempt to separate the combatants. The military action included bombing facilities around Cairo and elsewhere in the country as well as in the Canal Zone. There was heavy urban fighting as the Allies fought their way down the Canal. Resistance groups, sometimes organised by Muslim Brothers or Communists as well as by the government, fought back.

American pressure soon led to a halt to the invasion and what became a demeaning withdrawal by Britain and France. Israel had hoped to add territory it had occupied in Sinai[33] to the Jewish state and also to expand into Jordan. It took slightly longer to leave Sinai and Gaza, and this involved a pragmatic compromise by Nasser. He agreed that UN observers would be stationed in Sinai with Egyptian consent, and that he would allow Israeli ships to pass round the southern tip of Sinai through the Straits of Tiran. Nevertheless, these were mere points of detail compared with his triumph in standing up for Egypt and facing down Britain and France. Because Britain had broken its treaty with Egypt, it lost its right to station troops in the Canal Zone in wartime: the last trace of almost three-quarters of a century of occupation.

In retaliation for what had happened, Nasser sequestrated British, French and Jewish property in Egypt. The extension of the sequestration to Jewish property showed how blurred the distinctions between 'Jewish', 'Zionist' and 'Israeli' had now become in both Israel and the Arab world. After the 1952 revolution, the Free Officers had taken tangible steps to reassure the Egyptian Jewish community[34] but its situation remained precarious. In 1954, terrorist attacks, including bombs in cinemas, were made against British and American establishments by Egyptian Jews recruited as Israeli agents in Zionist youth clubs. The intention was to make the work appear to be by Egyptian nationalists and disrupt relations between the Egyptian military regime and the West, not least by causing the collapse of negotiations between Britain and Egypt over the withdrawal of British troops from the Suez Canal Zone. Although nobody was hurt in these outrages, two of the perpetrators were hanged for treason and others received lengthy prison sentences. When pleas for clemency were made to Nasser, he is said to have retorted that he had just hanged some Muslim terrorists and that he could not be expected to treat Jewish terrorists differently.

Nevertheless, it was widely assumed in the West that the perpetrators were innocent victims of trumped up charges, and public figures campaigned to pressurise the Egyptian government into releasing them. In these campaigns, Egypt was frequently portrayed as an anti-Semitic, quasi-Nazi regime, something all too many Westerners seemed prepared to accept unquestioningly and which elements in Israel encouraged. It would only be in 1975 that the truth finally came out. The surviving perpetrators were released in a prisoner exchange and three of them confirmed on TV that they had acted on orders from Israel.[35]

Nasser believed that the bloody Israeli raid on Gaza in 1955 was Israel's response to the sentences passed on the perpetrators of Operation Susannah, to give the terrorist operation its Israeli codeword. Both these events must be seen as part of the background to the sequestration of Jewish property. Even Jewish communities like the Karaites, whose language and traditional dress were indistinguishable from other non-Westernised Egyptians, now found themselves excluded from the new Egypt that was emerging. In 1956 there were still 50,000–55,000 Jews in the country. The overwhelming majority now emigrated or were forced to leave. It was the Suez/Sinai conflict, not the fighting of 1947–9, that tore the heart out of the Egyptian Jewish community.

VI

Nasser was now the hero of the Egyptian masses, and had an appeal in other Arab countries. Before he emerged as the leader of Egypt, the ideals of pan-Arabism were already widespread. They had been systematised in a revolutionary framework by the Ba'ath party,[36] which Michel Aflaq, an Orthodox Christian, and Salah al-din Bitar, a Sunni Muslim, had founded in Damascus during the Second World War.

The idea of One Arab Nation with an indivisible homeland is the central tenet of Ba'athism. There is a coercive element in this, since no part of that homeland may be allowed to go its separate way. Yet the ideals contained in the party's constitution are high:

only the Arabs have the right to manage their nation's affairs and resources and to channel its potential. The Ba'athist state should have freedom of speech, assembly, belief, artistic expression and full rights for women. It should have a parliamentary system for a single, decentralised state, equality before the law and an independent judiciary. The constitution also provides for a socialist system, including central planning and the nationalisation of banks and industry, as well as equitable distribution of farmland. Ba'athism is aggressively secular, but Aflaq, the ideologue of the movement, stressed the importance of Islam in Arab identity. The mission of Muhammad and the establishment of a society based on Islam had been the key historical experience of the Arabs, and the positive values that flowed from this should be their inspiration today.

Ba'athism was attractive to Arabic speakers from religious minorities, such as Shi'ites, Christians, Druze and Alawis, as well as to many Sunnis. The party was also adept at recruiting among the officer class in newly independent states. The new generation of nationalists tended to be intellectuals with a Western education, to whom the Ba'athists were well placed to appeal. They included those from aspiring families who found themselves in positions of power of which their fathers or grandfathers could never have dreamed. This was especially significant in a country like Syria where the broad masses now looked to the officer class for leadership.

The thrones of Arab monarchs and other leaders aligned with the West wobbled. In the late 1950s, democratic elections would probably have brought pro-Nasser governments to power in many Arab countries. It is difficult today to understand just how strong and widespread were the feelings he aroused. In Saudi Arabia, for instance, he inspired revolts in the army in 1955 and 1956. When he visited Riyadh in 1956, he was mobbed by tens of thousands of Saudis, and in 1962 air force pilots from Saudi Arabia and Jordan defected to Egypt. As late as 1967, when Saudi Arabia's monarchical and conservative regime was Nasser's chief Arab opponent, there were riots by his supporters in Dhahran and other Saudi cities in the run-up to the Six Day War.

Nasser did not provide the backing which might have enabled attempted coups in his favour to succeed in Iraq and Jordan, and the moments at which these might have been possible soon passed. Not only did he lack the Bismarckian ruthlessness, efficiency and diplomatic skill which would have been prerequisites to unite the countries of the Arab world into a single state or federation (assuming the USA and USSR would have permitted this), but he had no plans to do so.[37] What he wanted was the end of foreign influence and the overthrow of rulers who collaborated with it. Free of their shackles, he believed Arabs would then establish unity of their own, spontaneous accord. However, it was also important to him that everyone accepted his position as the great leader, the champion of the oppressed Egyptian and Arab nations and the embodiment of their collective wills. The radio station Voice of the Arabs and the rest of his propaganda machine constantly poured scorn and vitriol on all who stood in his way, while his intelligence services tried to subvert them.

In February 1958 the Syrian Ba'athists succeeded in uniting Syria with Egypt as a single state under Nasser's leadership. The USA and the West allowed it to go ahead because it forestalled a possible Communist coup in Syria. Although he enthusiastically adopted the merger, Nasser's initial instinct had been that the move was premature and too sudden. He had believed unification would require at least five years of preparation if it was to work, and was against attempts at unity imposed from above. When a coup in Damascus in 1961 led to Syria breaking away again, Nasser initially rushed troops to Syria to contain the rebellion but withdrew them because it had become clear that they would have had to fight the Syrian army, and he was not prepared to shed Arab blood.

The beginning of this short-lived union was not the most momentous political event in the Arab world in 1958. On 14 July the Iraqi monarchy was toppled in a bloody coup led by a group of 'Free Officers' in which both the King and Nuri Said, the veteran prime minister, were killed. Panic now gripped the pro-Western regimes in Lebanon and Jordan, leading to the landing the next day of American marines in Beirut and British paratroops in Amman at the request of the two governments. In Jordan, the new, young King Hussein was only twenty-two, and a cousin of the murdered King Faisal II of Iraq. He was now in a very precarious position.

Lebanon had been in the throes of a constitutional crisis. It was a democracy, but one marred by electoral corruption, the deeply antagonistic conceptions of the country's identity held by the Maronites and the predominantly Muslim 'pro-Arab' groupings, and the tendency of foreign interests to meddle in Lebanese affairs by using opposing factions as their proxies. Its various communities have been described as doing no more than 'cohabiting': living side by side and working together when their interests coincided, but always retaining their own, competing perspectives. In this way, they had failed to build a spirit of trust and harmony or the shared perspective which are vital to a nation.[38] In 1958 there was a risk that the country might dissolve into local units controlled by militias, but in the end compromise won through. The inherent instability of the country was patched together for the time being.

The new Iraqi regime was led by Brigadier Abd al-Karim Qasim, an officer who, like Nasser, was from humble origins by the standards of his country's elite. His background (half Sunni Arab and half Shi'ite Kurd) arguably qualified him to unite Iraq more than almost any other ruler before or since. There was a brief period during which the prize of Iraq joining the political union with Syria and Egypt dangled before Qasim's eyes, but he wisely concluded that Iraq was not ready to take part. It would also have meant sharing the fate which Syria suffered as a result of its union with Egypt: control from Cairo and domination by Nasser's towering colossus. On the domestic front, Qasim carried out land reform (although not altogether effectively), took the first steps towards establishing Iraqi control over the oil industry, and invested government revenues in social housing and education to an unprecedented extent.

The complex nature of Iraqi politics is demonstrated by the manner of his downfall, which duly came in 1963. The Kurdish Democratic Party, which was fighting a guerrilla war in the north, persuaded officers in the military to overthrow him in exchange for a cease-fire. His bullet-ridden corpse was shown on TV to prove that he was dead and resistance by his supporters futile. This may be evidence of his popularity. Well after his death, it emerged that the ascetic Qasim, who had never married, had slept next door to his office on an ordinary army bed and paid his salary to an orphanage.[39]

As regards Egypt's internal politics, Nasser saw the country in a paradoxical situation. On the one hand, it required national unity. On the other, it needed a social revolution which meant class conflict – the very antithesis of national unity. But he thought he had a solution. In the army, there was a tool to hand which he believed could deliver both. In the aftermath of the Suez crisis, a new direction appeared. All foreign manufacturers and exporters were 'Egyptianised' by law. Unfortunately, this turned out to be an opportunity for cronyism among army officers and other members of the new elite.

In the early 1960s, after Syria had left the union, Nasser concentrated on this ideal of a social revolution. Private property was never abolished, and agriculture and land remained in private hands. Yet more and more sectors of the economy were nationalised. Even the banks and insurance companies set up by Egyptian economic nationalists of an earlier generation fell under the yoke of a state bureaucracy. Monopolies were established and the stock exchange abolished. Imports of foreign capital, except for aid with no strings attached, were actively discouraged except as a last resort. Emphasis was placed on the rapid development of heavy industries for strategic reasons, as well as manufacturing aimed at import substitution. For a few years the economy boomed, but then slowed drastically.

In retrospect, it is easy to see how Nasserist and Ba'athist ideas led to economic sclerosis caused by the strangling of competition, the growth of bureaucracy, distortion of markets, reliance on subsidised prices to fight poverty, the destruction of national currencies and increased opportunities for corruption. Entrepreneurs found themselves treated almost as criminals, and successful private firms were impounded by the government, leading to the flight abroad of the cream of the nation's commercial talent. However, it took a while for the effects of such policies to become apparent. At that time in Europe and other parts of the West, there were many ministers in democratically elected centre-left governments who espoused much the same economic philosophy.

The wish to develop strategic industries in an Arab country was understandable, given the practical restraints which their absence put on political independence. The emphasis which the revolutionary regimes placed on such matters as public education, healthcare, social services and rural electrification was unprecedented in Arab states. It had a lasting impact, even though it was often accompanied by a decline in standards because there were insufficient trained teachers and doctors.

There was now a power vacuum in the region which only the USA or USSR could fill. While Nasser disputed this on principle – arguing that the Arab countries were attaining complete independence and should fill any vacuum themselves – the reality was that they would henceforth be faced with choosing between the carrots each superpower might offer, while at the same time dodging the blows of its stick. Yet for the time being there was plenty of unfinished business for Arab nationalists.

In 1962, a coup in North Yemen, perhaps the most reactionary state in the Arab world at that time, led to a civil war. This was fought between republican forces inspired by Arab revolutionary ideologies which transcended divides between the Sunni and Shi'ite groups which made up the population, and tribes loyal to the imam from the old ruling family who was also a religious leader for the Shi'ites. Nasser, for the one and only time in his career, broke with his reluctance to send troops to intervene in a struggle in another Arab country and despatched an expeditionary force. Despite various military surges by the Egyptians (and the use of poisoned gas by their air force), a stalemate ensued, although the republicans and their Egyptian backers destabilised the neighbouring British colony of Aden from which Britain made an undignified exit in late 1967. But by then, as will be seen in the next chapter, another event had changed the direction of the region.

VII

The era of Nasser saw the eclipse of political movements based on Islam. The Muslim Brotherhood had initially welcomed the Free Officers' coup of 1952, but was brutally repressed in 1954 after an alleged attempt on Nasser's life. Yet it was the appeal of Nasserism, rather than repression, that was the reason for its decline over the following years, since the constituencies from which the Brotherhood recruited its members became Nasser's most enthusiastic followers. It would only be when Nasserism failed to deliver its promises that the Brotherhood would come out the other side of that eclipse, and its ideas would once again become significant.

In the early 1950s, the Brotherhood had a new recruit called Sayyid Qutb. Qutb was born in 1906, the same year as Hassan al-Banna. Like him, he was a teacher although he went on to become a ministry of education bureaucrat. He was more highly educated than Hassan al-Banna, and was an intellectual rather than a populist. Rashid Rida had belonged to the last generation in which it was possible for a Muslim intellectual to be educated entirely within the traditional Muslim system and to think unselfconsciously in terms which owed nothing to the modern West. It may be no coincidence that the following generation spawned a thinker who rejected the West in its entirety, even if he used Western categories of thought while doing so.

One of the interesting things about Sayyid Qutb is that he could easily have gone in a very different direction. Before he became an Islamist, he was a writer and a literary critic who admired the first novels of Naguib Mahfouz. He recorded his boyhood affectionately in his autobiographical work *A Child from the Village*, which paints a picture of the gradual and chaotic spread of modernisation into a remote, rural community. The book shows he was a devout child, but contains no clue about the turn his life would subsequently take.

Significantly, it is dedicated to Taha Hussein, who had also published an autobiographical account of growing up in a village in Upper Egypt a few years earlier. Although a practising Muslim who – like Sayyid Qutb – memorised the Qur'an as a child, Taha Hussein was one of Egypt's foremost secular intellectuals of his generation. He abandoned the Azhar in favour of Egypt's first modern, secular university and rounded off his studies with a doctorate in France. Before Sayyid Qutb dedicated his memoir to him, Taha Hussein had published a book in which he hinted that the Qur'an might be analysed with the same literary tools as other texts, causing an uproar which forced him to withdraw it and make changes. As his thought developed, he would become a passionate advocate of values which he saw as both European and integral to Islam: an educated and humane culture, the virtues of civil society and genuine democracy. He was one of a group of respected intellectuals who argued that Egypt should consider itself part of Europe through a shared Mediterranean culture to which it had made a very substantial contribution.

Such positions were anathema to the Sayyid Qutb of later years, who came to perceive the West and 'Westernisers' as threatening his identity as a Muslim. This is what led him to set out on his new road in the very opposite direction from Taha Hussein who, by contrast, rose to the top of Egypt's literary establishment and became the first rector of Alexandria University and a reforming minister of education.

Sayyid Qutb's thought brings us to the violent streak in militant Islam today. For him, the word of God contained in the Qur'an and *hadith* is a self-contained universe of thought as well as a programme for action with which there could be no compromise, since true sovereignty belongs to God alone. Like Hassan al-Banna, but in contrast to Muhammad Abduh and Rashid Rida, Sayyid Qutb did not have the in-depth background in the religious sciences to address other Muslims in an authoritative fashion on Sharia. Whenever possible he availed himself of those arguments in classical sources which might be pleaded in support of his views, but his source for guidance was the subjective one of his own heart.[40] Like the Rashid Rida of later years, he also picked up anti-Semitic ideas from the West, such as the existence of world-wide Jewish conspiracies.[41]

For Sayyid Qutb, Islam is a way of life based on action. There should be no separation between politics and religion. Alongside writers in the Indian sub-continent, Mawdudi and Nadwi, the Arabic translations of whose works seem to have influenced him,[42] he focused on the concept of the Jahiliyya, which had originally meant the ignorance of the pagan Meccans and pre-Islamic Arabs. Jahiliyya was now extended to include what Sayyid Qutb conceived to be the forces working against Islam in the modern world: capitalism, communism, nationalism, secularism and whatever else led believers to contravene Sharia. Even Muslim reformers who tried to reconcile Islam and the modern world had been insidiously subverted by this new Jahiliyya, which was in essence an entire culture that was systematically hostile to Islam and suffocating it. This culture had to be repudiated and then dismantled, by violent means if necessary and without any compromise. This was the challenge for Muslims in the modern world. In Sayyid Qutb's eyes, Nasser, the religious establishment and, indeed, many ordinary Muslims were not true believers.

He spent most of the last ten years of his life in gaol. He was only released briefly then rearrested and hanged in 1966, following another alleged attempt by the Brotherhood to assassinate Nasser. It was from his prison cell that he formulated most of his programme for action in his very angry, paranoid and sometimes naive book *Milestones*. Muslims should strive to create a new 'Qur'anic generation' that is imbued with true Islam and its values, and will reorder society accordingly through a passionate faith like that of the first converts to Muhammad's message. This struggle should begin with the conversion of individuals whose task will be to fight for a righteous society, attacking the false gods of Jahiliyya until a just Islamic order prevails across the world. Islam came to free man from subservience to other men and his own desires. An Islamic system should therefore be erected to replace the Jahili system, and freedom of belief would then be possible for those who obeyed the law of the land which would flow exclusively from that Islamic system. He cites the Qur'anic dictum that there should be no compulsion in religion, but believes that force must be used to remove the obstacles the Jahili system puts in the way of people deciding with an open mind whether or not to accept Islam. A Muslim's only nation is the Muslim community, the *umma*, and his only country the land where this Islamic system has been established.

In his view, Muslims who did not accept his programme were not true Muslims but unbelievers. This led naturally to the concept of *takfir*, the declaration that a person who on the surface claims to be a Muslim may actually be an infidel. Although Qutb had not elaborated this concept at the time of his execution, *takfir* would soon enable others to find a theological basis to justify acts such as the assassination of President Sadat in 1981 and, since the invasion of Iraq in 2003, sectarian attacks on Shi'ites.

But what lay behind Sayyid Qutb's ideology, and why did he go off on such a very different trajectory from Taha Hussein? It is all too easy for Western commentators to snigger at passages Sayyid Qutb wrote following a visit to America which confirmed his views about the West. He attacks the mixing of the sexes in American society and what he considered to be the unrestrained behaviour of American women:

> They danced to the tunes of the Gramophone, and the dance-floor was replete with tapping feet, enticing legs, arms wrapped around waists, lips pressed to lips, and chests pressed to chests, the atmosphere was full of desire[43]

or

> The American girl is well-acquainted with her body's seductive capacity. She knows it lies in the face, and in expressive eyes and thirsty lips. She knows seductiveness lies in the round breasts, the full buttocks, and in the shapely thighs and sleek legs. She knows all this and does not hide it.[44]

Sayyid Qutb may have been a prude, but his position was a passionate one of principle. He was a shy, sensitive man with poor health who came from a deeply religious background in rural Egypt, where men and women would not dance together, nor even eat together at Western-style dinner parties. He saw the West as a threat to the values of the Muslim family. Like Hassan al-Banna and many others, he believed Westerners lacked dignity and were promiscuous, and that this promiscuity was a corruption at the valueless heart of Western society. Yet this was only part of a greater picture. For him, America was a symbol of an attitude to life which was profoundly wrong:

> [The USA is a] country of mass production, immense wealth and easy pleasures. I have seen [Americans] a helpless prey in the clutches of nervous diseases in spite of all their grand appearances . . . They are like machines swirling around madly, aimlessly into the unknown

. . . That they produce a lot there is no doubt. But to what aim is this mad rush? For the mere aim of gaining and production. The human element has no place if their life is neglected . . . Their life is an everlasting windmill which grinds all in its way: men, things, places and time . . . What is the medicine to all this imbroglio? A peaceful heart, a serene soul, the pleasure which follows strenuous work, the relation of affection between men, the cooperation of friends.[45]

Sayyid Qutb's attacks on Western capitalism, lifestyles and sexual mores are inseparably linked: they are idols that lead the true believer away from God. Like 'Western promiscuity', capitalism and the cult of the individual suck the spiritual energy out of Muslim society and deprive it of the social justice that should be at its core. After some reflection, he came to the conclusion that the place for women was in the home, finding their fulfilment through nurturing the next generation of Muslims and avoiding the possibility that they would lead men astray. This meant that they should renounce the opportunities the modern world gave them in the workplace.

Sunni Islam teaches that revolt against a Muslim ruler is something only to be contemplated in desperate circumstances, since the *fitna*, the civil disorder, it produces is likely to be worse than tyranny. Nevertheless, Sayyid Qutb noticed there was one major figure, Ibn Taymiyya, who had once preached jihad against nominally Muslim rulers who did not enforce Sharia. Ibn Taymiyya had not made clear what degree of departure from Sharia amounted to apostasy. This left open a door at which those who followed Sayyid Qutb could push. Sayyid Qutb also had an answer to justify himself against the charge that his views would lead to *fitna*. When asked during the interrogation at his trial whether 'the establishment of a Muslim military underground may bring about a *fitna* or so serious a calamity that Islam may perish', he replied: 'It may well bring about *fitna*, but the blame should be placed at the door of those who interdict open Muslim Brotherhood activity thus pushing Muslims to underground action.'[46]

Only a year after Sayyid Qutb's execution, war would come to the Arab world with consequences that neither the victors nor the vanquished anticipated. One of those unforeseen consequences was that his ideas, which might have remained fairly obscure, would now become relevant for a significant number of people.

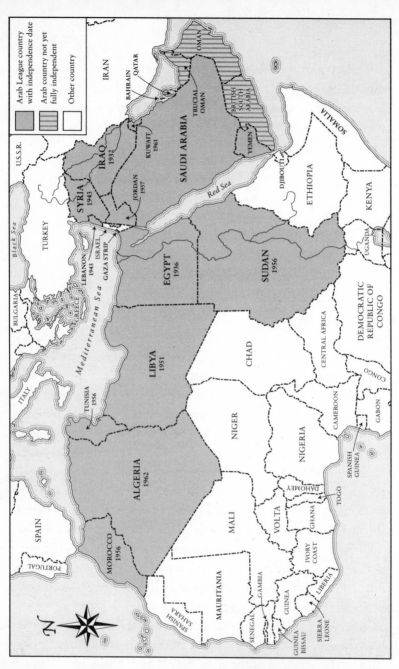

THE ARAB WORLD AT THE BEGINNING OF 1967
(DATES REFER TO YEAR OF LEGAL INDEPENDENCE)

CHAPTER SEVEN

THE SIX DAY WAR AND ITS CONSEQUENCES

I

It might have seemed to an observer at the start of 1967 that Nasser's dream that the Arab world would throw off the shackles of foreign control was fast becoming a reality. Surveying the scene broadly from West to East, Morocco and Tunisia had become fully independent in 1956 and France's protectorates over them had been terminated. Long ago, Algeria had been annexed as French sovereign territory and considered part of metropolitan France but it, too, became fully independent in 1962 after a bitter and very bloody war of independence. Britain had administered the former Italian colony of Libya after the Second World War, but it became an independent kingdom in 1951. In 1956, the shared Egyptian and British sovereignty over Sudan had also ended and Sudan, too, became a fully independent state. In the Arab East, Syria and Iraq now espoused forms of Arab socialism akin to that of Nasser, while Jordan and Kuwait were no longer tied to Britain by special treaty relationships and prudently hedged their bets. In South Arabia, Britain had decided to withdraw from its colony of Aden and the protectorates in its hinterland before the year was out. The only territories with which Britain still had a formal treaty relationship which gave it control over foreign affairs were Oman, Bahrain, Qatar and the small states that would form the UAE in 1971.

True, the forces that defied Nasser were far from dead. The main obstacle to revolutionary progress was King Faisal of Saudi Arabia. Faisal's support for reactionary and tribal elements in Yemen had bogged down the forces of the revolution and its Egyptian allies. But who knew at the start of 1967 how that conflict would end? Revolutionary forces were gaining the upper hand in Aden and its protectorates where British authority was disintegrating. Who could say this revolution would not spread to the Gulf? There was already an insurrection in southern Oman. History seemed to be on the side of the Arab nationalist revolutionaries.

Any such thoughts were hubristic. It was only possible to look at the Arab world in this way if the crucial realities of the unresolved Palestine problem and Israeli military superiority were swept under the carpet. Another full-scale war between Israel and its neighbours was the inevitable outcome of the failure to settle the dispute which the establishment of Israel had created in 1947–9. Israel's subsequent behaviour, especially its attack on Egypt in 1956 in collusion with Britain and France, had confirmed all the worst fears among Arabs. It was seen as the servant of the imperialism which still aimed to dominate and exploit the region.

Before Suez, Nasser had devoted little attention to Israel and had been in contact with figures in Israeli governments more than once, but the Israeli raid on Gaza in February 1955 and the Suez/Sinai war hardened his attitude. Palestine was also an issue that blended naturally with his pan-Arabism, an injustice that resonated deeply. This made it impossible for any Arab leader to be seen to compromise and provided a gift for demagogues of all political persuasions. Nasser began to indulge in extreme rhetoric. In 1962 he referred to 'the cancer in the Arab region that is Israel',[1] and in 1965 stated that 'progress for us is death for Israel'.[2] In 1963 it had been suggested he should meet Ben Gurion, but he turned the offer down because he saw Ben Gurion as untrustworthy. His reasons were the 1948 war, the attack on Gaza in 1955 and the Suez/Sinai war.[3] Nevertheless,

Egypt did put out a peace feeler in 1965 which came to nothing.[4]

The run-up to the Six Day War began with tension between Israel and Syria. Border incidents had occurred regularly along this front since the 1949 cease-fire, but the much more important question of the headwaters of the river Jordan was not limited to the border area. Israel had built a canal to divert water from the river and was determined to stop, by force of arms if necessary, any attempt by Syria or Lebanon to carry out their own diversion schemes further upstream. Israel's canal was a major threat to the water supplies of Syria and Jordan. When Israel completed its works in 1964, the Arab League responded with a programme for action that was prefaced by a formal declaration on behalf of its members which made the destruction of Israel an ultimate goal.

Israel's military operations deterred Syria from completing its own diversion works, but in retaliation Syria encouraged pin-prick raids into Israel by Palestinian guerrillas. These included acts of sabotage aimed at Israel's new water carrier as well as attacks on civilians, many of which were carried out through Jordanian territory despite Jordan's best attempts to prevent them. International tension mounted as the Israeli government used its military superiority to begin a strategy of escalation on the Syrian front in the spring of 1967. This included initiating artillery duels and air strikes, and the use of bullying and inflammatory rhetoric. The Israeli chief of staff, Yitzhak Rabin, gave a newspaper interview in which he said Israel should occupy Damascus and overthrow the Syrian government if it did not end its support for Palestinian guerrillas. The prime minister, Levi Eshkol, and other figures made statements in which they pointedly did not disassociate themselves from such thinking.

By contrast, Nasser had kept the guerrillas in the Gaza Strip on a tight leash so that Israel's borders with Egypt and Gaza were quiet. He did not want war with Israel at this stage, and had warned the other Arab states not to allow a military confrontation with Israel to occur until they had built up their armed forces. His military commitments in Yemen were substantial, and the Egyptian armed forces were not prepared for another campaign. Yet he had to be seen to act by supporting Syria in some tangible way. At the same time, the Jordanians were taunting him since he had not done anything in response to Israel's raid on the West Bank village of Samu the previous November, which Israel had virtually razed to the ground, killing twenty-one Jordanian soldiers and wounding thirty-seven.

His response was to send a large force of troops into Sinai, to exercise his right to demand the withdrawal of the UN force which had been stationed there with Egyptian permission since Israel withdrew in 1957, and to prevent access to the Israeli port of Eilat on the Red Sea by blockading the Straits of Tiran. In a speech on 26 May he said that if Israel 'embarks on aggression against Syria or Egypt, the battle against Israel will be a general one . . . and our basic objective will be to destroy Israel'.[5] The following day he spoke to the National Assembly, and said that he was not just trying to restore the situation to what it had been before 1956 but to that before 1948. Egypt's radio stations, which were aimed at Arab and international opinion as well as home consumption, broadcast claims that Egypt was about to liberate Palestine.

Nasser's rhetoric terrified the Israeli public and gave Israel what seemed to most Western opinion and many people all over the world a perfectly justifiable excuse to attack Egypt, while Israel's earlier threats against Syria were hardly noticed in the Western media. In fact, Egypt was intent on resolving the crisis through negotiation at the UN and via the Americans, but the Israeli military and much of the country's governing establishment was itching for war and the conquests that would follow. Israel's main aim was the destruction of the Egyptian army, and it began this process by launching a surprise air attack on the morning of 5 June which destroyed Egypt's air force on the ground and effectively decided the outcome of the conflict. The Egyptian response was to claim great successes in the war that had just begun and which Israel easily portrayed to the world as an attack by Egypt. One result was that Jordanian military air traffic controllers actually thought Israeli planes which they saw returning to base on their radar screens were Egyptian bombers attacking Israeli airbases. They were not the only ones deceived. To this day it is widely believed in the West that Egypt either started the war or was about to do so.

The Israeli military knew they were superior to the combined armed forces of their neighbours and that, even if Egypt attacked first, Israel would win.[6] They were anxious to strike at some point before the Arab states were able to level the playing field. If, as in 1956, Jordan had been able to stay neutral (it had just entered into a defensive alliance with Egypt), Israel might not have seized East Jerusalem and the West Bank as well. But the political reality for King Hussein was that he had no choice but to be seen to be supporting Egypt. With the gates of the temple of Janus opened once again, Israel took full advantage of the situation as it developed. It pushed with alacrity all the way to the Suez Canal and the Jordan valley, then seized the Syrian Golan Heights, turning a deaf ear to calls for a cease-fire until it had achieved its objectives. By the time the guns fell silent, Israel was in belligerent occupation of very substantial extra territories. These included those parts of the Palestine Mandate it had not seized in 1947–9: the West Bank of the Jordan, including East Jerusalem, and the formerly Egyptian-occupied Gaza Strip. In addition, it now had possession of the entirety of the Sinai Peninsula and the Syrian mountains that rose to the east of the Sea of Galilee. The Suez Canal ceased to be an international waterway and was transformed into a defensive ditch, while Israeli observers could now look down on the plains of Damascus and southern Syria from the peak of Jebel al-shaykh at a height of over 2,800 metres.

II

Although Israel's victory dazzled the world and changed the face of the Middle East, it made yet further conflict inevitable. It can also be seen as the start of a new era. The departure of the colonial powers was nearly complete before the war began, but Nasser's hope that the Arabs could fill the vacuum they left was now dashed beyond any possibility of repair. The Six Day War ended any doubt that the Arab world would be a front line in the Cold War and a theatre for wars by proxy.

The war also ensured that a specifically Palestinian identity would prevail among the inhabitants of the newly occupied Palestinian territories. This made the moral legitimacy which Israel craved above all else a yet harder objective to achieve. In 1974 the Arab League would pass a resolution making the Palestine Liberation Organisation (PLO) 'the sole legitimate representative of the Palestinian people' which would one day compel Israel to accept the Palestinians as a nation.

The PLO had been set up by the Arab League in 1964 with the object of establishing a secular state between the Jordan and the Mediterranean. This would end the territorial division caused by the establishment of Israel and, of necessity, lead to the end of the Jewish state. Nasser intended the PLO to be a symbolic body without any teeth, but following Israel's conquests in 1967 it escaped from his control. The largest movement affiliated to it was Fatah, which was led by the PLO's chairman, Yasser Arafat. His designer stubble and trademark Palestinian *keffaya* headdress soon made him a figure recognised all over the world.

The PLO gradually became 'a state within a state' in Jordan, which they used as a base for raids into Israel and the occupied West Bank. By the summer of 1970, a showdown with King Hussein was inevitable. After several bloody days of fighting, his army pushed the Palestinian militias out of the country. They made their way to Lebanon, a state with a much weaker government, where they were able to resume their attacks on Israel from the south of the country.

This, coupled with the inevitable Israeli counter-strikes, was a major factor leading to the destabilisation of Lebanon and the beginning of its sectarian civil war that started in 1975.

In September 1970, Nasser died suddenly from a heart attack at the age of fifty-two. The style of his successor, Anwar al-Sadat, was very different. Sadat had also been one of the Free Officers, although a relatively junior one. He seemed cautious, but as soon as he had a chance he set about trying to find ways to open up the economy to foreign investment. He also made a point of displaying his sympathy with the traditional values of rural Egypt, a populist move with a conservative emphasis that was different from that which Nasser might have shown. His forehead carried the *zabib* or 'raisin', the mark of hard skin formed by a devout Muslim saying his daily five sets of prayers, and he allowed a greater degree of religiosity in public life.

Whether his policy towards Israel was a departure from Nasser's is another question, for on this issue both men were ultimately driven by pragmatism, and it is impossible to say what course Nasser would have followed if he had survived. What the record does show is that Sadat was quite prepared to make peace in exchange for a complete Israeli withdrawal from Egyptian territory. At the time Sadat came to power, however, Israel wanted the border between the two countries very substantially redrawn in Israel's favour and its possession of the other occupied territories consolidated. The new status quo after 1967 meant that the passage of time could only reinforce Israel's position, and that the international community would increasingly acquiesce in it. Once again, Israel did not need peace and was not prepared to offer to return its spoils of war in order to achieve it.[7]

On 6 October 1973, it was the turn of Egypt and Syria to launch their own attack without warning. The Egyptians crossed the Suez Canal in dinghies along its entire length and established a defensive line a few kilometres to the east. The first Israeli counter-attacks were cut to pieces, but then forces led by General Ariel Sharon found a weak point in the middle of the front, punched their way across and wheeled south to encircle the Egyptian Third Army around Suez. Although from a military perspective Israel finished the war as clear victor on both fronts, it had suffered heavy losses and did not succeed in destroying the Egyptian army as it had done in 1967. On the Golan Heights, the initial Syrian onslaught had thrust deep into Israeli-held territory, nearly taking possession of the crest that looked down onto the Galilee before being pushed back. Israel ended the war with a greatly expanded area of Syrian territory under its control.

Under American pressure, disengagement soon followed. Israel evacuated the territory it had occupied during the fighting, and had to make withdrawals from its pre-war front lines. In the Golan Heights, an area including the summit of Mount Hermon and the town of Quneitra were restored to Syrian civilian control. In Sinai, Israel withdrew sufficiently for Egypt to reopen the Suez Canal. However, hopes for a more comprehensive peace soon ran into the sand. Attempts to draw Jordan into disengagement negotiations foundered as Rabin, the Israeli prime minister, promised that any withdrawal on the West Bank would be subject to a referendum of the Israeli electorate. He contemptuously told the Jordanians that the disengagement principle did not apply to them because they had not taken part in the attack. Over the next couple of years further steps were taken between Israel and Egypt which led to an additional Israeli withdrawal in Sinai. An increasing rift opened between Egypt and Syria, as no similar negotiations were facilitated between Syria and Israel. If there was a chance to negotiate a comprehensive peace it was soon lost. The diplomacy of Henry Kissinger, the US Secretary of State, seemed in the words of a leading historian of the period to have been aimed at 'dividing the Arab world, avoiding the core issues of the Arab Israeli conflict and frustrating the search for a comprehensive settlement',[8] while the efforts of King Hussein of Jordan to work out a peaceful solution to the conflict 'were met, for the most part, with ignorance and indifference on the part of top American policy makers and dishonesty and deviousness on the part of the Israeli ones'.[9]

III

Simultaneously, tensions between the different religious factions in Lebanon were bubbling to the surface in a dangerous way. As was seen in Chapter 4, the country had originally been created as a Maronite Christian enclave which took in sufficient of the neighbouring areas and their inhabitants to form a viable sovereign state. The idea had been that the Maronites would be able to dominate, but this had become less sustainable as different religious groups in Lebanon increased in population at varying rates, which reflected both natural increase and emigration, and had made the government too nervous about the political consequences of a census to hold one since 1931. Now everybody knew that the Muslim groups, when added together and including the Druze, formed a majority of the population while the Maronites were not prepared to sacrifice their leading position. Factions on all sides had militias, sometimes several competing ones. These were significant enough for outside parties that wished to influence Lebanese affairs to back them as proxies. There was an additional complication in the south, where large numbers of Palestinian guerrillas were now carrying out operations against Israel. Lebanon's weak government was the product of compromises which gave no opportunity for strong rule of the kind which enabled King Hussein to drive the PLO out of Jordan.

Fighting broke out in 1975 between various 'right-wing' Christian militias and 'left-wing' Arab nationalist and predominantly Muslim forces. The PLO became involved on the left-wing side, earning Palestinians the hatred of right-wing Maronites. The conflict soon developed a disturbing feature on both sides: sectarian massacres carried out solely for revenge, on some occasions killing hundreds of people. When it looked as though the largely Muslim, left-wing militias and their PLO allies were winning, the Ba'athist Syria of Hafez al-Assad supported the Christian militias and entered the country at the invitation of the government to restore the status quo.

This began a period of Syrian domination of Lebanon that would last for some thirty years. Now that it had a hegemonic position in the country, Syria's concern would be to ensure that no Lebanese faction could become strong enough to displace it. The alliance with the Christian militias was one of expediency, and Syria would not hesitate to turn against them when circumstances dictated. For its part, Israel let it be known quietly that it would allow the Syrians to intervene to save Israel's clients and restore the balance of power, provided they did not advance south of Sidon or use their air force.

Some in Israel remembered an old Zionist dream of a Christian Lebanon that would be its ally, an idea which had always had influential advocates in the Maronite community. The paradox was that, while Israel allowed Syria to shore up the elements in Lebanon it felt were most sympathetic to it, the PLO was able to take refuge from the Syrians in the buffer zone south of Sidon which Israel would not allow Syria to penetrate. Strife-torn Lebanon was now ripped to shreds because of its strategic position between Israel and Syria.

In Israeli elections in 1977, the Likud party became dominant and its leader, Menachem Begin, the prime minister. Likud and Begin openly preached an ideology under which Zionists had the right to all the land between the Mediterranean and the Jordan. On the other hand, Jimmy Carter, the new president of the USA, was more committed to the search for peace between Arabs and Israelis than any previous US president, and even – to Begin's fury – spoke of 'the legitimate rights of the Palestinian people'.

When attempts at establishing multilateral talks failed, Sadat visited Jerusalem in November 1977, where he courteously and eloquently put the Arab case in his speech to the Knesset, the Israeli parliament. He made it clear that peace would require Israel to return in full the territories it had occupied in 1967. However, while he was prepared to make peace for Egypt on the basis of Israel's withdrawal from occupied Egyptian territory, he had no control over the actions or tactics of other Arab states, or over Israel's. The other Arab states were devastated. In particular, Syria, which had lost its vital military ally, felt betrayed.

The peace treaty Egypt and Israel eventually signed on 29 March 1979 provided for full normalisation of relations, a complete withdrawal by Israel in stages from occupied Egyptian land, and detailed arrangements for security in the Sinai peninsula where Egypt's military forces would be restricted. But the arrangements for Palestinian autonomy which Sadat negotiated in the accompanying Camp David Accords were vague, and Begin found ways to ensure they were stillborn. He not only stepped up settlement activities, but established Israel's first settlement in the Gaza Strip. Peace between Egypt and Israel did not, therefore, prepare the way for general peace or the integration of Israel into the region. By splitting the Arab states, it arguably made this goal harder to achieve.

On 6 October 1981, while taking the salute in a parade celebrating the eighth anniversary of Egypt's triumph in crossing the Suez Canal, Anwar Sadat was assassinated by militants inspired by Sayyid Qutb's ideology. He joined King Abdullah I of Jordan and possibly Husni Zai'm of Syria in paying the price for trying to reach a settlement with Israel. His funeral was attended by three former American presidents: Jimmy Carter, Richard Nixon and Gerald Ford, but not a single Arab head of state.

IV

There was one other consequence of the Arab defeat in the Six Day War which took some time to become apparent. Throughout history, people have turned to God in repentance for their sins after they have suffered some calamity. The Six Day War of 1967 was certainly the kind of event likely to provoke such a response. Said Aburish, a Palestinian intellectual from Bethany outside Jerusalem, wrote in 2004 that the war 'resembled an act of mass suicide' which prevented anybody

speaking of the dignity and pride of the Arabs. An entire generation
of Arabs had egged their rulers on, pushing them into postures which
enabled Israel to go to war even though the leaderships knew they did
not have the military strength to resist an Israeli attack.[10]

It would not have been surprising if, in their despair and humiliation, some conservative Arab Muslims saw the military disaster of the
Six Day War as punishment for their sins and the neglect of religious
observance. This coincided with a shift in the balance of power in the
Arab world towards the oil-rich, Wahhabi monarchy of Saudi Arabia.

When the Organisation of Petroleum Exporting Countries,
OPEC, was founded in newly revolutionary Baghdad in 1959, three
of its four initial members (Iraq, Saudi Arabia, Iran and Venezuela) were from the Middle East, and two of them were Arab. OPEC
helped its growing number of members use their muscle to raise
revenues. In the early 1970s, producing states began nationalising
their oil industries or acquiring majority stakes in the operating companies. The key moment was the series of production cuts during
the 1973 war which included a temporary embargo on sales to the
United States. This quadrupled prices and triggered a recession in
the West. Although the producers could not maintain control of the
market, international dependence on Middle Eastern hydrocarbons
made the region ever more important strategically.

Saudi Arabia led the embargo in 1973 and was by far the most
powerful of the Arab oil states. It was the one major Arab country
that had successfully resisted Western ideologies, although Arab
nationalism had a strong impact in the 1950s and 1960s. As we have
seen, King Faisal, who came to power in 1964, was Nasser's principal
Arab opponent. He seems to have considered Nasser an apostate
driven by a desire for power and appealed for a much greater emphasis
on Islam as a force to bind Arab and other Muslim countries together.
Faisal's moment came in 1969 when an Australian Christian fanatic
tried to burn down the al-Aqsa mosque in Israeli-occupied East
Jerusalem, destroying the pulpit Saladin had presented to it nearly

800 years earlier. Predominantly Muslim states joined together to establish their own international body, the Organisation of the Islamic Conference. An agreement to campaign to restore the rights of the Palestinians was written into its charter, thus making Palestine explicitly a Muslim as well as an Arab issue.

Egyptian migrant workers and pilgrims who went to Saudi Arabia saw a society at which, until recently, they had been able to laugh because of its Bedouin values and general lack of sophistication. The Wahhabi kingdom had always been arrogant, but that arrogance was no longer a joke at which they could scoff. New highways and clean cities of glass and marble were rising with breathtaking speed from the bare desert. It often seemed as though these cities had barely been completed before they were knocked down and rebuilt on a brighter and even more expansive scale, a process that was sometimes repeated every few years. The place of Islam in the life of the kingdom was a direct challenge to secularism in every predominantly Muslim country, and visitors from poorer Arab countries were impressed by the way in which it (and the other Gulf states) began spending massively on healthcare, education, housing and other services for ordinary people. This munificence may have been inspired by fear of revolution, but it had its roots in traditional patronage by the tribal shaykh, not in some Western-inspired, socialist ideology, and was financed by oil money. It was thus authentically Arab. And all this was possible while the royal family lived lavishly and there was ample spending on defence.

By contrast, there was an atmosphere of despair in those Arab countries that did not have massive oil revenues. The Arab world was experiencing an intensifying population explosion as migrants flocked to the cities and medical care improved. The war with Israel had devastated the economies of Egypt, Syria and Jordan, while Nasser's economic policies were now shown conclusively to be disastrous. Not only was there now no hope of a balance of power between Israel and the Arab states, but the balance of power within the Arab world itself had changed.

CHAPTER EIGHT

IRAQ, ISRAEL, MILITANCY AND TERRORISM

I

1979 was not only the year of the Egypt–Israel peace treaty. It saw two events which were of huge significance for the growth of political Islam although both took place outside the Arab world. The first was the Islamic revolution in Iran. The second was the Soviet invasion of Afghanistan. Both were also episodes in the Cold War between the West and the Soviet bloc which dominated the geopolitics of the era. In the Arab world, the West had the upper hand and all the monarchies and Egypt were firmly in the Western camp. But there were also states which inclined towards the Soviet bloc, especially those with an Arab socialist ideology such as Syria, Iraq, Algeria and South Yemen. The PLO under Yasser Arafat also fell into this category. At the time, it would have been a brave observer who hazarded that no more Arab monarchies would be overthrown by a group of free officers with nationalist and socialist views. Egypt's shift from Soviet to American ally had demonstrated how Arab allegiances were based on self-interest and not ideology. Further shifts by Arab states were possible, and they might be in either direction.

At that time, predominantly Shi'ite Iran was ruled by the Shah, Muhammad Reza Pahlavi, the son of an army officer who had seized power in the 1920s and proclaimed himself emperor. The Shah owed his position to support from America and Britain and used symbols from Iran's ancient, pre-Islamic past to provide a nationalist narrative for a modernising nation. He bullied his smaller neighbours and maintained that security in the Gulf was the responsibility of the local states alone, with the strong implication that the whole area with its vast oil resources should be an Iranian sphere of influence. The threat which many Arab countries feel today from Iran can be traced back to these policies.

When his regime collapsed in February 1979, the ideology that replaced the Shah's nationalist vision of Iran was a revolutionary form of Shi'ism. This was formulated by the spiritual leader of the revolution, the Ayatollah Khomeini, whose thought included a new concept: the *velayat-e faqih*, literally 'Government of the Sharia Jurist'. Under the watchful guidance of learned religious teachers who would play a role unprecedented in the history of Islam, Iran would adapt whatever it considered good in the modern world but otherwise re-establish the purity of a truly Muslim society.

Ayatollah Khomeini was revered for his consistency in opposing the Shah at great personal cost. Unusually for a revolutionary, he was able to appeal to devout middle-class merchants and those who felt they had lost out during the Shah's rule, as well as to radicals and unemployed young men from the slums. *Velayat-e faqih* was controversial among Shi'ite religious leaders, and there was no inevitability that it would be implemented if the revolution succeeded. In fact, it was far from certain that the revolution would be Islamic. The forces which opposed the Shah were diverse and included very substantial non-Islamic elements, such as mainstream secularists, social democrats and Communists who found themselves ruthlessly purged once the Shah had fallen.

II

Islam now became the obvious rallying point for those who wanted to fight for justice in conflicts which could be seen as attacks on Muslims by non-Muslims. It was a time of great optimism for Islamists, although the triumph of a Shi'ite revolution would now widen the distance between Sunnis and Shi'ites which had been narrowing in earlier decades. Among Sunnis, appeals could be made to the theology of jihad whenever it was argued that war was needed to liberate a Muslim people oppressed by non-Muslims. Palestine was just one of a number of examples. Others were causes outside the Arab world such as secessionist movements in Kashmir, Chechnya, parts of the southern Philippines, and Bosnia at the time of the horrors of the dissolution of Yugoslavia.

The most significant of these conflicts for the development of political Islam was Afghanistan. Afghanistan was a pre-industrial, tribal society divided among different ethnic groups, none of which constituted a majority in the country as a whole. Originally a monarchy whose light rule survived because it understood how to compromise with local interests, it fell to a Marxist coup in April 1978 after a brief period as a republic under a member of the royal family who had seized power. When a Marxist faction attempted to impose socialism, widespread rebellion broke out. Although this was ethnically and tribally based, the factions united behind Islam as the core of Afghan identity. When the Soviets intervened in December 1979, the rebellions expanded to involve the majority of the population. Supported by money and arms from the Americans and Saudis, as well as a trickle of volunteers from Arab and Muslim countries, the resistance finally forced the Soviets into ignominious withdrawal ten years later.

This provided another enormous morale-booster to Islamists. Most observers believe that the Arab and other Muslim fighters who travelled to Afghanistan to take part in the jihad against the

Soviet invaders were of little military significance, but they left with a sensation of victory. Some went home proud that they had done something good and resumed their lives as ordinary people, but a significant number were determined to find other conflicts in which to fight jihad. Perhaps, after all, it was Islam, not secular nationalism, that was on the right side of history. The Soviet withdrawal was swiftly followed by the collapse of Communism in Eastern Europe. If Islam could slay that great behemoth, might it not also prove to be the force that would finally defeat America and its capitalist ideology? Resentment and hatred of the West had been one of the spurs behind the Iranian revolution.

With the invaders gone, Afghani politics became more complex. The lack of unity among those who had fought the Soviets even allowed the Communist government in Kabul to survive for a short while before it was replaced by coalitions of brutal and feuding warlords. It would only be in September 1996 that a Wahhabi religious movement called the Taliban (literally, 'the students of religious practice') took Kabul. Their control spread so that by late 1998 they were in control of 85 per cent of the country, although in some areas it was fiercely contested. The Taliban were sympathetic to Islamists who sought to use teachings such as those of Sayyid Qutb to establish Islamist states in other Muslim countries. They would harbour Osama bin Laden and al-Qa'ida, the organisation he established.

But before turning to these, and to the topic of terrorism generally, two key sets of conflicts which dominated the central lands of the Arab world into the twenty-first century must be examined. The first set revolves around the ambitions of one man, the Iraqi dictator Saddam Hussein. It comprises the Iran–Iraq War of the 1980s, the invasion of Kuwait in 1990 and the 2003 invasion of Iraq by a US-led coalition and the ensuing period of chaos. The other set consists of the ongoing Arab–Israeli dispute and the conflicts in adjacent Lebanon, into which the Arab–Israeli dispute continued to intrude.

III

Not all oil-rich Arab states were conservative monarchies. In Iraq, the secularist Ba'ath party under Hasan al-Bakr took power in a coup in 1968. Although its power base consisted of Sunni Arabs from his own part of the country, the Ba'athists found followers among all Iraq's communities and the party had many Shi'ite members. Nevertheless, the loyalty of the Shi'ite majority was always suspect, and there was open rebellion in Kurdistan. Iraq also came under pressure from Iran, its large and powerful non-Arab neighbour to the East.

In 1969, the Shah tore up the boundary treaty with Iraq dealing with the Shatt al-Arab waterway. Iraq had no real political choice other than to bow to his demands, but the crisis had serious internal repercussions. When Hasan al-Bakr failed to persuade the country's leading Shi'ite religious leader, Ayatollah Muhsin al-Hakim, to condemn the Iranian government's position, he was alarmed to see the Ayatollah receive support from some Sunni religious leaders.

The result was a repression of the public expression of Islam reminiscent of the Soviet hostility to religion and unparalleled in an Arab country. As government alarm at a possible united front of Sunni and Shi'ite opposition activity deepened, religious instruction in schools was ended and the Qur'an no longer recited on state broadcasting networks. The outrage this provoked was brutally put down. Shi'ite unrest eventually led to Saddam Hussein replacing Hasan al-Bakr in 1979. A purge of elements which might be a threat to the new leader followed, with possibly 500 being executed – a foretaste of what was to come.

Saddam Hussein was a civilian from a landless peasant family. A second cousin of Hasan al-Bakr, he started his rise to power without influence of his own or the possibility of joining an influential clique of officers in the army. Despite these major handicaps, he was to rule Iraq for longer than anyone else, through what Charles Tripp has called a 'disconcerting combination of charm, generosity and ruthless terror'.[1] He established his own version of Iraqi identity, looking back to the greatness of the ancient peoples of Mesopotamia and recreating them as proto-Arabs then drawing an unbroken line of greatness from them to the Abbasids and, ultimately, himself. Fear was the basis of his rule, but he also took the patronage which his predecessors had exercised to its ultimate conclusion. The fear and patronage were two sides of the same coin, as he ensured that the holder of every significant position of authority in Iraq only enjoyed his post on sufferance from himself. He was the archetypal brutal dictator. As he put it in the late 1980s, it was for him to decide what Ba'athism meant and 'the law is anything I write on a scrap of paper'.[2]

The chaos in Iran after the revolution made the new regime vulnerable. The military was in disarray following purges, and Western countries ceased supplying spare parts for the equipment they had sold the Shah. If Iraq was ever to restore its rights in the Shatt al-Arab and wipe out its humiliation at the hands of the Shah, this seemed to be the moment. It could also force the Gulf states to line up behind it, as well as ensure once and for all that Iran stopped stirring up trouble among its own Shi'ites and Kurds. In September 1980, Saddam Hussein attacked. After advancing into southern Iran to remove the Iranians from the hinterland of the Shatt al-Arab and seizing a few strategic points further north, his army halted and dug in. It did not go for the Iranian jugular and destroy Iran's capacity to fight. Saddam Hussein believed his military superiority would persuade the Iranians to negotiate. Instead, with their country as well as their revolution under attack, the Iranians responded with all-out war.

In 1982 Iran recovered most of the territory it had lost, and Saddam Hussein was obliged to offer peace based upon a full withdrawal. Determined to force a change of government in Baghdad, Iran rejected the offer. However, now that Iraq itself was under threat, the rejection strengthened Iraqi resolve. Iran remained on the offensive, sending wave after wave of attacks against the Iraqis, including the *Basij*, soldiers in their mid-teens or even younger who advanced across minefields with a key to Paradise around their necks and a symbolic shroud as part of their equipment.

Eventually, the massive casualties such Iranian tactics required took their toll, as did the superior weaponry that Iraq procured abroad, especially from Russia and France. The Gulf states helped with money, while the Americans supplied satellite imagery and other support. An exhausted Iran accepted a cease-fire in 1988, but by this time at least 250,000 Iraqis had been killed – some estimates suggest double this figure. Perhaps 60,000 or more of these were Kurds who had died in uprisings during which the Iraqi forces used scorched-earth tactics, including chemical weapons which were also deployed against the Iranian front line. Large numbers of Iraqi soldiers, perhaps 60,000 or 70,000, had been taken prisoner. Iranian casualty figures are not known, but it seems safe to conclude that they were higher than Iraq's. A figure in excess of half a million is perfectly possible.

In 1980, at the height of the oil boom, Iraq had $35 billion in reserves. When the war ended, it was $80 billion in debt and close to insolvency. No peace treaty was signed. Iraq needed to maintain its large conscript army of a million men for the foreseeable future. Concerned with retaining his hold on power, Saddam Hussein purged the officer corps which had expanded as the army grew during the conflict. He even had to remove members of his close circle who must have noticed how questionable his judgement had been. The death of the minister of defence, his own brother-in-law, in a helicopter crash may not have been an accident.

Half of Iraq's oil revenues now had to be used for servicing its debt. When requests to Gulf states to cancel their loans or cut production to improve the market for Iraq's oil fell on deaf ears, Saddam Hussein's response was a military swagger coupled with attempts to induce guilt. After all, had he not blunted the Iranian revolution? Was this not something for which everyone – the Gulf states, all Sunni Arabs and, indeed, the West – should be grateful?

When these tactics achieved nothing, he played the military card once again and sent his army to occupy Kuwait in August 1990. His strategy seems to have been remarkably similar to that which led him so disastrously to invade Iran. This limited use of force would compel others to negotiate, and Saudi Arabia and the other Arab Gulf states would be put in a position where they had no choice but to accept Iraqi hegemony.

It was a monumental miscalculation. Iraq was condemned by the United Nations, which authorised the use of force to liberate Kuwait. Sanctions were imposed, and a powerful US-led coalition was soon in place to accomplish that liberation. As well as the USA, Britain and France, the coalition contained very substantial Arab elements, including Saudi Arabia and the other Gulf states, Egypt, Syria and many states from the wider Muslim world.

Saddam Hussein's political tactic was to link the Kuwait issue with that of Palestine. He suggested the two problems should be resolved together. Although this was obviously self-serving, it created genuine popular support for him throughout the Arab world except in the Gulf monarchies, whose peoples he had antagonised and terrified. The Palestinian leader Yasser Arafat flew to Baghdad and greeted Saddam Hussein in a manner that could only be construed as supportive, thereby alienating many in the Gulf from the Palestinian cause and increasing the divide between them and the populations of poorer Arab countries. Like Arafat and many other Arab leaders of revolutionary regimes in the second half of the twentieth century, Saddam Hussein had had little exposure to the West before he came to power and his understanding of it and its psychology was limited.

The American-led coalition pushed the Iraqis out of Kuwait after a six-week bombing offensive that shattered Iraq's civilian and military infrastructure. Saddam Hussein had placed himself in a position where he could not back down. When the inevitable came, he left his army to its fate and concentrated instead on preserving the Republican Guard units which he needed to keep his rule intact. He also ordered the igniting of the Kuwaiti oilfields: a monstrous act of frustrated power and vengeance. All it achieved, apart from massive environmental damage, was to burden the Iraqi state with further huge liabilities in the form of reparations.

The successful expulsion of the Iraqis by the American-led coalition left a bitter taste in the mouths of the many who had hoped for an Iraqi victory. If these events had occurred in the 1950s or 1960s, the reaction would have been an Arab nationalist one. Much of the reaction was still nationalist, but now it was expressed in Islamist terms. Struggles against invaders in the Arab world were seen as part and parcel of the struggle against secular Arab governments which were perceived as tyrants and collaborators with the West: a category which now included the very unsecular Saudi Arabia.

The Kuwait crisis made it fully apparent how the reaffirmation of Muslim identity was now centre stage. Saddam Hussein was an unlikely champion for Islam, but the charge stung when he accused the Saudi royal family of betraying Islam by relying on American and other Western armies to protect their kingdom. At the same time, he condemned them and their Kuwaiti counterparts for squandering the oil wealth of their countries, and claimed he would put it at the service of the 'disinherited'. In doing so, he tapped into the desire of many people to see fat cats get their comeuppance. Large parts of the masses in poorer Arab countries demonstrated in his support in many Arab capitals. They were often led by fiery Islamist preachers who saw the Saudis as stooges of the West.

Following the near destruction of Saddam Hussein's military power, there were localised uprisings in the Shi'ite south of Iraq, while in the north the Kurdish militias pushed the Iraqi army out of predominantly Kurdish areas. The Republican Guard had little difficulty putting down the uncoordinated rebellions in the south despite a no-fly zone declared by the UN which prevented Saddam Hussein using fixed-wing aircraft. In the north, however, a similar no-fly zone helped the Kurdish areas remain outside his control.

Initially, the Kurdish safe haven this created was marred by the tribal rivalry that had always bedevilled Kurdish political movements, but in 1998 America brokered a power-sharing arrangement between them. Although relations between the factions remained tense, democratic institutions were gradually created and the economy boomed as Iraqi Kurdistan took on more of the appearance of a separate state.

The sanctions the UN had imposed on Iraq remained in place. UN resolutions required Iraq to renounce weapons of mass destruction, recognise Kuwaiti territorial integrity and pay war reparations. Saddam Hussein's response was to dig in and survive, just as he had done during the long years of the Iran–Iraq War. He also conducted a cat and mouse game with UN weapons inspectors and looked for ways to split the coalition against him. The sanctions were draconian. Except for 'supplies intended strictly for medical purposes, and, in humanitarian circumstances, foodstuffs',[3] all trade with Iraq was banned. Iraq was already a devastated country, with its infrastructure and industrial capacity shattered. It did what it could to rebuild, but so long as the sanctions remained this could only be done to a completely inadequate extent. America (often, but not always, with British support) used its position on the Security Council and the relevant UN committees to ensure that even those medicines and foodstuffs covered by the exemptions would be blocked, delayed or bogged down in the bureaucracy.

Essential services such as water, electricity and transport systems could not be repaired, nor agriculture expanded to replace the food previously imported. The sanctions thus condemned Iraq to starvation and malnutrition, leading to disease and a sharp rise in infant mortality. The interpretation of the sanctions insisted on by America made this inevitable. The driving force behind American policy was the desire for regime change: an objective that lay beyond those intended to be achieved by the sanctions the UN had imposed. In fact, America was abusing the UN.[4] Comparisons with Palestine were drawn in the Arab media, which compared the suffering of

Iraqi children with that of Palestinians under Israeli occupation.[5]

Until 1996, Saddam Hussein resisted offers for Iraq to sell quantities of oil to pay for food and medicines, since the UN insisted on disbursing these funds itself. Then he acquiesced in the hope that Iraq's cooperation would be a step towards the end of sanctions and reintegration of Iraq into the world economy. He also used the destitution in which most Iraqis now found themselves as moral blackmail in the struggle to lift sanctions, while contriving to use whatever he could siphon off from the oil for food programme and sales of smuggled oil for the patronage networks which sustained his regime.

US-led attempts to reinforce implementation of sanctions met with an increasingly lukewarm response, not least because of the humanitarian crisis they had caused. At the same time, Saddam Hussein's refusal to cooperate with the UN inspectors made it plausible that he was restarting his weapons programmes. Nevertheless, the American strategy for dealing with Iraq was containment and deterrence until President George W. Bush came to power in 2001, and remained so until after 9/11. Over the course of 2002, a number of motives for invading Iraq were put forward by the US administration. These often varied according to the audience that was being addressed: to end the potential threat of an Iraq armed with weapons of mass destruction, to replace the rule of a bloody dictator and war-monger by democracy, and to remove a backer of international terrorism and threat to Israel.

When the USA with the support of Britain and other members of President Bush's 'coalition of the willing' invaded Iraq in March 2003, Saddam Hussein's contact with reality was sufficiently tenuous for him to hope that his army might hold the Americans and their allies off long enough to achieve a cease-fire. Within weeks Iraq was occupied, but the American strategy was confused, and the staggering lack of preparation to pacify a hostile country and prepare an administration to rule it also indicated a worrying degree of self-delusion. In the first weeks of their occupation, control passed from the grasp of the Americans and their allies as bemused soldiers witnessed looting and riots which they had no orders to control – although this was a legal obligation on the occupying powers. The result was inevitable. The occupation authorities lost the initiative and were even unable to restore the run-down electricity and water supplies.

As boiling summer temperatures came to the plains of Iraq, things went badly wrong. American decisions to 'de-Ba'athify' Iraq and disband the army deprived the country of its administrators and sent hundreds of thousands of men into unemployment with nothing to take home except their weapons. De-Ba'athification was used by mushrooming, power-hungry opposition groups as an excellent opportunity to settle old scores and remove opponents. It seemed as though no one in the American-led Coalition Provisional Authority which was meant to be administering the country had studied the history of insurrections in Iraq (or Palestine) during the British Mandate, or learned how in Syria during the French Mandate incensed but very diverse groups, often led by local men with military training, ignited much of the country. A bomb killed the UN envoy sent to coordinate reconstruction, forcing the UN and the development agencies to pull their staff out. The insurgency, as it came to be called, grew among Sunni Arabs who saw their position threatened by American encouragement of the hitherto oppressed Shi'ite majority.

Whatever claim America may have had to moral high ground was lost when news of torture and sadistic degradation of prisoners at Abu Ghraib prison seeped out in April 2004. Shi'ite militias also appeared, notably the Mahdi Army of Muqtada al-Sadr, although the most senior Shi'ite religious leaders carefully remained on the sidelines. Soon the Americans had overreached themselves. Riots erupted in the south which led them to lose control of Najaf at the same time as they were taking on the Sunni insurgent stronghold of

Falluja. As with the rebellions against the Mandates in Iraq and Syria in the 1920s, a dangerous point was reached as Iraqis began to feel it was possible to defeat the Americans. Only Kurdistan was quiet. The Americans and their allies were too thinly stretched to control the rest of the country, and it was becoming a dangerous gamble for Iraqis to support them.

Terrorism against Shi'ites escalated, as did reprisals. During 2006 alone, over 35,000 Iraqi civilians and members of the security forces are known to have died as a result of the violence. Areas of towns and villages were ethnically cleansed by rival factions, and several million refugees poured into Syria and Jordan, including many members of the small Christian minorities. The American leadership was forced to accept that purely military tactics would not defeat the insurgency. Perhaps the turning point came in September that year, when an alliance of Sunni tribal leaders in Anbar Province began to cooperate with the government in Baghdad and the Americans.

Since then, political progress has been slow and fragile but incremental. Iraqis are becoming used to elections to choose their rulers at both national and local levels – and to delays of months which threaten the country's stability while elected politicians haggle about the composition of the government. The Iraqi economy is at last being reconstructed, but the main political parties which rule in coalition wield patronage in the manner of all former rulers of Iraq. This poses subtle dangers, while terrorist outrages increasingly punctuate everyday life and the threat of civil war is only in abeyance. On the one hand, patronage may subvert the new democracy since there is a risk that no major elected faction will be able to play the role of an effective parliamentary opposition. On the other, the power of patronage may help the emergence of a new strongman, this time a Shi'ite who is backed by a sectarian majority in parliament achieved through the democratic process. This would be unlikely to lead to the reconciliation Iraq so desperately needs.

IV

Egypt's separate peace with Israel transformed the dynamics of the Arab–Israeli dispute by destroying any possibility of a military balance of power between the antagonists. Although Iraq built massive armed forces and aspired to take over the political space Egypt had vacated, it could do little more than fulminate against Israel from the safety of the far side of the Syrian desert. As has been seen, it was soon preoccupied with its war with Iran.

There was now no prospect of a coalition of Arab states deterring Israel from doing whatever it chose. The Jewish state had become a strategic partner of the USA and at some point surreptitiously acquired the atom bomb. Arabs noted how successive Israeli governments had no intention of negotiating over the rights of the Palestinians in good faith. In 1981, Israel annexed the Golan Heights, although this was a self-evident breach of international law. Then, using the shooting of the Israeli ambassador in London in 1982 as a pretext, it invaded Lebanon to attack the PLO's bases and embroiled itself in the smouldering Lebanese civil war in the hope of turning that conflict to its advantage. The invasion ratcheted it up to new levels of violence.

While a limited operation in the south of the country was all the Israeli cabinet had sanctioned, the minister of defence, Ariel Sharon, had a larger vision. If Israel could defeat the PLO and ensure that the Maronite militias with which it had formed an alliance controlled Lebanon, it would be well on the way to dominating the entire region. It hoped that destroying the PLO would cripple Palestinian nationalism. Jordan could become the homeland for Palestinians and the Occupied Territories could be absorbed into the Jewish state. A Christian-dominated Lebanon, from which all pan-Arabism had been expunged, would become the second Arab state to sign a peace treaty with Israel.

Soon the Israeli army was outside Beirut, cutting the highway to Damascus and linking up with its allies. After a bloody two-month siege of the city, Israel won its prize although the UN estimated that 17,000 Lebanese and Palestinians had died in the campaign and 30,000 had been injured, the majority of whom were children.[6] The PLO was forced to withdraw to Arab countries far from its borders. Yet the decision of the Arab League that the PLO was the 'sole legitimate representative of the Palestinian People' could not be erased on the battlefield. It now had diplomatic missions in over a hundred countries and observer status at the UN. The Arab summit at Fez that September proposed Arab recognition of Israel in return for a Palestinian state in East Jerusalem, the West Bank and Gaza.

Israel stage-managed the election of its Maronite ally, Bashir Gemayyal, as president of Lebanon, but he was assassinated three weeks later. The assassination led to the massacres of Sabra and Shatila, where militiamen from the Gemayyal faction slaughtered Palestinian refugees under the eyes and ears of the Israeli army as revenge for his death. Bashir was replaced by his brother Amin, who looked to Syria rather than Israel for support. Although Amin signed the peace agreement Israel had so coveted in May 1983, under which Israel would withdraw to within forty-five kilometres of the international border, the Syrians returned to the Beirut–Damascus road and the warring militias turned one by one against the Israelis. From that point onwards, Israel's position in Lebanon deteriorated. In May 1984, under Syrian pressure, Amin Gemayyal repudiated the agreement Israel had forced out of him.

Israel was now reaping what it had sown and its army was becoming the hunted rather than the hunter. In 1985, by which time Israel had suffered 660 fatalities in the campaign, it withdrew to a buffer zone in the predominantly Shi'ite south. Initially, many Shi'ites had welcomed the Israelis because the Palestinians had turned the area into a battleground. The Shi'ite masses had tended to support secular left-wing political groupings in the hope that socialism would improve their lot, but two changes had happened as a result of the civil war and the Israeli occupation. The first was that Palestinian fighters had departed, ending that particular cause of friction. The other was that Iran exported its revolution to the Shi'ite poor, many of whom now received weapons training and political education from Iranian revolutionary guards. The ultimate result of this was the appearance of a new political party with its own militia. It called itself Hizbullah, 'the party of God'.

Like the Muslim Brotherhood, Hizbullah believes in a state which would be ruled by Islam, except with a Shi'ite rather than a Sunni version of Islamic law. However, it acknowledges that Lebanon's diversity makes that impossible unless it can persuade Christians and non-Shi'ite Muslims that this would be in their interest (something it knows to be unrealistic). Ever since it first started to contest elections in 1992, it has shown itself able to compromise with political forces from other sects, including Maronites. Its electoral campaigns have been on issues such as economic exploitation, under-development, personal freedom and security, with a noticeable absence of talk about religious issues. In local government, it has been commended for providing low-cost housing for the poor and has shown itself prepared to accept tax revenues from alcohol sales.[7] Yet at the same time it considers itself the armed vanguard of an Islamic resistance movement. As it stated in its original 1985 programme, 'we have seen that aggression can only be repelled with the sacrifice of blood, and that freedom is not given but regained with the sacrifice of both heart and soul.' While most Lebanese may not accept its religious ideas, they cannot but feel pride in its success in eventually wearing down the Israeli occupiers and finally driving them, exhausted and demoralised, from Lebanon in 2000.

This occurred some ten years after the country's civil war had finally come to an end. The crisis caused by Saddam Hussein's invasion of Kuwait turned out to be the catalyst that enabled this to happen. Saddam Hussein was the mortal foe of Syria's Hafez al-Assad, and had done whatever he could to disturb Syria's hegemony over Lebanon. In 1988, the presidential term of Amin Gemayyal expired. This condemned the country to one of the most vicious rounds of fighting in the civil war when parliament was unable to produce a quorum to elect a successor. The Maronite commander of the army, General Michel Aoun, attempted to take over, but the veteran Sunni prime minister Selim al-Hoss also claimed the right to do so. He was backed by a coalition that wished to take sectarianism out of Lebanese politics, but this proved to be as unrealistic as Saddam Hussein's hope of ending Syrian domination of the country. As fighting devastated Lebanon yet again, the Arab League managed to broker a settlement in the city of Taif in Saudi Arabia. The sectarian basis of rule would survive, but would be adjusted in a way that would end domination by the Christians – something that Lebanon's demographics now unquestionably demanded. The Taif Accords also contained an endorsement of Syria's role in Lebanon. At the request of the new, legitimate Lebanese government that now took power, Syrian troops ended Aoun's resistance. Preoccupied elsewhere, Iraq was unable to help its protégé.

This ended the civil war but left Lebanon a shattered land with its problems of identity still unresolved. The country was rebuilt, and Beirut was given a new, showpiece city centre which was superficially designed to erase the old divides that had been so destructive. Yet the fault lines in Lebanese society remain. Syria was forced to withdraw its troops after the assassination of prime minister Rafiq Hariri in 2005, but the two countries remain closely entwined. The civil war that began in Syria in 2011/12 could all too easily spill over into Lebanon, where many fear it could reignite the flames of sectarian strife.

V

In December 1987, two years after Israel had been forced to drop its plans to achieve hegemony over Lebanon and had retreated to its buffer zone in the south of the country, something unprecedented happened in the Occupied Territories. Rioting in protest at the occupation spread like fire through the long grass of a dry summer and refused to die down. At first, there was no premeditation or coordination, although these appeared later. Protesters waved the forbidden Palestinian flag, blocked streets with burning tyres, and threw stones and Molotov cocktails at Israeli troops and settlers. Much of the activity was non-violent and some of it was no more than civil disobedience, but the Israelis responded to this, too, with tear gas, potentially lethal rubber-coated steel bullets, baton charges and gunfire. Israel was determined to teach the population a lesson: that concessions would not be won by protest and resistance. Yet the uprising stubbornly continued.

It became known as the Intifada, or the 'shaking off'. Although it did not shake off the Israeli occupation, the Americans realised that the current state of affairs was unsustainable, while the PLO came under pressure from Palestinians in the territories to move towards acceptance of a two-state solution based on the 1949 armistice lines. It accepted this principle in November 1988. Just before President Reagan left office, he recognised the PLO while simultaneously underlining the USA's commitment to Israel's security.

Eighteen months later, when Saddam Hussein invaded Kuwait, America needed Arab goodwill. President George H. Bush and his secretary of state, James Baker, tried to find a way to cut through the many facets of the Arab–Israeli problem and broker negotiations. Baker promised the Palestinians that, if they entered into negotiations, it would mean 'no more settlements'. There were reasons for cautious optimism. With the end of the Cold War, America had become the magnet to which all felt pulled. Syria, a staunch member of the coalition against Saddam Hussein, now accepted American invitations. Jordan, which had been perceived as sympathetic to Saddam Hussein and where public opinion had made it impossible for King Hussein to join the coalition against him to free Kuwait, was delighted to re-enter the fold of friends of the West, while Egypt received massive debt relief from Washington and its rehabilitation with other Arab countries was completed. The PLO had no choice but to acquiesce in what America was doing.

On the Israeli side, Yitzhak Rabin came to power with an almost unparalleled degree of support in the Israeli parliament for a platform of peace negotiations. Yet Israel continued to assert that it had the right to annex parts of the territories occupied in 1967 and to construct settlements. After Bill Clinton became president of the United States in 1993, American-sponsored negotiations remained deadlocked but a breakthrough occurred in secret talks between Israel and the PLO brokered by the Norwegian government in Oslo. Israel would turn over the Gaza Strip and a small area around Jericho to the PLO on the basis of interim self-government. This meant that Israel and the PLO would recognise each other. In doing this, Rabin seems to have believed he was throwing a life-line to the PLO which ought to make compromises in exchange.[8]

Such compromises were not forthcoming, for the Palestinians considered Rabin had no right to expect them. The basic problem was that each side had a different conception of what its rights were. For the Palestinians, the situation to be addressed was essentially ending a colonial regime: Israel should prepare the territories for independence, withdraw its army and settlers, and recognise the rights of the refugees it had displaced. The Israelis did not see it that way. They saw it as a question of redeploying their forces away from Palestinian urban areas while retaining ultimate control over land which they stubbornly maintained they had the right to claim.

Further interim agreements were reached. These were drafted to test the good faith of both parties, particularly the ability of the PLO to control terrorism. They gave the go-ahead for Palestinian elections for a self-governing Palestine National Authority (PNA) and the division of the West Bank into three zones: that under total Palestinian control, that under Palestinian civil control but with Israel retaining responsibility for security, and the remainder in which Israel retained full civil and military control. In Gaza, Israel remained in control of 35 per cent of the land, including the settlements for Israeli citizens. However, the fact that Israeli settlement-building continued meant that the question marks over its good faith remained. New obstacles to Palestinian economic growth and general wellbeing appeared in the form of the numerous checkpoints which now regulated access in the West Bank between the many enclaves into which it had been carved.

Rabin succeeded in agreeing peace with Jordan although King Hussein, understandably suspicious of Israeli intentions, delayed signing the treaty until Israel and the PLO had reached their agreement on Gaza and Jericho. Nevertheless, Rabin deftly refrained from crossing any Rubicon which would have meant the irrevocable abandonment of the Zionist dream of incorporating parts of the Occupied Territories into Israel.

Although there are serious grounds to suggest that he never intended such a step,[9] the fact that he appeared as though he might be about to take it led to his assassination by a Zionist militant on 4 November 1995. Ever since the establishment of Israel, many had feared recognition of Palestinian rights would lead to an inter-Jewish civil war. This fear had been a factor, for instance, in dissuading Israeli leaders from evacuating settlements in Hebron and elsewhere in the Occupied Territories which were illegal even under Israeli law. Rabin's assassination showed that such fears were not misplaced.

Shortly afterwards, in May 1996, another hardliner became prime minister of Israel. Benjamin Netanyahu now had the opportunity to redirect Israel's policy while maintaining an air of sweet innocence. For him, Palestinian and other Arab rights were essentially limited to concessions or privileges which Israel might be persuaded to grant if it was in its interest to do so. He would appear on Western television as baffled, pained and, above all, angered by Arab stubbornness, while he stonewalled on the next stages of negotiations. At the same time, he continued to expand settlements and demolish Palestinian houses in East Jerusalem that had been built without a permit from the occupying authorities. Violence returned, forcing the Clinton administration to take a new interest.

A protocol dealing with Hebron was signed in January 1997, but Israel remained in exclusive control of 71 per cent of the West Bank. Netanyahu indicated that he considered the Palestinians' share of the West Bank in a final peace settlement should be about 40 per cent of the occupied land.[10] In October 1998, after great pressure, he indicated he would be prepared for Israel to withdraw from a further 13 per cent of the West Bank as its second redeployment under Oslo, although the Palestinians had believed they had the right to expect that this redeployment would lead to Israel virtually leaving the West Bank in its entirety.

In the summer of 2000, during the last year of his presidency, Clinton made a final and much too hasty effort to broker a comprehensive settlement. Agreement proved impossible, and violence soon followed. The trigger was Ariel Sharon's visit to the al-Aqsa mosque in East Jerusalem that September. This was a symbolic act: a manifestation of power and a determination to show that the law would be as Israel dictated. The use once again of lethal force against demonstrators and rioters caused the situation to spiral out of control. This sparked the fires of the Second Intifada, known as the al-Aqsa Intifada, which was far bloodier than the first, since Palestinians now had light arms. Palestinian groups confronted the occupation with armed resistance, as well as suicide bombings and terrorism against Israeli civilians. Clinton scurried around trying to broker a cease-fire and a final settlement, but left office at the end of 2000 with the conflagration just getting worse.

George W. Bush, Clinton's successor, was wary of involving himself in attempts at Israeli–Arab peace-making, being mindful of his predecessors' failures. He initially had to do business with Ariel Sharon, whom the Israeli electorate elected to power in February 2001. Sharon maintained that Arafat, the president of the PLO, had turned on a tap of violence which he could also turn off at will. This was never true, not least because the source of the Palestinian anger which lay behind it was the failure of the Oslo process to deliver their rights, and also because much of the violence came from political opponents over whom he had no control and to whom he had to find ways of reaching out.

Yet Arafat tolerated and encouraged calls for the expulsion of the Israelis from the Occupied Territories by force, believing the violence was a warning to Israel of the risks it ran in not coming to an agreement and that it therefore strengthened his position. In fact, it had the opposite effect since it made Israeli opinion form up behind the hardliners and the large Israeli peace camp melted away. Ever since the First Intifada, the PLO had faced Islamist rivals, especially the movement known as Hamas which conducted its own resistance and terrorist activities and rejected PLO control. Israel's attempts to punish him for his inability to curb Hamas only strengthened the latter.[11]

When, on 11 September 2001, Arab suicide terrorists rammed hijacked airliners into the World Trade Center and the Pentagon, the Bush administration found itself forced to confront the problems of Israel and the Palestinians. Bush explicitly recognised the need for a Palestinian state but supported the Israeli refusal to negotiate with Arafat on the grounds that he was not doing enough to control terrorism. He also encouraged the American public's perception of Israel as an ally against terrorism.

Occasions that might have provided an opportunity to move forward on the diplomatic front, such as the reiteration in March 2002 by the Arab League of a Saudi initiative for a comprehensive peace based on the 1949 armistice lines, went unnoticed in the ongoing violence. In the same month, a particularly vicious suicide attack at a Passover dinner in the Israeli resort of Netanya killed thirty Israelis and wounded 140, triggering a huge military operation in reply. The Israeli army brutally reoccupied the areas on the West Bank under Palestinian control, killing nearly 500 Palestinians and besieging Arafat in the ruins of his offices in Ramallah. This completed the devastation of the infrastructure of the Palestine National Authority. Thenceforth Arafat was a virtual prisoner and arguably a hostage.

Israel has had considerable success on the security front since 2002. The Second Intifada tailed off and Israeli casualties dropped dramatically. A senior Israeli officer said at one point that Israel had eliminated all resistance organisations in the Gaza Strip except for the population at large.[12] This summed up Israel's dilemma. Successful counter-insurgency operations require a political strategy to win the hearts and minds of the population among whom the insurgents move. Zionism, the founding ideology of the Jewish state, made this difficult if not impossible. On the one hand, the days were long gone when Israel could shoo Palestinians en masse into Gaza, Lebanon or across the Jordan. On the other, Zionist ideology was such that no Israeli prime minister has yet been able to admit publicly that, morally and legally, Israel does not have the right to acquire whatever parts of the Occupied Territories it wished to retain. For its part, the Palestinian National Authority now found itself in an impossible position. It had been so weakened by Israel's attacks on its infrastructure that it could not restrain the Islamist movement Hamas and other groups. It now also lacked the credibility to do so.

Like Rabin and many other Israeli prime ministers before him, Sharon had won the trust of the Israeli electorate because of his known ruthlessness in confronting the Palestinians. While preserving his ideological position intact, he admitted that the Palestinian birth rate meant that demographics were now against Israel, and it could not hold on to the Occupied Territories in their entirety. Israel should therefore abandon some areas which were densely populated by Palestinians so as not to compromise its Jewish majority. He began building a barrier. Most of it was located inside occupied territory so as to enclose settlements and open land whenever possible. Although Israel insisted in public that the barrier was purely a security measure, it would have been naive, given Israel's previous record and the ideology of Zionism, not to see it as another attempt to add to the territory of its state. Bush helped, too. In April 2004 he referred obliquely to major Israeli settlements in the Occupied Territories as 'facts on the ground' that must be taken into account in any final settlement.

After Arafat's death in November that year, Israel was unable to come to an arrangement with his mild-mannered successor, Mahmoud Abbas. Sharon took yet another unilateral step, deciding that Israel would fix the limits of Palestinian entitlement without any negotiations. It was on this basis that Israel uprooted its settlements and withdrew its troops from Gaza in August 2005 without any coordination with the PNA. At the same time, he asserted that Israel would retain parts of the West Bank. We will never know what Sharon's next step would have been because he was incapacitated by a stroke the following January, the same month in which Hamas won the Palestinian parliamentary election.

The roots of Hamas lie in the Palestinian branch of the Muslim Brotherhood. As elsewhere, Islamist sentiment had gradually become more significant as disillusionment set in with secular nationalism. The strategy of the PLO after the 1967 defeat had been to emulate the Viet Cong in Vietnam and win back Palestine by guerrilla war. This was always unrealistic, and was frustrated after the PLO was driven first from Jordan in 1970 and then from Lebanon in 1982. Islamist groups slowly became important in the Occupied Territories, particularly in Gaza. The Israelis were fairly tolerant of them, and subtly encouraged them as a counterweight to the nationalism which they then saw as the challenge to the legitimacy of their state. In December 1987, as the First Intifada exploded, Hamas was established as a specifically Islamic resistance organisation to oppose the Israeli occupation.

It rejected the Oslo process on the grounds that Palestine was Muslim territory and therefore its ownership could not be compromised. This seemed to consign it to the margins. However, the failure of the Oslo process to deliver the results Palestinians had expected – and to which they were entitled in international law – left it as the natural opposition to the politicians in power. When Yasser Arafat, the chairman of the PLO, returned to Palestinian soil he behaved like other Arab autocrats. Responsibility for security was divided between separate organisations so that they would provide a restraint on each other, and aid funds were tapped for purposes of patronage, creating a PLO nomenklatura.

At the same time as the PLO was showing itself to be corrupt, elections by universal suffrage were introduced and great effort was expended by the international community to ensure that they were genuinely democratic. Once Hamas started to contest elections, it emerged as the principal opposition party. It surprised even itself when it won the parliamentary elections in January 2006. Yet its platform was unacceptable to America and Europe as well as to Israel.

Although it received support from the Palestinian electorate in reaction to corruption in the PNA, which contrasted with its own so-cial work to help the population, its support was also a consequence of Israel's enduring unwillingness to recognise Palestinian rights and the shattering of the infrastructure of the nascent Palestinian state. Hamas argued that its resistance to the occupation had at least caused Israel to give up Gaza, just as the militia of Hizbullah, the Shi'ite Islamist movement in Lebanon, had forced Israel to withdraw back to its border. As a matter of principle, Hamas refused to be bound publicly by the compromise the PLO had made in 1988 when it recognised Israel as a sovereign state without a reciprocal statement by Israel of Palestinian rights.

In early 2006, an impasse developed. Israel attempted to continue negotiations with Mahmoud Abbas but refused to do business with the Hamas-led PNA government. In June, a major Israeli invasion of the Gaza Strip took place in an attempt to free an Israeli soldier who had been abducted and to reduce the untargeted rocket fire aimed at neighbouring areas of Israel.

The ferocity and devastation of this campaign were to some extent obscured by the much bloodier campaign that took place that summer in south Lebanon, after Hizbullah emulated the Gaza attack and captured two Israeli soldiers. Israel's response included the destruction of much of the infrastructure of Lebanon which had been painstakingly rebuilt by European aid money in the years since the end of the Lebanese civil war. As before, Hizbullah showed itself a determined, disciplined and skilful foe, and succeeded in inflicting casualties on the Israeli army and peppering northern Israel with indiscriminate rocket fire before a cease-fire took hold.

Deadlock was now built upon deadlock. Attempts to broker a unity government for the PNA failed, and fighting broke out between the Palestinian factions. June 2007 saw Hamas drive Fatah from Gaza, while Fatah clamped down on Hamas on the West Bank. Since then, Israel has blockaded Gaza with Egyptian connivance. This has not entirely succeeded in stopping militants firing rockets from Gaza into Israel, something that bloody Israeli incursions into Gaza, including Operation Cast Lead over the New Year of 2009 which cost 1,300 Palestinian lives, and the blockade of the territory have failed to end completely.

Israel, now ruled once again by a right-wing coalition led by Benjamin Netanyahu, has refused to halt settlement building and continued its evictions of Palestinians from East Jerusalem. In response, Mahmoud Abbas adopted a new strategy: to insist on Palestinian rights under international law and to search for ways to enforce them. In September 2011, he applied for Palestinian membership of the UN as a sovereign state whose territory would be East Jerusalem, the West Bank and Gaza, those remaining portions of Palestinian land that were occupied by Israel in 1967.

In doing this, he was on ground that should have been solid. The indigenous Palestinians of the Occupied Territories now unquestionably had the right to a state comprising the Palestinian lands which Israel occupied in 1967. In these territories, the Palestinian National Authority had established the infrastructure of a state, so that Palestine, too, now fulfilled the four requirements set out in the Montevideo Convention which Israel fulfilled in the late 1940s. The PLO had also waived its claim to the lands Israel seized in 1948-9. Yet the Palestinian request for membership was not even voted upon in the Security Council. Israel had used its influence in America to procure the threat of an American veto of Palestinian membership, and its influence in Europe to persuade the European members of the Security Council to abstain in the vote – thus ensuring that the American veto was not even necessary.

Complying with Israel's wishes, America and other Western powers had repeatedly attempted to prevent the clarification of Palestinian legal rights. When Israel began constructing its 'security barrier' across the land of the Occupied Palestinian Territory – rather than along its border with the Territory, which is where Israel would have constructed it if it had been acting in good faith – the UN General Assembly asked the International Court of Justice to give an advisory opinion on the legal consequences of this barrier. A host of Western states, including the USA, the UK and the European Union, submitted written statements to the Court requesting it to use its inherent discretion not to hear the case. The Court turned these down, and in July 2004 clarified beyond any serious discussion a host of legal issues that Israel would rather had not been clarified: including the right of political self-determination for the people of the Occupied Palestinian Territory, the illegality of Israeli attempts to annex parts of the Territory, and the fact that the people of the Territory (as well as the land itself) were entitled to the full protection of international humanitarian law. This included protection under Article 49(6) of the 1949 Fourth Geneva Convention which, as the American judge Thomas Buergenthal – a Holocaust survivor – pointed out, made Israeli civilian settlements there illegal.

During the long years since the beginning of the Oslo process in 1993, frameworks which were meant to provide the basis for negotiations for a final settlement between Israel and the Palestinians, such as the 2003 'Road Map', made no mention of international law. It might have been thought that two parties cannot negotiate an agreement to solve their disputes unless they first establish each other's legal entitlements. Moreover, if, as Israel argues, Palestinian statehood can only come about through the reaching of agreement with Israel, how was Israel's statehood allowed to come about in 1948–9 without negotiations with Palestinian representatives?

In November 2012, Mahmoud Abbas received a consolation prize. The UN General Assembly voted to accept Palestine as a non-member observer state – explicitly recognising it as independent and fully sovereign, even though it was not granted the privilege of UN membership. Israel and the USA found themselves in uncomfortable isolation when, among major states, only Canada and the Czech Republic joined them in opposing the motion. However, Palestine's admittance to the UN and an end to the Israeli-Palestinian dispute remain distant goals.

Bernard Lewis, the originator of the phrase 'clash of civilisations', wrote in 1996 that the 'outside powers' defend 'the interests of the international community' in the Middle East. He defined these interests loosely as 'a decent respect for the basic rules of the United Nations'.[13] Because of the Palestinian issue, most Arabs see such a statement as nothing more than a cruel and cynical joke. Yet it is still representative of the views held by large segments of opinion across the West, especially in America. If, during Obama's second term, the Zionist lobby manages to frustrate any settlement which acknowledges the rights of the Palestinians in international law alongside those of Israel, they will have driven the final nail into the coffin of the legitimacy of the state of Israel in its present form. The

Palestinian struggle will then shift to creating a non-sectarian state for Palestinians and Israelis between the Jordan and the Mediterranean.

VI

It is often said that one man's terrorist is the next man's freedom fighter. A more subtle approach is to acknowledge that the freedom fighter is a terrorist but to accept his use of terrorism on the grounds that the greater good for which he is fighting justifies the means employed. Thus it was with the Jewish American writer Leon Uris whose hugely popular novel *Exodus*, which was published in 1958, included a thinly fictionalised account of the story of the Zionist groups that carried out such atrocities as the blowing up of the British army headquarters in the King David Hotel in Jerusalem, killing some eighty British, Arab and Jewish officials,[14] and the massacre of Deir Yassin, in which about 110 unarmed Palestinian villagers, many of them women and children, died.[15] Their terrorism was 'useful',[16] Uris wrote, because it helped persuade Britain to give up in Palestine.

Uris's book and the film version of it starring Paul Newman shaped Western attitudes to the Arab–Israeli conflict in the years running up to the Six Day War. Today the necessary role that Zionist terrorism played in the establishment of Israel is all but forgotten by most people in the West. Terrorism carried out by Arabs, on the other hand, stands tall and fearsome in the forefront of the popular imagination.

Fanaticism, cruelty, deviousness and greed have been stereotypical of Arabs in the way they are portrayed in much of the Western media and Hollywood for decades. The way in which the conflicts in Israel/Palestine and Lebanon were reported in the West had already done much to build up the unflattering image of Arabs as stereotypically terrorists well before 11 September 2001. Subsequent events, not least the many atrocities in Iraq since the invasion of 2003, just added to this perception during the long decades when the Arab world was dominated by autocrats. 'Arab terrorism', which morphed into 'Islamic terrorism' during the 1980s, needs to be examined in any discussion of the years leading up to the Arab Spring.

The key element in terrorism is the deliberate targeting of civilians. There have been many attempts to define it, but no definition seems to have gained universal agreement. One official US State Department document described it in 2002 as 'premeditated, politically motivated violence perpetrated against non-combatant targets'.[17] Yet this definition, like many others, overlooks two important categories of violence which most of us would label 'terrorist' because they are aimed at civilians and are perpetrated by groups fighting for a political cause. These are acts carried out with revenge or deterrence as the primary purpose, as opposed to the achievement of a specific, political objective. They occur all too often when violence is used in conflicts in the Arab world, and are therefore included as terrorism when the word is used in this book.

Prior to the 1980s, most Arabs who carried out terrorist atrocities were from nationalist groups influenced by Marxist and anarchist ideas. Terrorists like the 'Black September' group who massacred Israeli athletes at the Munic Olympics in 1972 were secular – if not positively atheistic. Such groups still operate, but since the 1980s those motivated by Islamist ideology have become the most numerous, and their attacks the most nihilistic. Juan Cole has drawn attention to parallels between Timothy McVeigh, the Oklahoma bomber, and the stories of some Islamist terrorists, particularly with regard to the paranoid milieux from which they sprang.[18] Arab terrorism is sometimes said to be comprised of two waves, the first inspired by secular ideologies and the second by ideologies based on an interpretation of Islam. Yet it can be argued that this distinction is illusory, since both waves stem from pain, rage and impotence which are essentially the same. Prominent terrorists from both waves have been radicalised by Israeli war crimes and torture or maltreatment in the jails of Arab governments. Many more have been brutalised by other conflicts, especially that in Iraq. It is too early to judge whether the violence in Libya and the civil war in Syria will have had a similar effect and produce new crops of terrorists, but history gives few reasons for optimism on this score.

Suicide is forbidden in Islam, as it is in Christianity and Judaism. That is why suicide bombing is such a modern phenomenon. Any precedents are from outside the world of Islam, such as the Japanese Kamikazes and the Tamil Tigers in Sri Lanka. The first Muslim suicide bombers appeared in the aftermath of the 1982 Israeli invasion of Lebanon. The initial targets were military. The first was the Israeli army's headquarters in Tyre in southern Lebanon, where seventy-two Israelis were killed on 11 November 1982. Within a year, 241 American marines and 58 French paratroopers died when their barracks in Beirut were also targeted by suicide bombers. The Americans and French were present with the consent of the Lebanese government, but were becoming sucked into the fighting between different factions.

The bombers were Shi'ites who took their inspiration from the martyrdoms of the first and third imams: the Prophet's nephew and son-in-law Ali and Ali's son Hussein. Soon suicide bombing was being used by a myriad of organisations in Lebanon with an anti-Israeli and anti-Western agenda. These ceased to be aimed at military targets and were intended to achieve political goals that broadly reflected those of the governments of Syria and Iran, which were prepared to sponsor them.

It was to be another ten years after those first Shi'ite attacks in Lebanon before the phenomenon of suicide bombing first appeared among Sunnis in Palestine. There had already been one isolated attack in which the bomber killed himself and wounded one victim, but it was the Israeli Baruch Goldstein's sacrilegious attack on civilian worshippers in the shrine of Abraham in Hebron in 1994, in which he killed twenty-nine men at prayer with an automatic weapon and wounded many more, that sparked the first wave of Palestinian suicide attacks.

The perpetrators hoped to deter Israeli attacks against Palestinians and end the occupation, while others were motivated by despair and the cold rage of premeditated revenge. Sometimes the targets would be military, but it has been those against civilians that have seared themselves onto international consciousness. Suicide attacks also became a potent weapon in the hands of those who wished to scupper a settlement. As the 1990s progressed, whenever the possibility of a break-through in negotiations seemed on the horizon, or if the Israeli electorate looked as though it might choose a less extreme government, suicide attacks seemed always to be launched in order to reduce the chances of a compromise being reached. Later, when Osama bin Laden decided to take jihad to 'the far enemy', suicide attacks against non-military targets became a way to instil fear and raise the perpetrators' profile. Yet there is a nihilism in such indiscriminate violence which is incompatible with Islam since, as was seen in Chapter 2, jihad does not condone attacks on civilians.

Not all Arab terrorists are Muslim. George Habash, an Orthodox Christian, was originally from the Palestinian town of Lydda. He was not born a terrorist. As a young medical student, he did what he could to help the people of his native town when the Israeli army ethnically cleansed them in 1948. (Glubb, whose soldiers received the 30,000 or so victims at the end of a march across open country on a pitilessly hot day, wrote that nobody will ever know how many children died in that dreadful experience.[19]) Habash went on to found the Marxist Popular Front for the Liberation of Palestine, the PLFP, which specialised in plane hijackings and calls for the overthrow of Arab governments as well as attacks on Israeli targets. 'The only language the enemy understands is that of revolutionary violence,' the group's inaugural statement maintained.

The Jordanian town of Zarqa' was once a small town beside a blue stream, but was overwhelmed and transformed for ever when thousands of those Israel evicted from Lydda and neighbouring Ramle arrived and were placed in camps. The small Jordanian economy was quite unable to integrate them, and the majority of the refugees were forced to rely on handouts and casual work such as share cropping. Some twenty-two years later, in 1970, Habash's PFLP fighters landed hijacked planes there at the nearby airstrip known as Dawson's Field. Is it just a coincidence that Abu Musab al-Zarqawi, a man who would become truly infamous, had been born there in 1966? Although he was not a Palestinian himself, he would have grown up witnessing the hopelessness of the situation of the refugees.

When the secular nationalists of the PLO and the PFLP managed to achieve nothing, Zarqa' became a hot-bed of Islamist extremism. It provided a large number of foreign fighters who went to Iraq to fight the American occupation,[20] including Abu Musab himself. Abu Musab's formation included a period in a Jordanian jail where he was tortured. Interviews with former 'jihadis' show that many of them were brutalised by their treatment at the hands of the security forces of Arab states. Those to whom this happened included Osama bin Laden's successor as leader of al-Qa'ida, Ayman al-Zawahiri. It has been suggested that the writings of Sayyid Qutb himself became angrier and more extreme as a result of his treatment in prison.

Since the 1990s, international 'Islamic' terrorism has occurred against Western targets across the world, as well as within the Middle East. The prime motivation behind it has been to alter the policies of Western governments, although a symbolic repudiation of Western lifestyles has also been an ingredient. Qutb's view of Western capitalism would have had a place in the mindset of those who attacked the World Trade Center in New York in 1993 and on 9/11 itself. Similarly, the kind of attitude he displayed towards Western women may have influenced those who bombed the discos in Bali in October 2002, killing 202. Nevertheless, by far the greatest spur to such activity has been the perception that the West, led by America, has dominated and occupied the heartlands of Islam and the Arab world.

VII

Until he was killed by American special forces in 2011, the bogey man behind international Islamist terrorism was Osama bin Laden. His father was a building contractor from the Hadramawt in southern Yemen who settled in Saudi Arabia and established a firm known for its solid workmanship and fidelity to its contractual obligations. He became a friend of the king and one of the kingdom's richest men. Bin Laden was born in 1957 and grew up as a member of the kingdom's elite. His father, who seems to have been a very distant figure for the boy, lavishly entertained pilgrims who came on the Hajj from all over the world, and it would have been only natural for the boy to love the brotherhood and unity which is a feature of Muslim culture in so many lands. This, together with the perception that wealth and exposure to Western ways were tearing his generation away from its traditional values, may provide keys to understanding his subsequent career – although not the methods he employed. Like Hassan al-Banna and Sayyid Qutb, his credentials as a scholar of Sharia were unimpressive. The certainty of his views stemmed from the marriage of Wahhabi sternness and neuroticism to Qutbian subjectivity, rather than the wide reading and reflection on the arguments of jurists throughout the ages which are the hallmarks of genuine religious scholarship.

By 1986, bin Laden was in Afghanistan, showing courage in battle against the Russians and setting up his own camps. Within a couple of years he was also establishing his own database of activists, which became the origin of the network known as al-Qa'ida. Returning home to Saudi Arabia just in time for the crisis caused by Saddam Hussein's invasion of Kuwait, he offered his network of fighters to repel the threat of Iraqi invasion. Although the rejection of his offer was polite, he was enraged by the arrival of American forces to defend the kingdom. From that point he went his own way.

He initially set himself up in Sudan, but in 1996 travelled to the Afghanistan of the Taliban after the Sudanese authorities succumbed to pressure to expel him. Attacks organised by members of his circle began in Saudi Arabia around this time, and he issued a tract in which he condemned the Saudis for collaborating with the 'Crusader-Zionist alliance' and called on Muslims to perform their duty of jihad to expel them. This was followed two years later by the covenant of 'the International Islamic Front against Jews and Crusaders' which included a fatwa providing that

> killing the Americans and their allies – civilians and military – is an individual duty for every Muslim who can carry it out in any country where it proves possible, in order to liberate al-Aqsa Mosque [in Jerusalem] and the holy sanctuary [Mecca] from their grip, and to the point where their armies leave all Muslim territory, defeated and unable to threaten any Muslim.[21]

In 1998, the seventh anniversary of the arrival of American troops in Saudi Arabia was marked by bomb attacks on the American Embassies in Kenya and Tanzania. Other attacks on US interests followed, notably the suicide bombing of the USS *Cole* in Aden harbour and, on 11 September 2001, the most shocking attack of all. By the end of that year, as the Americans and their Afghan allies ejected the Taliban from Kabul, he was a fugitive.

Cassettes containing his speeches appeared mysteriously from time to time. To Westerners, the image these showed of him was truly bizarre. There seemed to be a calmness and gentleness in his manner, as he raised his hand to admonish or even to bless. Were it not for the turban he wore and the automatic weapon by his side, this man who masterminded mass murder seemed almost to have modelled his image on a sentimentalised portrayal of Jesus Christ.

His prominence and leadership came from his personal charisma, prestigious position in Saudi society, wealth and genius for publicity. He was a naturally austere man who obtained the consent of his first wife, whom it seems he truly loved, to take additional wives so that he could beget more children for Islam. His son Omar recalls his father making the family sleep on the bare ground to train them for the existential conflict with the West, which he knew was coming. Osama bin Laden also forbade his children from smiling too broadly, as it was unseemly, but Omar envied Christian children their fun dressing up at Halloween even though his father would never have allowed him to join in something so frivolous.[22]

Osama bin Laden showed the integrity of someone who renounces the world in order to put his ideals into practice. To understand him, one has to accept that he saw himself as fighting evil. His seductive appeal, like that of extreme left-wing and right-wing splinter groups everywhere, began with the fact that he had some fair points to make: it was a humiliation for the House of Saud to rely on American troops against Saddam Hussein; and Israel could only come into existence as a predominantly Jewish state by the doing of grave wrongs to its indigenous, Muslim majority.

He believed symbolic attacks on the West would have two consequences. First, they would galvanise Muslims across the world behind his movement and its objectives, especially in reaction to America's inevitable response. Secondly, attacks such as those of 9/11 would lead to the disintegration of the USA by building up pressure from individual states to secede from the Union. He had little excuse for such profound ignorance of the West, and even less for misreading the Muslim world, but he consistently misjudged both. He also rewrote history to fit his ideology, and resurrected the long-dead propaganda of Abdul Hamid II. He considered the Ottoman Empire to have been a true caliphate, and that the rebellion against it by Ibn Saud which led ultimately to the establishment of Saudi Arabia caused its collapse and the submission of the Muslim world to the West.

Marwan Bishara has summed up al-Qa'ida's paradoxes. It has 'limited capacity and unlimited megalomania, modern organisation and medieval agenda'.[23] Like some of the terrorist splinter groups that the West has produced, bin Laden and his colleagues know what they want to overthrow and have used modern technology and organisational skills in their attempts to achieve their objective. Yet they seem to have made no preparations for the day after they take power. They have not developed institutions but rely purely on the ancient idea of loyalty to a shaykh: a personal bond that can supplant that of the family, but leaves the followers rootless on the shaykh's death. It is also likely to discourage the followers from having the confidence to question what the shaykh tells them, and risks playing to any tendency he may have towards hubris. The opinions of Muslims who disagree must be rejected. It is thus scarcely surprising that the leaders of al-Qa'ida implored Muslims to have nothing to do with democracy, as when they begged Iraqis not to take part in elections and excoriated movements such as the Muslim Brotherhood and Hamas for doing so. One can sense real fear behind the anger in their attacks on 'parliaments of idol worshippers' in their sermons,[24] as democracy might make their potential constituency slip away from them. The Tunisian Islamist leader Rached Ghannouchi has optimistically claimed that al-Qa'ida is 'finished', thanks to the transition to democracy in his country.[25] The killing of Christopher Stevens, the US ambassador to Libya, on 11 September 2012, the appearance of al-Qa'ida affiliates or imitators in a number of countries including Yemen, Mali and, above all, in Syria, as well as the continuation of sectarian bombings in Iraq all show that his words were premature.

CHAPTER NINE

THE AGE OF THE AUTOCRATS
AND THE RISE OF ISLAMISM

I

Until what is still generally called the Arab Spring began at the end of 2010, the problems of the Arab world over the previous thirty years had seemed intractable. Westerners dismissed it as frozen in an amalgam of despotism, corruption and an ever more archaic and hypocritical religiosity. Many felt instinctively that its disputes were petty-minded and caused by dictators exporting terrorism and manufacturing anger to distract the public from grievances at home. This period was the age of the Arab autocrats. They came in various shapes and sizes but were all successful in keeping the hatches battened down at home, despite a little water seeping through the cracks here and there. Sometimes greater press freedom was permitted or a constitutional concession was made, although care was taken to ensure that such changes did not lead to genuine empowerment for Arab electorates. The people might be allowed to let off steam and vent some anger, but nothing they could possibly do would topple the regime. Or so it seemed. One day change would come. On that, almost everyone agreed – but it seemed too hazardous to predict what form it would take or when, where or how it would come about.

How did this grimly stable world of Arab autocracy come into existence? And what kind of people became autocrats? How, once in power, did they manage to stay there? And what effect did power have on them? Much important information that would be needed to answer such questions in a comprehensive fashion isn't readily available. Little is made public about the activities of the *mukhabarat*, the security agencies which spied on the general population and were well shielded from public view. Such organisations do not publish an annual report accompanied by a set of audited accounts. Autocracies lack transparency, and significant decisions are always taken behind closed doors. Furthermore, every Arab state has had a different historical experience from its neighbours. There are enormous variations between Arab countries in such basic matters as area, size and diversity of population, system of government and availability of resources. The path followed in one might not be replicated next door, although rulers often copied techniques used by each other.

In a recent study of the phenomenon of Arab 'presidents for life', Roger Owen has managed to divide most of the Arab republics in this era of autocrats into two main categories. The first consists of those with strong, centralised governments led by a powerful president, such as Egypt, Syria, Tunisia and Algeria. The other category contains those which history had left with a weaker central authority like Libya, Yemen and Sudan. In each of these last three, despite the great differences between them, the government's difficulty in asserting its authority over a diverse population spread across geographically remote areas required the president to exercise 'a much more elaborate practice of accommodations, negotiations and compromise'. This made him perforce a kind of manager.[1] Nevertheless, as will be seen, accommodations of various sorts had to be made by all Arab rulers, and some similarities between their regimes are striking. This also applies to the surviving Arab monarchies. Some of them are ruled by a king with powers similar to an autocratic president. Morocco, Jordan and Oman are good examples. In these states, the king – or the sultan, in the case of Oman – has much the same position as a powerful executive president, except that he does not need to perform acrobatics with the constitution in order to legitimise his position on the throne. In other monarchies, most notably Saudi Arabia, the king is far more than a figurehead but in an important sense the country is ruled by the family rather than by him alone in person. The number of legitimate, male lineal descendants of King Abdul Aziz, who reigned until his death in 1953, runs well into five figures. In theory, any one of them could be chosen by the family to succeed the present king.

II

There was a time when military takeovers seemed to be about to become the normal way of changing governments in the Arab world. In the 1960s, Syria, Iraq and North Yemen appeared addicted to regime change by coup, an illness that was prevalent in some other parts of the Third World and which it was feared might spread to other Arab countries. In fact, the reverse happened. Monarchies, once overthrown in Egypt, Tunisia and Libya, were replaced by regimes that endured. In Saudi Arabia, Oman and Abu Dhabi, palace coups removed the monarch and installed a brother or a son who was judged to be more likely to procure the royal family's continuation in power. In each of these cases, the new monarch proved successful in doing so. The Arab world became characterised by the lengthy reigns of monarchs and presidents.

The officers who conducted the coups that overthrew monarchies were junior enough to have direct command of troops, such as Colonel Nasser and his colleagues in Egypt, Brigadier Qasim in Iraq and Major Gaddafi in Libya. They came from the new middle classes to which modern education had spread only fairly recently. This meant that their knowledge of English or French and exposure to the wider world beyond their own country was often limited, and they had no real reason to be sympathetic to the West. They bitterly resented the humiliations the Arabs had suffered during the colonial period and the destruction of Palestine in order to create Israel. Above all, they blamed the former ruling elite for failing to protect and advance their country's people so as to create a modern nation state. They were idealistic, motivated and angry. That was how Nasserism came into existence in Egypt and Ba'athism was adopted in Syria and Iraq. Yet once in power, and apparently in a position where they could set out to right all the ills they detested, would they be able to do much better than their aristocratic and urban notable predecessors?

Take Hafez al-Assad and his son Bashar, who between them ruled Syria from 1970 until the country descended into civil war in 2011-2. Hafez was born in 1930 into a leading family in a remote and poor village in the mountains of north-west Syria, which were dominated by the Alawi peasantry to which the Assads belonged. A combination of hard work, intelligence and sheer good fortune enabled him to attend the secondary school in Lattakia, the only one at that time in the entire coastal region of Syria between the Lebanese and Turkish borders. As a boy he resented the favouritism shown to classmates from well-off backgrounds, who felt free not just to bully the poorer boys but even expected deference from the teachers. Some of them put little effort into work at school because they could decide themselves what marks the teacher should award them at the year end. Because of the eminence of their families, it was difficult for a teacher to stand up to them. One day the young Hafez saw a teacher snap. 'You can't buy my dignity for a few liras,' he said, then walked out of the class and never came back. Hafez admired that teacher. It has been suggested that it was this incident that turned him into a revolutionary.[2]

The patronage of the notables, which had been the glue of provincial society under the Ottomans, continued during the Mandate and after independence. But another Ottoman tendency also continued in Syria: the sons of the notables joined the administrative class, and thus left opportunities for bright boys from the countryside or the urban petty bourgeoisie to get ahead in the armed forces. Hafez al-Assad joined the air force and in time rose to be its commander. He was involved in a coup in 1966 which finally ended the power of the old elite, then became head of state in another coup in 1970. Now that he was in power, and subject to all its pressures – not least the huge international pressures on Syria because of its pivotal position in the Arab–Israeli dispute – his rule developed features that were common to many other Arab regimes, both monarchical and republican. Sadly, history suggests that the revolutionary rulers of Arab countries, despite their ideals, would suffer from many of the same vices as the old elite once their power was consolidated. But there was one big difference. Perhaps because they had themselves seized power, they were more conscious of security than their predecessors, and by and large built more repressive states than those they had taken over.

In Syria, economic booms favoured those close to the Ba'athist regime. The careers and businesses of party members flourished. There were kickbacks and privileges for relatives and friends, all based on new networks of patronage. This intensified after the 1973 war. In time, what Patrick Seale has called a 'merchant-military complex' developed, a new wealthy class who lived ostentatiously at the pinnacle of society and depended entirely on the regime for their meteoric rise and sometimes for virtually all that they possessed. They forgot the socialist ideals on which they had supposedly tried to build the Ba'athist state. Business partnerships between senior military figures who belonged to the same Alawi sect as the president and the country's Sunni merchant elite became so frequent that they have been described as a 'central mechanism'[3] for bridging the gap between the members of the two sects.

Corruption was rife among the poorly paid bureaucrats of Syria, as it was in the other secular republics. Governments were well aware of this problem but found it difficult to confront. Shortly before the Arab Spring reached Syria in 2011, a minister publicly expressed the hope that the increasing use of online forms in government departments would gradually replace the need for the public to meet officials face to face in their offices, and thus reduce the opportunities for corruption.

If low-level corruption added to the inefficiency of a bloated bureaucracy which suffered from hardening of the arteries, the crony capitalism and blatant nepotism at the top of government made corruption a straightforward economic issue, as well as a criminal one. It slowed the growth of the economy, stifled entrepreneurship, created monopolies and carved up markets in a cosy fashion. *Wasta*, 'corrupt influence' or, more literally, 'intermediary-ship', the trading of favours up and down the hierarchies of power, cemented the culture of deference natural in a conservative society and made systems of patronage dominate politics, the economy and just about everything else.

The cult of Hafez al-Assad's personality began to grow, with the corollary that he became more remote. Trusted advisers whose loyalty was to him personally remained in place as years turned into decades and controlled access to him. Now his power was consolidated, he could change his ministers at will and none of them could challenge his authority. He had a tendency to micro-manage and also the insecurity of a ruler who comes from a minority.

There was a reaction. Islamists had always hated the Ba'ath party because of its secular ideology, and Hafez al-Assad had taken part in street fighting against youths from the Muslim Brotherhood as a teenager. Now urban guerrilla warfare appeared in Syria, beginning with a massacre of eighty-three Alawite artillery cadets in Aleppo in 1979 and unleashing a cycle of repression by the regime and terrorist response. This culminated in the 1982 massacre at Hama in which perhaps anything between 5,000 and 20,000 people were killed by the regime when militants seized control of the city as a step towards an Islamist revolution. The insurgency was ruthlessly stamped out by forces commanded by the president's brother Rif'at as the regime strengthened its control across the entire country.

It was also a catalyst in making the attitudes of the new, Ba'athist elite increasingly conservative. The feelings of the masses came to be seen as something to be controlled rather than mobilised. In these circumstances, it is scarcely surprising that many ordinary people became disillusioned with the ideals of the revolution. They also became politically apathetic, aware that they could change little and seeking just to get on with their lives. It was too dangerous to do anything else. An Emergency Law passed in 1963 had given the police and various security services unfettered powers. It remained on the statute book until 2011. Today a Syrian would have to be nearly seventy to have a clear recollection of the time before it. Ba'athist Syria seems to have had no less than seventeen different *mukhabarat* agencies. Their jurisdictions overlapped in mysterious ways not known to ordinary people, and almost certainly not to many of those who worked for them. It was far from clear to whom they were accountable behind the scenes, or to what extent their task was to spy on each other as well as on the general population. If someone was taken away for questioning there was no certainty when he would be released, whether he would emerge from custody beaten black and blue, or if he would just never be seen again.

The best way for the relatives to find out would be to approach a *mukhabarat* officer, who might well expect some favour in return. Ordinary *mukhabarat* officers were not well paid, were not necessarily very intelligent and were frequently venal. When they made their rounds, some expected to be tipped. If a shopkeeper or householder happened to have no money to offer, some officers were bold enough to look around and point at something they could see, which might be as unlikely as a canary in a cage or the secateurs the caretaker was using to prune the plants on the roof terrace, and demand it as a present. The number of people employed by the *mukhabarat* was not known, but there was no doubt it was a substantial proportion of the workforce, very possibly 10 per cent or more. Syria was one of the worst cases in this respect, but in most Arab countries the activities of the *mukhabarat* placed a drag on business activities and stifled personal freedom to a greater or lesser extent.

When Hafez al-Assad's son Bashar took over the presidency after his father's death in 2000, what seemed to be tentative attempts at political liberalisation were soon smothered, although a considerable measure of economic liberalisation was achieved. The Syrian economy and many ordinary citizens certainly benefited from this, but the liberalisation had a less savoury side. Opening up the economy enabled the elite to enrich themselves at the expense of the country and to keep the regime in place at times when other streams of revenue, notably from oil, were declining. In 2011, when the demonstrations of the Arab Spring spread to Syria, they were violently repressed by forces led by the president's brother Maher. One of the targets of the demonstrators was the president's billionaire cousin Rami Makhlouf who, according to some estimates, controlled up to 60 per cent of the Syrian economy and was the prime beneficiary of the new economic liberalisation. Ruling cliques look after themselves, and recent events have shown that they are right to fear the loss of power because of the vengeance that might be taken on them.

Hafez al-Assad grew up in a cottage with a dirt floor and no plumbing or electricity. His successor son was a doctor who had been training as an ophthalmologist at the prestigious Western Eye Hospital in London before he was summoned back to Damascus to learn the ropes of government as his father's health declined. This just shows how much had changed, and how far the al-Assads and their relatives had travelled. 'Makhlouf', the family name of Bashar's cousin Rami, means 'rewarded by God'. It had been given to his ancestors during the First World War at the time of the great famine which wartime conditions brought about with the aid of drought and a plague of locusts. Hundreds of thousands starved to death. Rami's ancestors used their savings to feed as many as they could, and earned the family its name because of their generosity. By contrast, long before the Arab Spring reached Syria, Rami was detested as 'the big thief'.

Other countries may not have had as many as seventeen separate security services, but it was the general practice to establish several competing ones so as to make an attempt at a coup very risky. Rulers of republics and kingdoms alike also retained power by keeping close to their armed forces, feeding them choice morsels as one might to a pet. In some countries, the armed forces became almost a state within the state. In Egypt, for instance, they became major actors in the economy and as remote from accountability as the Mamluks of yore. The armed forces could also be, as in Saudi Arabia, a vehicle for the distribution of patronage and largesse.

Rulers could be sheltered from unwelcome news by sycophantic or timorous courtiers. Some such as Saddam Hussein, Muammar Gaddafi, Hosni Mubarak and Bashar al-Assad seem sooner or later to have passed through a dangerous threshold and come to believe their own propaganda, making them unable to grasp the extent of the opposition to them. This is one reason why they found conspiracy theories attractive ways to explain discontent. But it should also be remembered that foreign powers had frequently conspired against Arab countries.

III

Hosni Mubarak was born in 1928 in the small provincial town of Kafr al-Masalha in the Nile Delta, two years before Hafez al-Assad. He joined the air force, where he gained a reputation for competence, and eventually became its commander. Sadat selected him to be his vice-president, and he stepped into Sadat's shoes as president of Egypt after his assassination. While Hafez al-Assad kept close to the people of his native mountains, and today his body lies in a magnificent marble mausoleum in his home village of Kardaha, Hosni Mubarak seems to have had little contact with his home town after he became president of Egypt. He had moved on to greater things.

The problems Egypt faced when Hosni Mubarak took power were vast. They included finding gainful employment for hundreds of thousands of new school leavers and graduates every year, as well as for the existing unemployed and those underemployed in the bloated public sector which dominated the economy. There was an ever-growing urban underclass which could not share in the nouveau riche, glitzy world of villas in gated compounds and ostentatious wedding receptions in five-star hotels which symbolised the economic prosperity of the new elite which Sadat had created and would expand greatly under Hosni Mubarak's rule.

Autocratic Arab rulers did not have unrestrained freedom of action. This applied to economic matters as well as in the political arena. The patronage designed to inculcate loyalty required them to favour those on whom they relied and provide education, healthcare and tarmac roads, as well as affordable water and electricity, to win the loyalty of the people at large. Economic reform in Egypt under Hosni Mubarak was intermittent, generally half-hearted and almost always patchy. Cutting subsidies on staple items such as bread, heating oil or fuel for the car was encouraged by economic reformers and the IMF, but it went against the grain, as did restructuring state-owned industries and government departments to reduce the number of public-sector employees. According to Ahmed Nazif, a technocrat and economic reformer who was then prime minister, in 2006-7 the government was spending LE100 billion annually on direct and indirect subsidies. LE40 billion went on subsidised energy and half the fuel sold to the public at subsidised prices was imported. To put this into perspective, the combined government health and education budgets amounted to approximately LE30 billion.[4]

Political restraints on the government, particularly fear of the mob which the twentieth century showed many times can rampage in the streets in times of crisis or in protest at rises in the prices of staples (which now included fuel for the car as well as bread for the stomach), often led to weak governmental decision-taking, as did *wasta*. A regrettable example of government weakness in Egypt was the lack of enforcement of planning controls, especially when bribes were on offer. In the 1970s, the Pyramids were approached across several miles of green fields. Today, urban sprawl virtually undermines the feet of the Sphinx.

Yet Hosni Mubarak found Egypt struggling with a debt and foreign exchange crisis which, over time and despite a number of mistakes, his regime was able to solve. Much of the country's infrastructure is still inadequate and ramshackle, but during his years in power it improved considerably. Egypt's private sector expanded while Cairo was even developing an embryonic world-class financial community. It seemed perfectly possible that millions were about to rise out of poverty and into the middle classes – as was happening in other 'Third World' countries such as India and Brazil.

The reasons this did not happen were the cronyism which slowed the growth of the economy and the consequent repression and political corruption. It had become what the Nobel economics laureate Gunnar Myrdal calls a 'soft state'. This concept has been explored by the veteran Egyptian commentator and economist Galal Amin:

A soft state is a state that passes laws but does not enforce them. The elites can afford to ignore the law because their power protects them from it, while others pay bribes to work round it. Everything is up for sale, be it building permits for illegal construction, licences to import illicit goods, or underhand tax rebates and deferrals. The rules are made to be broken and to enrich those who break them, and taxes are often evaded. People clamour for positions of influence so that they may turn them to personal gain. Favours are sold or dispensed to protégés, relatives and sycophants. Travel grants and foreign currency are handed out to those in power and to those close to them. Token-interest bank loans are granted to the non-creditworthy and then the interest payments are waived, and even the principal may not be repaid since the borrowers are often allowed to leave the country and are never forced to repay what they have borrowed.

In the soft state, then, corruption is generalised and the payment of bribes is widespread; the weakness of the state encourages corruption, and the spread of corruption further weakens the state. Corruption spreads from the executive power to the legislative, and from there to the judiciary. To be sure, some corruption exists in one form or another in all countries, but under the soft state it becomes a way of life.[5]

Galal Amin examines how corruption has grown in Egypt. By contrast with what would come later, the level of corruption under the monarchy was low. It grew during the Second World War, but the relatively small size of the government before the 1952 revolution meant that there was much less opportunity for corruption than would later be the case. Amin points the finger of blame for its growth at Sadat and the conspicuous consumption that became socially acceptable under his economic reforms. There were increased 'opportunities for wealth enhancement' at the top levels of society, while prices rose faster than wages at a time of inflation. The gap widened between rich and poor and squeezed those in the middle.[6] This was followed by the era of Hosni Mubarak from 1979 which combined an increasingly soft state with more repressive government.

Like the Assads in Syria, Hosni Mubarak ruled under a state of emergency throughout his thirty years in power although, unlike them, he did not have the excuse that his country was still at war. Totalitarian rule was not new to Egypt. It had existed under Nasser, but if Sadat enabled the growth of corruption in Egypt it should also be acknowledged that he allowed Egypt to become a freer place. He envisaged the country becoming a democracy – albeit after his time – and allowed the formation of political parties.

Manipulation of elections had a long tradition in Egypt which dated back to parliamentary life under the monarchy. Nasser had abolished the party system as socially divisive and incapable of producing the strong leadership Egypt needed, and the country became a one-party state under his Arab Socialist Union. Sadat replaced it with the National Democratic Party (the NDP) which would be a tool for his authority and ensure that opposition forces (such as those who opposed his peace treaty with Israel) could not gain control of parliament. Mubarak inherited what has been called a 'non competitive multiparty system' which resembled a patron–client arrangement.[7]

The NDP had no real ideology except to support the president and ensure that he stayed in power. There were many contrasting platforms within the party which ranged from socialist through moderate Islamist to liberal and capitalist. This had the effect of depriving the party of any chance of standing for a particular ideology or becoming a power base in its own right which might one day call the president to account or decide to replace him. In 1985, Egypt's private sector overtook the public sector as the provider of more than half of Egypt's gross national product. As Mubarak's rule continued, prominent businessmen with an interdependent relationship with the regime increasingly joined parliament. They were unlikely to play a significant part in opening up the economy in a way that might threaten their own interests.

As was happening elsewhere, economic reform was used for an ulterior motive. Under Mubarak, membership of parliament has been described as 'the best investment in Egypt'. For every million Egyptian pounds spent on an electoral campaign, the dividend would be ten million.[8] No Egyptian minister was ever forced to resign as a result of parliamentary pressure, and MPs had immunity from prosecution. The electoral laws for selecting MPs might be enacted by parliament, but the decision as to what they contained was a matter for the president.

The management of parliamentary elections was apparent to anyone who cared to look. When the NDP did badly, successful independent candidates who had defeated the official government candidate would flock to be admitted to the party after the results were declared. In this way, in the 2000 elections, the NDP only won 172 seats (38.5 per cent of the total) at the ballot box, but the party's tally rose to 388 seats (85.5 per cent) as it mopped up successful independent candidates afterwards. The official parliamentary opposition from other registered political parties was small and fragmented. These parties never succeeded in combining together in an effective way. They sometimes suffered from the dictatorial, narcissistic leadership of powerful personalities who were unable to compromise, and became ensnared in the web of regime patronage.

When, in the first two rounds of the 2005 parliamentary elections, it became apparent that independent candidates backed by the Muslim Brotherhood had won seventy-six out of the 111 seats declared,[9] voters in constituencies thought likely to elect further candidates opposed to Hosni Mubarak were intimidated from going to the polling stations by the security forces and plain-clothes thugs carrying batons suspiciously similar to those of the riot police. There were some notorious instances of ballot stuffing. Even so, the final tally of MPs linked to the Muslim Brotherhood was eighty-eight seats, a six-fold increase in their representation and 20 per cent of the total.

Next time Egyptians were due to elect a parliament, in November and December 2010, the government was prepared. In the first round of voting, not a single independent backed by the Muslim Brotherhood succeeded, while the NDP took 209 seats outright. The electoral fraud was so blatant that the Muslim Brotherhood and the Wafd party boycotted the rest of the polls. Mubarak now had a parliament which he not only controlled but which had almost no opposition voices.

Thoughts began to turn to the presidential election which would fall in 2011. Last time, in 2005, Ayman Nour the main opposition candidate had been convicted of forging signatures on his nomination papers – a rather improbable charge – and was thrown into gaol where his health suffered permanent damage. Now, however, the president had turned eighty. Would he stand again? The spotlight focused increasingly on his family. In an innovative use of a modern communications medium, a Facebook campaign had been started for his son Gamal to stand as his successor. As a prominent Egyptian lawyer said at the time with breathtaking cynicism, 'Who will come after Mubarak? It might be the army, which would be a disaster. Or it might be the Islamists, which would also be a disaster. And then there is Gamal. So I find myself asking, "why not?"'

But he never had to decide whether to vote for Gamal Mubarak. Within weeks of the declaration of the results in the 2010 parliamentary elections, history would intervene.

IV

The monarchies of the Arabian Peninsula also had aspects of the soft state, but there was an important difference between these monarchies and those overthrown in Egypt and Iraq. They owed their existence to indigenous families, not a colonial or mandatory power. None of them was founded by an Ottoman adventurer or a figure for whom the British created a throne in furtherance of their own imperial policies. With the exception of Saudi Arabia, these countries – Oman, Bahrain, Kuwait, the UAE and Qatar – had been under British control, but with a much lighter touch than had been the case in Egypt, Palestine or Iraq. They were each founded by a tribal notable who might be a warrior, as in Saudi Arabia, or a wealthy merchant, as in Qatar. These families had legitimacy in the eyes of a sizeable part, frequently the majority, of the indigenous population. As the twentieth century wore on, symbols of national sovereignty were created: a national flag – sometimes the banner of the ruling tribe[10] – was adopted, and a stirring national anthem composed. Brightly coloured postage stamps were issued, coins minted and a national day celebrated every year with the pomp of military parades and the most spectacular firework displays money could buy.

The ruling family presented itself as the embodiment of the state and the nation, something that was sealed by the omnipresent pictures of the ruler and key close relatives such as the crown prince and, very often, the prime minister. Government stemmed from the ruler, who was the shaykh, the sultan, the amir or the king. His followers had been able to approach him directly. A substantial proportion of them had known him personally and might drop by for a chat at a formal *majlis* held once or twice every week. But as their numbers increased naturally over several decades as a result of the healthcare and prosperity now arranged for them, the personal contact with the ruler was inevitably diluted, while society became increasingly urbanised and literate.

In 1981, these Arab oil monarchies grouped themselves together as the Gulf Co-operation Council (GCC). It was an agreement to act together on matters as diverse as economic policy (a customs union, single market and common currency were ambitions) as well as on defence and internal security issues. It was also an acknowledgement of how the members of this rich men's club composed of largely tribal societies were faced by similar dilemmas. For centuries before the exploitation of hydrocarbons – and even before the advent of Islam – rulers in the Arabian Peninsula needed to nurse the loyalty of their followers carefully if they were to maintain their power. There was no entrenched system of primogeniture like that of the European monarchies. The choice of ruler reflected power politics within the family. Frequent first-cousin marriage could give a powerful father-in-law immense influence and make sure the family's wealth and power were not diluted, while the polygamy permitted under Sharia allowed a multiplicity of dynastic alliances with important tribes. There was a tipping point at which loyalty would be lost. When that occurred, a ruler might be replaced by another member of his family, or else his followers might leave by exercising their traditional right of *hijra*, 'emigration', an event which would humiliate him. If too many of his followers 'emigrated', this could drain away his power and even dissolve his polity. The move by Muhammad and his followers from Mecca to Medina is only the best known example of this.

Any successful ruler had to be perceived as generous to his followers if he was to survive and thrive. When the oil era arrived, this meant a corresponding expectation of greater largesse. This led to the ultimate culture of entitlement, which the fear of revolution encouraged the ruler to indulge. The benefits of the modern world had to be given to the 'citizens' or 'nationals' (*al-muwaatinoon*) of the state, into which the traditional 'followers' (*al-taabi'oon*)[11] of the ruler gradually metamorphosed in the second half of the twentieth century. All the monarchies had seen what happened to the last kings of Egypt and Iraq. Slightly more recent and very salutary examples were the overthrow of the newly oil-rich Libyan kingdom by Muammar Gaddafi's revolutionary regime in 1969 and the attempts of the Marxist regime, which took over from Britain in South Yemen after independence in 1967, to ignite flames of revolution in Oman and the Gulf in the late 1960s and 1970s. The result was that the provision of education, healthcare, housing, subsidised water and electricity soon came to be expected as a matter of course, even though the monarchies had not made the same rash promises to provide them that were typical of the revolutionary republics. Young people also came to expect well-paid job opportunities to be created for them by the government when they finished school or university, and frequently a grant of land to build their own house.

The solution to the aspirations of the *muwaatinoon* was to grow and diversify the economy, but the traditional system of patronage cut against an open market. Restrictions on foreigners doing business were borrowed from revolutionary regimes so as to promote local commerce. Industry was also encouraged, with a strong governmental guiding hand and plenty of soft finance. Goods were manufactured to world-class standards by expatriate labour, usually from South Asia and the Far East under international management.

But the people who benefited most were the powerful merchant families who were best placed to take advantage of the laws limiting commercial activity by foreigners, as well as members of the ruling family and favourites of the ruler who used access to the government as a commodity with which to win commissions from their clients. At the same time, foreign labour was imported to carry out the work for which the *muwaatinoon* either lacked the expertise or perceived as demeaning. All this slowed the development of a genuine, independent middle class while encouraging the *muwaatinoon* to continue to look to patronage of the ruler as the source and guarantor of their welfare.

At first glance, the non-oil states which had been partly seduced by the economic and political systems of Eastern Europe during the Communist era could not have been more different from the oil-rich monarchies. Yet, as we have seen in the case of Syria and Egypt, the patronage of the soft state – exercised by the ruling party or the armed forces and, of course, the kinship networks of leading personalities in these groups – was of supreme importance. It is scarcely surprising that none of these states came close to breaking through the economic ceiling to catch up with the West in the way that some countries in the Far East have done. Industrialisation was seen as a top–down process, the product of national plans and state investment. Sometimes, wonderful economic opportunities were lost because of ideology which, it soon transpired, could so easily be blended with corruption. The magnificent port of Aden, for instance, could have become a regional hub for trade, finance and service infrastructure at the time of South Yemen's independence in 1967. It might have risen in tandem with Hong Kong and Singapore and achieved similar importance on the world stage, but the opportunity was driven away and it became a derelict backwater where Saddam Hussein's merchant fleet would rust away when UN sanctions were imposed on Iraq.

V

The solution – or at least a major element in the solution – of the problems that beset a developing country lie in education and the acquisition of knowledge and skills. According to a 2004 census, Morocco still had a literacy rate of only 52.3 per cent for those aged fifteen and above. For women, the figure was 39.6 per cent. In Yemen, a 2003 census gave the comparable percentages as 50.2 and 30 per cent.

Only slightly less shocking are recently available figures for Egypt, Syria and Iraq. For total literacy over the age of fifteen, the percentages are 71, 79.6 and 74.1, while the percentages for females are 59.4, 73.6 and 64 respectively. The oil-rich states of the Gulf do better but that is only to be expected, given their wealth. Yet by 2005, only Kuwait had literacy rates that were unambiguously over 90 per cent for both men and women. Saudi Arabia's figures, 78.8 per cent for total literacy and 70.8 per cent for women according to an estimate made in 2003, are a scandal when the vast resources of the kingdom are taken into consideration.[12]

The lower literacy rates for women do not, as is sometimes mistakenly assumed, stem from a hostility to female education like that of the Taliban in Afghanistan (except in some remote areas and among some Bedouin tribes). On the contrary, there is abundant evidence that female education is encouraged and appreciated – not least by females themselves. The twenty-first-century phenomenon of girls outperforming boys in exams is as much a feature of Arab countries as it is of many other societies. Slowly but incrementally, women do seem to be moving up the ladders of the professions and middle management. Female cabinet ministers are increasingly common, but the fact that women have not yet been appointed to key posts shows that there are still limits to what old-fashioned attitudes will allow them to achieve – and to what is publicly acceptable. Many Islamists oppose in principle the idea that a woman could rule a

Muslim country. On the other hand, they generally join others in calling for campaigns to achieve universal literacy. Apart from anything else, literacy enables an Arabic-speaking girl to read the Qur'an.

The causes of the slower spread in female literacy are social and economic, not religious or political. In a poor and traditional family, possibly one with many children, priority will be given to sending boys to school. It may also seem the natural order of things for a girl, rather than a boy, to be kept at home if there is need for extra help in the house or in the fields. Above all, perhaps, it may be assumed that a girl will be married at a very young age – well before the end of her teens – and that this will lead to her being taken out of school in any case. A poor, rural family may therefore question what point there is in their daughters spending much effort on their education. At all levels of society, there can also be cultural resistance among men to marrying a woman who is their intellectual equal – a phenomenon hardly confined to Arab society. Working against this, however, is the increasing realisation that an educated woman is likely to have better earning prospects, and that a sensible husband should appreciate this.

To be fair, it should also be noted how recently the drive for mass literacy has begun in Arab countries. At the time of the 1958 revolution, Iraq had a literacy rate of only 15 per cent while a figure of 10 per cent has been estimated for Egypt at the end of the First World War. Considerable credit is due to nationalist governments like those of Nasser and the Ba'athists for policies that spread education. During the ten years after the 1952 revolution, for instance, the size of the Egyptian education system was doubled. This was noticed in other countries where revolutions had not yet occurred, and provided a spur for oil-rich monarchies to turn their attention to public education.

But the problem is much greater than eradicating illiteracy. During the age of the autocrats, many intellectuals sensed a general dumbing down that permeated society throughout the Arab world. All too often, schools and universities in Arab countries are factories for cramming their students with lists of facts, rather than unlocking minds. Sometimes, paucity of resources could be pleaded and standards might slip as the number of students increased. The ever-increasing religiosity was hardly a process calculated to encourage independent ideas, and helped to make it even harder to tackle subjects which society considered taboo. The greatest factor, however, was the wish of authoritarian rulers to discourage critical thought. For instance, during a cultural crackdown in Saudi Arabia in 1980, topics such as the history of civilisation and of Europe were removed from schools. Everywhere, a particularly watchful eye was kept over the teaching of history to ensure that it reinforced the approved national narrative which would be that of the ruling party or dynasty. As the 2005 UN Arab Human Development Report put it with masterful understatement: 'school systems under authoritarian rule rarely give sufficient encouragement to initiative, discovery or the development of creative and critical faculties or personal aptitudes.'

VI

The Islamic revival which took place during these decades was the most noticed response by ordinary Arabs to the unattractive situation in which they found themselves. Some were inspired by the Iranian revolution which showed that Islam could be a more powerful way to move millions than a secularist ideology born in Europe. Two factors led to the revival. The first was the need of a rapidly urbanising society that was no longer pre-industrial to find a response to the modern world. The other was a crisis of identity caused by the political, economic and cultural domination of the West. This made it imperative that the response came from within Arab society's own traditions.

The revival happened gradually, and many aspects of it had nothing to do with politics. It became hard to speak against anything that was claimed to be a reassertion of Muslim values. To do so was likely to be perceived as disloyal or 'letting the side down' or, perhaps, 'politically incorrect'. Some people took to asking others about their religious observance in a way that would once have been considered bad form, not least because every Muslim knows that only God can see into the hearts of men. This enabled the more literalist interpretations of Islam to have more influence on the way people lived their lives as they tried to emulate the practice of the very first Muslims who had known the Prophet and his companions, *al-salaf al-salih*, 'the righteous forefathers'. At its extreme, this led to an inward-looking attitude of mind that became known as 'Salafism': a Wahhabi quest for authenticity that rejects whatever came from the Jahiliyya, the West or any other non-Islamic source – although technology was acceptable, since it was morally neutral.

Salafis became a common sight in most Muslim countries and in Muslim communities elsewhere. The men are distinguished by their bushy beards modelled on that of the Prophet and the women by the black wrappings which swathe them from head to toe, allowing only their eyes to be seen. The face veil is even retained when they eat or drink in public, so that no man outside the permitted degree of kindred may see their faces as they lift a cup, a spoon or an ice cream to their lips. But Salafis are at the end of a spectrum. Many more Muslims modified aspects of their behaviour to comply more closely with traditional interpretations of Sharia. Most women adopted the hijab, or Islamic headscarf. Sometimes this was a proud expression of faith and belonging, but it could also be the result of social pressure designed to remind women that they should not set their hearts on all the things that were open to men. There were also contradictions in its spread. The popularity of pretty, colourful headscarves which became items of fashion could negate their ostensible purpose as a sign of modesty and religious observance, something that thoughtful observers like the Iraqi intellectual Ali Allawi did not hesitate to point out.[13] Alcohol was ever more frequently shunned in polite society. Moves were made to ban it, especially in places where it might be consumed in front of women and children, and there was pressure for it to be outlawed altogether. This probably had the unintended side effect of encouraging smoking. Once, pious imams had argued that smoking was *haram* by analogy with alcohol, but this attempt at prohibition was now generally forgotten – as was the even earlier attempt to declare coffee *haram*.

But there was much more to the reaffirmation of Islam than a concentration on appearances and public behaviour. There was a genuine thirst to establish a feeling of brotherhood and shared social responsibility among Muslims so as to attack the increasing disparities in wealth, while honesty and justice were Muslim virtues which seemed conspicuously absent from public life. The world had changed; social bonds that had existed from time immemorial were being weakened, reducing the cohesion of traditional society. If capitalism of the crony and vulture varieties was one threat to Islam, Western ideologies such as class-based socialism, the best known secular movement opposing it, were others.

Back in the 1890s, Jamal-al-Din al-Afghani had already spoken of Islam as providing a 'true socialism' which contrasted with the Western variety. Brotherhood and cooperation would be its hallmarks, which would flow from the inspiration of the Prophet's example and be buttressed by religious principles and observance. A generation later Rashid Rida had argued that a society which obeyed the proper interpretation of Sharia would be able to resist the excesses of both capitalism and the disorder that was the natural consequence of class-based socialism, because it would be immune to their temptations.[14] By the early 1980s, some economists were looking for ways to apply the principles of Sharia to modern economics and build a fairer society. Here, however, literalism frequently intervened. The work of Muhammad Abduh, who had reflected on the purpose behind the

Qur'anic prohibition of interest and suggested that interest did not always amount to usury when it served a socially useful purpose, was sidelined. Instead, a multi-billion-dollar Islamic banking industry developed which concentrated on formality rather than substance, and produced sophisticated banking products that conformed to the letter of the strictest interpretations of those provisions of Sharia which forbid speculative transactions and the payment of interest.

Islamic sensitivities stood ready to be roused against government corruption and oppression, especially if it was by secularist regimes in states like Egypt, Syria, Iraq and Algeria. Rulers began to make accommodations with Islamists, giving them an access to the public sphere that they had previously been denied. In the early years of the revival, it seemed sensible to relax restrictions on organisations like the Muslim Brotherhood in the hope that they would provide a counterweight to Marxist and other groups. Successful Islamist candidates in elections to student and professional bodies soon developed a reputation for a lack of corruption and a concern for their members, which helped them rout their left-wing opponents and build up their own support. Islamist organisations sometimes offered regimes a political quid pro quo. In 1970, Jordan's Islamists backed King Hussein when he cracked down on the secular nationalists of the PLO in what became known as Black September. But secularist republics and conservative monarchs soon found that advantage was being taken by militants who used ideologies like that of Sayyid Qutb to try to overthrow them. This led to crackdowns, and provided an excuse to curtail all serious political opposition.

We have already seen how a major Islamist insurrection broke out in Syria in 1979–82. The heroism and perceived success of militants returning victorious from Afghanistan at the end of the 1980s led to new attempts at armed struggle to establish Islamic states. Egypt and Algeria had been two of the countries of which the returning fighters had the highest hopes, but by the late 1990s it had become apparent that attempts to bring about an Islamic revolution through violence led the militants who initiated it to lose their popular support. Their tactics were thwarted by a quasi-mathematical formula: the more successful they were in destabilising a regime by violence, the more that violence alienated the host population whose support they thus failed to gain. In Egypt, attacks on foreign tourists, Copts and secularists declined as they damaged the economy and gave the government an extra excuse to stifle opposition activity. In Algeria the army took control of the country after it looked as though Islamists were about to win an election, leading to a bloody civil war from which the country eventually emerged deeply traumatised.

There were exceptions to this rule but they reflected particular circumstances. In Lebanon and Palestine the militias of the Islamist movements Hizbullah and Hamas played the role that normally belongs to a conventional army resisting an invader. Another exception applied in the divided society of Iraq, where suicide bombing and other terrorism against civilian targets was a big factor in setting Sunnis and Shi'ites against each other after the removal of Saddam Hussein.

Regimes all over the Arab world also attempted to move in directions which would diffuse Islamist hostility to them. There was a way they could do this which seemed at first sight to be relatively painless and appealed to both conservatives and radicals: giving support to, or at least not objecting to, measures which cemented Islam at the centre of national life. Nasser and others had resisted attempts to import references to Islam into constitutions. This changed. After Nasser's death Sadat, who branded himself 'the believing president', increasingly let religion slip back into Egyptian public life. He tolerated Muslim Brotherhood activity in mosques, which the organisation turned into an opportunity to set up a country-wide political organisation and build political support by providing services to the poor. He also made a bow in the Brotherhood's direction by amending the constitution to make the principles of Sharia 'a main source' and then 'the main source' of legislation.[15]

Judges with Islamist sympathies sometimes used this to interpret the law against secular practices. In a notorious case in the mid-1990s, a Cairo Court of Appeal ordered the dissolution of the marriage of Professor Abu Zaid on the grounds that he had allegedly left Islam and could therefore no longer be married to a Muslim woman. The couple was forced to flee abroad. The incident demonstrated the coercive impulse behind much Islamism, as well as the unintended consequences of making concessions in its direction.

The autocracies had a kind of symbiotic relationship with Islamism, which allowed each to feed off the other. In Egypt, the regime's relationship with Islamism and the Muslim Brotherhood was complex. In the 2005 presidential campaign, posters for Mubarak appealed jointly to Christian and Muslim voters as fellow Egyptians, and the regime presented itself to the West as a bastion of secularism. On the other hand, in the course of the same campaign it persuaded imams to preach against some human rights and democracy activists on the grounds that they were pawns of foreign, 'infidel' interests.[16] The Muslim Brotherhood had its uses, not least because its political organisation and grass-roots activity helping ordinary Muslims – most notably during the 1992 earthquake in Cairo – meant that it was harder for secular parties like Nasserists and the Wafd to make an impact.

The test of Islamism would only arrive when it acquired real power at the ballot box. While the autocrats held sway, that would not happen.

VII

In 2002, Alaa al Aswany published *The Yacoubian Building* which became the best-selling Arabic novel both in his native Egypt and throughout the Arab world for several years. A film version was released in 2006. The message of book and film was that there was something very rotten indeed in the state of Egypt, and that this went right to the top and infected the whole of society. It showed what life under a dictatorship does to people.

The novel tells the tale of a group of disparate characters living in an ornate but decayed block of flats in what was once the Khedive Ismail's 'European' Cairo, and is now known in English as 'Downtown'. Aswany lets the novel have a happy ending for two of them. One is the Francophile Zaki Bey, an ageing and dissolute relic of the ancien regime who laments that, but for the 1952 revolution, he might have been a cabinet minister. He provides a contrast to the much more sinister people who now wield the power and influence that was once the prerogative of his class. The other happy ending is for Busayna, a poor girl whose family live in a hovel on the roof of the building, who once went out with Taha, the doorkeeper's son. She gets to know Zaki when another denizen of the roof, a Christian tailor called Malak, temporarily suborns her to take a job with Zaki as part of a conspiracy to defraud him of his flat. The plan is for her to persuade Zaki to sign papers while he is drunk or stoned, but she is overcome with remorse and angrily rips them up after he has signed them. Zaki treats her well and behaves honourably towards her, a striking contrast to her previous employer who used to rub himself against her to achieve sexual release. She falls in love with Zaki and they marry, despite an age gap of at least thirty years. But there is no other way out of poverty for her.

The fate of some of the other principal characters is grim. Taha, the doorkeeper's son who once hoped to marry Busayna, works hard at school but is rejected for the police because of his father's lowly position. He goes to Cairo University, but his poverty and the holes in his socks exclude him from the life of the bright young things from Egypt's upper crust who dominate life on campus. Naturally devout, he falls into extremist Islamist company and is tortured by the police after being a ringleader in a demonstration. This radicalises him. He receives weapons training, and is married to a beautiful Islamist bride who gives him the briefest but sweetest of honeymoons before joyfully letting him go off to his death, which he meets while assassinating the man who had coordinated his torture.

Then there is Hatem, the homosexual editor of a French-language newspaper. The child of a glacially remote law professor and a neglectful French mother, he was befriended and then seduced as a boy by the family's (male) Nubian cook, whose affection he still craves. Hatem seduces Abduh, a Nubian policeman, although he knows that Abduh is married and has a child. When the child dies, Abduh sees the death as punishment from God for his sin, and breaks off the relationship. When Hatem seduces him again, Abduh strangles him.[17]

The final main character is Hagg Azzam, who has risen from shoe-shine boy to great wealth and has built a commercial empire which includes distributorships for major Japanese car manufacturers. He portrays himself as a scrupulously devout Muslim but is rotten to the core. Not only is his fortune built on drug money, but he enters into what should be, for a believer, an unconscionable bargain. In response to a late flush of sexual energy, he secretly takes a second wife, a poor widow from Alexandria whom he separates from her child. He insists she should not allow herself to fall pregnant, but when she does he has her abducted and the foetus aborted while she is sedated. Then he repudiates her, believing himself to be generous because he pays everything she is due under Sharia and a bit more. Not content with his wealth, he has political ambitions and enters into a corrupt deal with the ruling party to become the local member of parliament, signing over half the profits of his new Japanese car dealership in return.

It may well be asked: why did Mubarak's government allow such a novel to be published and turned into a film? The answer is contained in one word: arrogance. It thought that the Egyptian people could let off a little steam and vent a little anger, but nothing they could possibly do would topple the president.

CONCLUSION

SOMETHING SNAPS: THE ARAB SPRING AND BEYOND

I

The match which lit the Arab Spring was struck on 17 December 2010 by Muhammad Bouazizi, a vegetable seller in the depressed, dusty town of Sidi Bouzid in central Tunisia, when he turned himself into a torch outside the municipal offices. Protests had spread across the country before he died in hospital on 4 January 2011. The harshness of his life, his strong sense of family and the lack of economic opportunity open to him made him a figure millions of young Arabs could identify with, from Agadir to Aden. His father, a migrant worker on construction sites in neighbouring Libya, had died when he was three. His mother married his father's brother, but Bouazizi's uncle had poor health which prevented him from doing regular work. Bouazizi was one of seven children and the main breadwinner for his family. He left school without qualifications but supported a sister to go to university. Unable to find a decent job, he sold vegetables from a cart and was harassed because he did not have the required permit. He had not been a political activist, but he took his complaint to the authorities when officials overturned his cart and confiscated his weighing scales. They showed no interest, so he poured paint thinner over himself and ignited it. He was twenty-six.

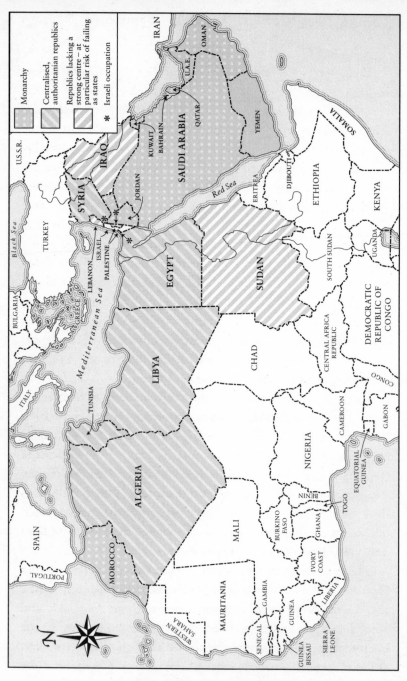

THE ARAB WORLD ON THE EVE OF THE ARAB SPRING

There were voices that said it was only a matter of time before an explosion happened in the Arab world. Many people in the region sensed an ever more stifling atmosphere that seemed to call for some violent resolution, if only to purge the electricity in the air. Yet another Israeli pulverisation of Lebanon was one possibility that was frequently mentioned; a conflict with Iran that closed the sea lanes in the Gulf and brought in the Americans was another. There had been other incidents that might have provided the same sort of spark as Bouazizi's death. In Egypt, solidarity with strikers at textile factories in April 2008 and the death in police custody of a young man called Khaled Said in Alexandria in June 2010 both led to protest movements in which the organisers made use of Facebook to spread their message. Yet the question why one incident sparked a revolution while another did not is as futile as asking why a global crash which revealed that the financial system was unstable happened sooner rather than later, or later rather than sooner.

Ten days after Bouazizi died, Tunisia's president Ben Ali fled. His position became untenable once the army command refused to use lethal force to quell the demonstrations which the self-immolation had triggered. On 11 February 2011, President Mubarak of Egypt also relinquished power. On 25 January, crowds calling for the fall of the regime had succeeded in taking over Tahrir Square, the communications hub in the centre of Cairo, effectively paralysing the centre of the city. Despite their best efforts, the police could not shift them. The Egyptian generals followed the example of their Tunisian colleagues and refused to do so.

The demonstrators who forced these two regimes from power had no political leaders and acted spontaneously, often responding to calls for freedom and dignity plastered over Facebook and YouTube. Much greater numbers who did not have access to the internet followed them, and the crowds taking to the streets grew as they developed a natural sense of solidarity and faced down the violence of the security forces. Social divides and other divisions were temporarily bridged, as happened in European revolutions in the nineteenth century when gentlemen in silk top hats and street urchins in rags jointly manned the barricades against the dragoons and artillery of a reactionary regime.

Spontaneous demonstrations, strikes and riots now rippled across other Arab countries, whether monarchies or republics, oil states or non-oil states. Riots hit some Moroccan towns and the Omani port city of Sohar. In both countries constitutional concessions were promised, but the fact that the grievances were in large part economic was underscored by a pledge the Moroccan government made to double food subsidies and an undertaking by Sultan Qaboos of Oman to create more jobs. In the same way, demonstrations in Jordan also demanded the reduction of food and fuel prices, as well as democracy and more freedom. Flickerings of discontent in two oil-rich states, Saudi Arabia and Algeria, seemed to be nipped in the bud by promises of massive government spending.

Egypt and Tunisia soon seemed to be tentatively on the path to a more democratic future. In Tunisia, a constituent assembly which acted as a transitional parliament was elected (27 per cent of the deputies were women). A coalition government was appointed and work on a new constitution began. Casually watching the country's parliamentary TV channel, you are struck by how normal proceedings in the new, freely elected Chamber of Deputies seem. An impassioned orator addresses rows of half-empty, green leather benches, as the Speaker tells him it is time to sit down. The members present yawn and look at the ceiling in boredom: just like Westminster or any other Western parliament.

A memorable slogan of the crowds in Tahrir Square which overthrew Hosni Mubarak in Egypt was "*iyd wahda*", "one hand": an ecstatic call for national unity and an appeal to the possibly wavering generals not to order their troops to open fire. It also predated the revolution as a call for brotherhood between Egyptian Muslims and Christians, a promise that in those heady days the demonstrators seemed determined to fulfil. Yet three years later Egypt has fresh scars from the brutal excesses of a largely intact security state and mounting sectarian hatred. It was never meant to be like this.

The well-organised Islamists won Egypt's first elections after the revolution and dominated the country's politics when the Muslim Brotherhood's candidate, Muhammad Morsi, narrowly defeated a representative of the old regime for the presidency in June 2012. Although Morsi had campaigned with a promise to be a president for all Egyptians, his regime soon showed a streak that was not just socially conservative but misogynistic. It also tolerated religious hate speech and did little to stop increasing attacks on Christians and other groups which were not Sunni. In one particularly horrific episode, a mob murdered four men in a village outside Cairo who had converted to Shi'ism. As with many attacks on Christians, the police pleaded that the crowds were too large for them to intervene, and just stood idly by.

Morsi took steps to impose an Islamist agenda on the country – something for which he did not have a clear mandate. When this was coupled with economic incompetence, massive demonstrations against him and the Muslim Brotherhood led to a military coup in July 2013. Subsequently, however, civil liberties were cut back. Violence tarnished the reputation of the military and its backers, especially when possibly a thousand people were killed as protest camps set up by Morsi supporters were cleared.

Egypt now seems likely to be pulled in three ways against a backdrop of identity politics: between supporters of military rule, those who want an Islamist future for their country, and those who wish to adopt Western liberal values to a greater or lesser extent. The overthrow of the elected Morsi government shows that for a while to come real power will not lie exclusively within the constitutional order, although this may eventually become possible if the country manages to pass through the stormy weather which unquestionably lies ahead. The events since the fall of Mubarak show how easy it is to manipulate a poorly educated population for which genuine discussion of live political issues is still new.

Things became bloody and messy in Libya, Bahrain, Yemen and Syria. The Libyan dictator Muammar Gaddafi proved to be a colossus with clay feet. Nevertheless, he would almost certainly have reasserted his control if the uprising which seized Benghazi and the main towns of the eastern region of Cyrenaica had not been aided by air power provided by NATO and one or two Arab League states under a UN Security Council resolution. Bit by bit, his grip on the country loosened and the insurgents finally took the capital, Tripoli, in August 2011. He fled to his home town and last stronghold, Sirte, but was captured and killed on 20 October. By then, the institutions of the Libyan state had been virtually destroyed and the number of people who had died in the conflict had almost certainly risen into the tens of thousands. Libya is a sparsely populated country where population centres are separated by immense expanses of desert and there are strong regional and tribal loyalties. Gaddafi's regime was largely overthrown by militias which came from different towns and were only loosely allied together. They proved reluctant to disarm once he was overthrown. This made the establishment of central control and the path to a democratic future slow and problematic.

In Bahrain, demonstrators tried to take over the Pearl Roundabout on the outskirts of the capital Manama and turn it into Manama's version of Tahrir Square. The roundabout owed its name to the giant replica of a pearl featured in its centre. It had been built as a celebration of the days before oil when such wealth as the island state possessed came from the Gulf's pearl trade. The security forces cleared the area one morning before dawn, killing several people. The monument was demolished so as to prevent it being transformed into a symbol of revolution. The government was able to keep the situation under control but at the price of considerable violence. It also received tangible military and moral support from Saudi Arabia and the other members of the GCC, which had no wish to see a Gulf monarchy sucked down the road to what had happened in Tunisia and Egypt. Bahrain is a divided society, split between Sunni tribes who conquered the country in the late eighteenth century and now constitute an aristocracy which makes up perhaps 30 per cent of the population, while the rest are the urbanised descendants of the Shi'ite peasantry who feel excluded despite the educational opportunities the country's wealth has now given all Bahrainis. The brutality with which the monarchy confronted pro-democracy protests in 2011 risks cementing a status quo that is unsustainable in the long term.

Before the Arab Spring reached Yemen, many already feared it was a slowly failing state. It was riddled with secessionism in the south and faced a rebellion in remote parts of the north as well as an active al-Qa'ida affiliate. In many areas tribal authority had always been stronger than that of the elected government, which could only administer by negotiation and compromise. President Ali Abdullah Saleh presided over one of the most corrupt regimes in the Arab world and had some thirty close relatives in key positions in the army and security services. Like the rulers of Tunisia, Egypt, Bahrain and many others, he presented himself as a bulwark against Islamist terrorism to attract support from America and the West. It took a year to dislodge him, despite demonstrations and the defection of part of the army which took the country to the brink of civil war. His resignation was finally brokered by Saudi Arabia and the other GCC states in exchange for immunity from prosecution. For decades many observers have said that it suited Saudi Arabia to keep Yemen stable but weak, so that one set of forces in the country might be played off against another and it could not provide a threat to its wealthy neighbour. The rewards of this policy are now clear.

In Syria, President Bashar al-Assad believed that his regime's strong Arab nationalist stance on the Palestinian issue would save him from the storm. This might not have been self-delusion if his regime had moved swiftly with reforms, but it soon showed that it was incapable of introducing any reform process that risked the loss of power or the introduction of accountability, and that its police did not know how to control a peaceful protest calling for democracy without responding with violence. The Arab Spring reached Syria in March 2011 when trivial incidents, such as children scrawling anti-regime graffiti on walls in the southern town of Der'aa, were met with a response designed to instil fear. The body of Hamza al-Khateeb, a thirteen-year-old boy who had gone missing on 29 April, was returned to his family grotesquely mutilated. Although the authorities tried to deny that they were responsible, ordinary Syrians found the accusations all too credible. Soon large parts of the country were aflame with anger. An insurgency took root in the city of Homs and many small towns and villages, as well as the semi-rural suburbs of the Ghutah around Damascus. The areas of the country which retained a superficial normality shrank steadily until by the summer of 2012 even Damascus and Aleppo had become battlegrounds. Deaths climbed well over a hundred thousand, while those who had been displaced either within the country or as refugees who had fled to Lebanon, Turkey or Jordan numbered in the millions.

Comparisons with the insurrection of the early 1980s that led to the destruction of Hama sprang to mind. Some of the regions affected were the same, such as the area around Idlib and parts of the Orontes valley, including Hama itself. The repression with which the earlier rebellion had been met would have added revenge to the factors motivating some of those who rose up in 2011. But while the early 1980s rebellion had been led by a group with a specific religious vision of what they wanted Syria to become, and which by definition excluded many Syrians, the protesters and rebels in 2011 were brought together by something quite different: the wish to replace a corrupt and repressive regime with democracy and freedom.

Telling comparisons can also be made with the great Syrian rebellion of 1925, which its historian Michael Provence has described as 'the largest, longest and most destructive' of the Arab revolts against the Mandates.[1] That revolt also spread across large parts of the country. Some localities which rebelled in 1925 did the same in 2010-11. The Damascus suburb of Midan, the Ghutah, Hama and the countryside of the Orontes valley are names that resurface eighty-six or so years later. Many of the rebels in both insurrections had received military training: in 1925 it came from their time in the Ottoman army, in 2010-11 from Syrian national service. Both were rebellions of the urban and rural poor, and of the young, while the elites frequently tried to stand to one side for as long as they could. The Ba'athist regime's response mirrored that of the Mandatory authorities in its use of violence, including the brutal shelling of urban areas intended to terrorise the inhabitants and force the rebels to withdraw. Guns boomed once again from the heights of Mount Qasyoun above Damascus, just as they had done in 1925. The predominantly Alawi bully-boys of the Shabiha, the ill-disciplined and thuggish pro-government militia, had their counterpart in the Circassians and Armenian refugees recruited by the French to carry out atrocities in areas sympathetic to the rebels. It was as though the Ba'athists had replaced the French, and were determined to follow their example in finally crushing the rebellion by terror and overwhelming fire-power.

Nothing could show more clearly than the civil war in Syria that what the Arab Spring has unleashed is unfinished business. It would be hazardous to predict where it will end in any country. There is little point in trying to give an account of a journey which has not reached its destination. Its immediate causes are obvious. There has been a reaction against the repressive and corrupt cliques which ruled 'soft' states. These cliques looked after their relatives and friends and failed to develop policies that would provide adequate employment opportunities and enable their people to live decent and reasonably free lives. They tolerated an ever-widening gap between rich and poor. Emergency laws that allowed the security forces to use violence without fear of being called to account and the curtailment of political freedom were the preferred methods of staying in power. Very often the regimes managed to enlist American and European support – or at least toleration – for the less savoury aspects of their rule. Whatever the future of the Arab world may be, a genie has popped out of a bottle and cannot be put back. Yet where does the Arab world go from here? And how can the long history of the Arabs help answer this question?

II

Perhaps the first question that has to be asked is what role will be played by Islamism. The appeal of Islamism is that it is a quest for authenticity and identity which is at the same time a rallying cry against corruption, injustice and subservience to foreign interests. Now that Islamists are being elected to parliament, forming governments and controlling ministries of education, they will no longer have the luxury of a podium without responsibility.

What do Islamists want? Is it a reversion to an idealised version of the Middle Ages made possible by modern technology and generous dollops of oil wealth? This was the vision of Osama bin Laden, but its appeal goes much wider than him and his followers and does not imply resorting to violence. It is characteristic of what Irshad Manji calls 'Desert Islam', the Salafi literalism that has spread across the Muslim world. When Egyptian Salafis formed their own political party, the Hizb al-Nur or 'Party of Light', to contest the country's first parliamentary elections after the fall of Hosni Mubarak, street preachers urged their followers to vote for it. Sometimes claims were made that greater religious observance would lead to a reward from God in the form of wealth from the discovery of vast oil resources – as, it was asserted, had happened in Saudi Arabia because of its people's piety. Some who voted for Hizb al-Nur benefited from the charitable actions of Salafi groups during the Mubarak era, and it managed to garner 27 per cent of the vote at the ballot box in November 2011. This was very impressive for a party that had only been formed six months earlier, and shows a bedrock of support for the essence of its message.

Yet literalism can only have a certain appeal. At the other end of the spectrum lies an alternative vision: a quest to build a just society that will be based on the spirit of Qur'anic revelation and the ideals of the Prophet. It is the struggle between these two visions that is likely to preoccupy Islam in the immediate future, both of them influencing a centre ground which contains the broad mass of Muslims. One crucial battle between them is likely to be over the position of women.

In the classical formulations of Sharia, which date from the eighth and ninth centuries, there are many rules which baldly restrict the autonomy of a Muslim woman. She may not marry a non-Muslim. Her testimony is worth half that of a Muslim man. A man may marry as many as four women at any one time, and may also take slave concubines. Although Sharia specifies a rather vague obligation on a man to treat his wives equally, and co-wives have certain specific rights, a husband does not necessarily even have to inform his first wife that he is taking a second. He may also divorce a wife purely because he wishes to make a vacancy among the four for another. The husband has 'a limited right of correction'[2] and may restrict his wife's right to go outside the home. The marriage contract itself is entered into on her behalf by her male guardian – her father or, if he is not still living, her adult son or grandfather. This contract is designed to protect her by stipulating the payment her husband must make in the event that he repudiates her by divorce. The agreed amount will then become her property, but it is sometimes only a nominal sum and divorce will traditionally lead to her returning to her father's family.

The husband may divorce her at will without needing to go to court, while the circumstances in which a woman may divorce her husband are often so limited or complex that her best recourse may be to try to persuade him to divorce her. Suggestions that women should be given equal rights to divorce are met with the retort that this would lead to the collapse of the family. The husband is responsible for the upkeep of the children, but this is an acknowledgement that they belong to his family rather than hers. One consequence is the father's right to care and control over the children from a young age which is often nine, seven or even younger. Although judges have some discretion, they must follow the basic principle that the father should have custody of a daughter before she comes of marriageable age, and of a son once he is old enough to need 'to learn the ways of men'.[3] Daughters inherit a portion of a parent's estate, but their fixed share is half that of a son.

Many of these rules are designed to reinforce ancient cultural practices. The age of majority under the classical formulations of Sharia is puberty (with a presumption of puberty at the age of fifteen lunar years). Traditionally, it is common for a daughter to be married as soon as possible after reaching this age and engagement contracts are frequently made by parents years beforehand. The reason is the fear that an unmarried daughter may compromise the family's honour. It is difficult for her to leave home on her own. Indeed, in pre-industrial Arab societies many people would assume that the only possible reason women might choose to live away from their families was that they were engaging in prostitution.

Unspoken assumptions about the position of women are deeply entrenched. They are found among secularists as well as the devout. It was an Egyptian army general, not an Islamist, who was reported by CNN to have justified virginity testing of young female protesters in Tahrir Square on the grounds that these women 'were not like your daughters or mine. These were girls who had camped out in tents with male protesters. We didn't want [them] to say we had sexually assaulted or raped them, so we wanted to prove they were not virgins in the first place.' There is strong cultural resistance to a woman leading a completely independent life. Marriage partners are frequently introduced by the family, especially mothers conferring together. Although this applies to sons as much as daughters, and leads to many happy marriages, traditionally a married woman is often expected to come second to his mother in her husband's affections.[4]

Although polygamy is incompatible with Christianity, and is therefore illegal and virtually absent in the West, many of the other cultural and legal features of traditional society mentioned here once had counterparts in Europe and America. The custom of the father giving the bride away at the altar is a dim echo of the idea that the marriage was the seal of an alliance between two families, as well as a public assertion that the husband now takes over the father's responsibilities towards his daughter. Long ago, a husband had the right under the English Common Law to beat his wife and, until very recently indeed, their marriage was an automatic defence to a charge of rape brought by a wife against her husband. Until the Married Women's Property Act of 1882, a husband had the right to dispose of his wife's property without her consent. This last had no direct counterpart in Sharia, since the wife always retained legal control over her own property.

These abuses have been tackled in Western countries by changes to the law passed by parliaments. Yet can changes be made to Sharia in the same way? Those who idealise a vanished world of Islamic authenticity like the religious establishment in Saudi Arabia, Salafis and large elements in the Muslim Brotherhood, base their views on a literalist reading of texts and will instinctively reject such a notion. On the other hand, when governments have succeeded in reforming aspects of Sharia to bring it in line with modern conditions, public opinion has sometimes swung behind the reforms.

Turkey today is governed by a coalition dominated by the AK party which has its roots in political Islam and takes the opportunity to show pride in the country's Ottoman heritage and reaffirm its Muslim identity whenever it has the chance. Yet in the 1920s, the secularist leader Ataturk removed Sharia from the legal system lock, stock and barrel. Turkish family law today is based on that of

Switzerland and men and women are equal in matters such as divorce and inheritance rights. There is no desire in the mainstream of the Turkish electorate to change this, although the reforms had been achieved by uprooting Sharia, not reforming it, and illegal Sharia practices such as polygamy still linger on in remote areas. Similarly, there is no appetite whatsoever among Islamists to reintroduce slavery in Muslim countries. Not even Osama bin Laden or the Taliban called for this, although when slavery and the slave trade were abolished in the nineteenth and twentieth centuries, slavery itself was defended by some religious scholars on the grounds that it was wrong to make unlawful something that was *halal*.

In reforming Sharia, the rethinking of its rules and principles by modern, liberally minded Sharia scholars is often more effective than the stroke of a secularist ruler's pen signing a decree. If care is not taken to advocate changes in this way, there is the risk that they will be perceived as tainted with the brush of Western hostility to Islam and rejected at a popular level:[5] a consideration which the spread of democratic elections may make even more important. There have always been female religious scholars, but generations of women who are literate to an extent unparalleled in Arab history now produce their own experts on Sharia, some of whom search for ways in which Islam can be reinterpreted to enforce and extend women's rights. Moreover, in every Arab country where there are elections, women have the vote. In time, the effects of this are bound to shine through. Women have played major roles in the Arab Spring, and even when attempts are made to reduce their access to the public sphere, they have shown that they can make their voices heard online.

An example of successfully working within the framework of Sharia to modernise the law is the abolition of polygamy in Tunisia in 1956. Despite strong opposition from Sharia judges, the secularist ruler Habib Bourghiba was able to present the change to the law as complying with Islamic jurisprudence and in accordance with a demand that had for long been made by many Muslims. There is little appetite for putting the clock back, and it has been agreed that the new Tunisian constitution will not contain an article making Sharia the source of legislation. A more recent example is the reformed Moroccan law of 2004 which, while not outlawing polygamy, circumscribes it with conditions and formalities to such an extent that it has now been described as 'almost impossible'.[6]

It is a paradox that, while Islam attempted to replace tribalism with a shared identity focused on religion, tribalism remains alive and well throughout the Arabian peninsula and in many other places in the Arab world. The teachings in the classical formulations of Sharia on women and the family have inadvertently encouraged this. The root of tribalism is the extended family descended from a common, male ancestor. Sharia rules were crafted to preserve the cohesion and property of this extended family in a pre-industrial society, something that is reinforced by its tolerance and approval of first cousin marriage. This remains widespread in those Arab societies which are tribal. It is legitimate to ask whether the preservation of such rules should be the true purpose of Sharia today.

It should also be noted that tribalism does not fit easily with democracy. Members of tribes may tend to vote *en bloc* in support of the tribal candidate, thereby frustrating the growth of healthy political parties. A decaying tribalism can even acquire new vigour when central government is unable to carry out the functions expected of it. It can then be fostered and manipulated – as Saddam Hussein did so successfully after the imposition of UN sanctions on Iraq.

III

Ali Abd al-Raziq, an Azharite and one of Muhammad Abduh's many influential pupils, wrote a book in 1925 containing some radical ideas: Muhammad's role was purely spiritual; God did not send him to exercise political authority; the community he established was not a state in any recognisable sense, for it had no budget or administration. The book was condemned by the authorities at the Azhar and banned,[7] with the result that the author retired permanently from public life.

Nearly ninety years later, however, a theology has finally developed which rejects the concept of an 'Islamic' state. In a nutshell, it goes like this. During the early Meccan period of the revelation, Muhammad and his followers were persecuted. It was only after Muhammad escaped to Medina that he established a polity to defend Islam against its enemies and to allow the community to build itself up and the religion to spread. The use of warfare by the Prophet's followers was defensive, since it was aimed against those who wished to destroy Islam. The same is sometimes even argued with regard to the great conquests which took place after his death. They were intended to do no more than make sure the message of Islam would not be erased by mighty foreign powers and to 'open'[8] the conquered countries, making their peoples aware of the light of Islam and giving them the choice to accept or reject it.

Those crucial early years of the new faith occurred in a world that lacked the modern concepts of human rights, freedom of conscience and equality before the law. Today, whenever these become the law of the land, they allow Muslims to practise their faith freely. Because these concepts reflect values which should be those of Islam, Muslims should uphold them. Islam no longer requires the special protection of an 'Islamic state' which, it ought to be acknowledged, has led to much injustice. Indeed, justice and fairness should matter to Muslims above all else.

Many of the thinkers who expound such ideas today – like Abdulaziz Sachedina, Abdullahi al-Na'im and Khaled Abou El Fadl[9] – live in America or other Western countries. Al-Na'im left Sudan after the execution for blasphemy in 1985 of Mahmud Muhammad Taha, who had advocated a fresh look at the Meccan and Medinan verses of the Qur'an. Much of the timeless message of Islam is set out in the former, whilst the latter – which contain detail that is at the heart of the classical formulations of Sharia – are often concerned with problems specific to the circumstances of the Prophet in Medina. Taha had suggested that this shows that Sharia should be reinterpreted in the light of Islam's progressive message and in a way appropriate to different times and places.

Al-Na'im, who has translated some of Taha's thought into English, is concerned by the way authoritarian rulers can use Sharia for nefarious purposes, such as suppressing dissent, and has come to argue that 'historical' Sharia must be done away with or revised. For him, an Islamic state is 'a dangerous illusion'.[10] Indeed, the state must be religiously neutral because pious intention, *niyah*, is required for compliance with religious precepts and obligations, and coercive enforcement of these by the state negates that compliance.

This theology is likely to be attractive to the ever greater number of Muslims following in the steps of the late nineteenth century reformer Muhammad Abduh and choosing to live as part of the modern world while finding ways to remain good Muslims. They value modern education and want their children – including, it should be stressed, their daughters – to succeed in exactly the same way as parents do everywhere. Other Muslims aspire to join them. Whenever opportunity allows, they do so in droves.[11] When it comes to politics, they want democracy. They have role models in the socially conservative 'post-Islamist' elected politicians of Turkey and now, possibly, in some Arab countries as well.

In Tunisia, the Islamist Nahda party led that country's first democratically elected coalition government. It has publicly repudiated the idea of an Islamic state. The party's president is Rached Ghannouchi. Born in 1941 and educated in Cairo, Damascus and Paris as well as Tunisia, he was initially a follower of Nasser's ideas and became a socialist before moving in the direction of a non-violent Islam concerned with social justice. He lived as a political refugee in Britain for many years. For a time, he was a member of the Muslim Brotherhood but left its ranks. On 2 March 2012, he gave a speech on secularism and the relation between religion and the state as perceived by the Nahda party.[12] This was delivered against the background of the debate over drafting the country's new constitution and encapsulates years of reflection on the relationship between these topics.

In Ghannouchi's view, Muhammad was a political as well as a religious leader. Yet the state he established in Medina included Jews and other non-Muslims, implying that politics and religion were distinct even if that distinction was not always clear cut. It was reason and independent judgement (*ijtihad*), not revelation, that governed the political sphere. Reason teaches us technical matters, even those of government, while the role of religion is to answer the big questions of our existence and purpose, 'and to provide us with a system of values and principles that would guide our thinking, behaviour and the regulations of the state to which we aspire'.

Rached Ghannouchi relates the distinction between religion and politics to that made by classical scholars between the rules of worship and of behaviour, and which had already been reprised by a chain of modernists going back to Muhammad Abduh. The former is unchanging, 'the domain of creed, values and virtues which represent the public constants', while the latter 'is constantly evolving and represents the sphere of variables'. He then argues with regard to the latter that there has always been freedom of thought and diversity of interpretation in Islam. Islam needs to be kept free from the control of the state, and the way to achieve this is democracy. Indeed, 'the democratic mechanism is the best embodiment of the Shura [consultation] value in Islam'. In Tunisia, Islam is the people's religion, not that of the elite, and should not be imposed. The people, the elite and the media should debate and decide what is *halal* and *haram*.

The state's task is not to control people's minds but to serve the people: specifically by creating job opportunities, health and education. He also argues that: '[the state] should not be subject to the tutelage of any religious institution for there is no such thing in Islam. Rather there is a people and a nation who are the decision makers through their institutions.' He concludes with a call to freedom based on his understanding of Islam:

> The fact [is] that our revolution has succeeded in toppling a dicta-tor, [so] we ought to accept the principle of citizenship, and that this country does not belong to one party or another but to all of its citizens regardless of their religion, sex or any other consideration. Islam has bestowed on them the right to be citizens enjoying equal rights, and to believe in whatever they desire within the framework of mutual respect, and observance of the law which is legislated for them by their representatives in parliament.

We have seen in Chapter 3 how Albert Hourani noted that in intellectual debates in Egypt at the turn of the twentieth century 'the Islamic scaffolding' sometimes collapsed, and that arguments based on the Qur'an and Sunna continued instead with appeals to Western concepts such as freedom and progress. It might be asked: is the reverse happening today, and is an Islamic scaffolding being re-erected to advance what are essentially Western values such as democracy and full rights for women? It is not quite so simple. Ghannouchi, like many other modern Muslim (and Christian) thinkers, sees religion as having a vital contribution to make. For him, there are dangers in taking it out of the public sphere entirely, because it is religion that guarantees freedom and rights. Remove it, he is saying, and you risk dictatorship – a form of government of which he has had more than enough personal experience.

He sees secular democracy as it has been practised in the West as inadequate. Have not the Western democracies allowed an immoral accumulation of power and wealth when half the world is starving? Has not liberal democracy allowed itself to be influenced and even steered by ideas taken from thinkers like Darwin, Hegel and Nietzsche, which have been interpreted to justify the powerful oppressing the weak? In his view, democracy in the West is to a large extent based on utilitarian ideas which he calls 'the values of hedonism and power'.[13] He is not surprised that Western democracies have done terrible things. He is also very conscious of the role of the rich and powerful in democracies, particularly in America where big money, media empires and lobby groups have a stranglehold on the political process. That is why he calls for democracy to be infused with an 'Islamic contribution' which, in the words of Azzam Tamimi, would be

> primarily in the form of a code of ethics, a transcendant morality that seems to have no place in today's democratic practice . . . What Islam provides is not only a set of values for self-discipline and for the refinement of human conduct but also a set of restrictions to combat monopoly and a set of safeguards to protect public opinion.[14]

Whether Rached Ghannouchi's vision of Islam can protect and enhance true democracy in Tunisia and inspire the same in other Arab countries remains to be seen, but he rules out the option of using coercion to uphold the position of Islam, which he sees as incompatible with Islam as well as self-defeating. There is no reason why an Arab state with a Muslim population cannot develop into a full democracy.

IV

Sectarianism is a problem which emerging Arab democracies with mixed populations have to confront. Ghannouchi's idea that the Prophet's polity in Medina could inspire a modern state in which different communities live side by side in harmony and democracy, yet within a framework that is authentically Islamic, has also been expressed by other eminent Islamist intellectuals, some of whom, such as Yusuf al-Qaradawi and Tariq Ramadan, are relatively well known in the West. It can also be traced back to the reformers of the late nineteenth century. Yet some historians may raise an eyebrow. The so-called Constitution of Medina which established this polity was ultimately a failure. As was seen in Chapter 1, two of the three Jewish tribes were eventually exiled while the men of the Qurayza were executed, save for two who converted to Islam, and their women and children were enslaved. The reply would be that in the seventh century this was no more than customary punishment for treachery, and that the story of this treachery and its punishment does not invalidate the principles which underlie the Constitution of Medina.

Sectarianism in predominantly Muslim societies can be traced back to the disabilities which Sharia placed on Christians, Jews and others and which we looked at briefly in earlier chapters. It is reflected in the disdain which the three communities have shown to each other throughout the history of Islam, and of which we had a fleeting glimpse in Abu Nuwas's poem 'The Jewish Wine Seller'. When reporting to his Egyptian readers on the wonderful achievements of the Christian French, Tahtawi felt impelled to add how different they were from the lowly Egyptian Christians whom he despised. Today, sectarian problems with political dimensions that imperil democracy in the Arab world can be divided into two main categories: relations between Muslims and Christians, and the Sunni–Shi'ite divide.

Lebanon may still be as much as 40 per cent Christian. Christian minorities of up to 10 per cent of the population exist in Egypt and Syria, and smaller ones in the Palestinian territories, Jordan and Iraq. Is the best guarantee for their future the secularisation of the societies in which they live?[15] Many members of these communities – and many Muslims – certainly think so, but it is also important to note that there is sometimes resistance to Western-style secularisation among some Christians.

Parallel to the reaffirmation of Muslim identity in recent decades, there has been a reaffirmation of historic Christian identities in Arab countries. This does not apply only to the Maronites. Before the 1952 revolution, Copts participated much more in Egyptian political life than at any subsequent time. The foreign minorities which had controlled so much of the commercial and financial sectors had looked to their own communities to provide the management of their businesses. They frequently paid workers who were members of their community more than ordinary Egyptians, whether Muslim or Copt. This had tended to bring Muslims and Copts together. But one of the unforeseen consequences of Nasser's abolition of parliament, and his land reform programme and gathering of power into his own hands was the emigration of much of the Coptic political and commercial elite alongside many of their Muslim colleagues. Ordinary Copts came to rely more on their church which, under the vigorous leadership of Pope Shenouda III who reigned from 1971 to 2012, jealously represented them in dealings with the state. This was almost a re-emergence of the old *millet* system and, as Rachel Scott has pointed out, was probably both an effect and a cause of the re-Islamisation of society. In Mubarak's Egypt, Islamists successfully persuaded many Muslims to vote for Muslim candidates standing against a Christian as a matter of principle, so that hardly any Copts were elected to parliament and many became politically apathetic. Pope Shenouda negotiated a kind of informal pact with the government. Individual Copts could be sidelined, marginalised and discriminated against in many ways, but as a community they had a powerful church which looked after their interests and into which they could withdraw. The church strongly supported the Egyptian practice of identity cards stating the religion of the bearer.

In all Arab states (and Israel), the personal status law which applies to marriage and divorce, and sometimes to inheritance and guardianship of children, is that of an individual's religion, even if it is now frequently administered by the courts of the state. Because

Christianity does not have a specific law of inheritance, across the centuries Arab Christian communities have tended voluntarily to adopt Sharia rules which apply to Muslims, although there are now moves among some of them to move away from the rule that a sister inherits only half the share that goes to her brother. Some Christian clergy have as patriarchal an attitude to women as their Muslim counterparts, while marriage and divorce do not exist outside a religious context. Some conservative Christians share common ground with Islamists in fearing secularism may merely lead to the melting away of their communities. They would agree with Ghannouchi that the secularism of the West fails to show due respect to religion and rejects the important role they believe it should play in public life. For them, and for many Arabs generally, the Western cult of the individual and atomisation of society have gone much too far. The family is the basic unit of society, and the decline of the family in the West is seen as a slow, cultural suicide. The taboos on homosexuality and couples living together outside marriage have not waned in Arab countries over the last half century as they have in the West. Many Arabs are also keenly aware that sex tourists (heterosexual and homosexual alike) from Europe have been travelling to countries such as Egypt and Morocco since at least the time of Flaubert's visit to Egypt and the Levant in 1849–50.

But the divide within Islam between Sunnis and Shi'ites, not that between Muslims and Christians, appears to be the most explosive sectarian fissure in Arab societies today. For years there has been excited talk of a Sunni/Shi'ite religious war, and of the threat of a Shi'ite crescent that would stretch from Iran to Lebanon by way of Iraq and Syria, and simultaneously destabilise Saudi Arabia, Kuwait and Bahrain. Where an Arab state has substantial Sunni and Shi'ite populations, there is the risk that people will retreat into their religious identities in a way that provides plenty of opportunity for extremists to make mischief and for foreign powers to pressurise governments and conduct proxy wars. This book has shown how this has happened in some countries, and how the horrors of war and *fitna* can polarise communities.

As was seen in Chapter 8, this occurred in Iraq which had been one of the most secular Arab countries. Under the Ba'athists, intermarriage between Sunnis and Shi'ites was commonplace and unremarkable. Now intermarriage has become difficult, and the Iraqi Shi'ites use their numbers to dominate the country. Yet it is improbable that Iraq will become a client state of Iran in some grand alliance. Their interests are too different, although there will be issues on which they may work together – like opposing Saudi Arabian soft hegemony over the Gulf. Furthermore, even if the Iraqi Shi'ites were to establish a theocracy, which seems highly unlikely, they would choose Iraqi rather than Iranian Ayatollahs to guide them. If anything, the Islamic Republic of Iran is poised to be a net loser from the de-secularisation of Iraq, since the Iraqi shrines to Imam Ali and Imam Hussein at Najaf and Kerbala are the holiest places in Shi'ism and major centres for religious learning. As time passes, these are likely to give Iraqi Shi'ite religious leaders a prestige which their Iranian counterparts cannot match.

Suggestions that Syria under the Assads could be part of a Shi'ite crescent demonstrate a lack of understanding or wilful, possibly mischievous, blindness. The Ba'athists of Syria are completely secular. Syria is the one Arab state in which identity cards do not state the bearer's religion. Before Syria was engulfed by civil war in 2011–12 which brought sectarianism to the forefront of everybody's mind, many Syrians did not know the religion of work colleagues and thought of it as irrelevant. What happened in Syria is that the secular nature of the Ba'athist state enabled a member of the Alawi minority, Hafez al-Assad, to become president. This would have been impossible in any Arab state that was not militantly secular. But once at the top of that very greasy pole, Assad inserted people he could trust, frequently relatives and co-religionists from his native province, into the upper echelons of government, the army and the security services. Under the country's secular ethos, they mixed naturally with colleagues from the majority Sunni community and the other minorities, the Christians and Druze, and came to predominate.

Religious differences have always provided dangerous fault lines in Arab societies. Nevertheless, the story of the Syrian Ba'ath and the al-Assad's is primarily a case study of the negative effects of the culture of patronage in Arab societies, in which the traditions of democracy had been shallow before they were uprooted entirely a generation earlier. The Syrian alliance with Iran which grew stronger – and less equal – under Hafez's son Bashar was one of convenience and mutual interests, not ideology. Although Alawism has Shi'ite roots, Alawis are heretics in the eyes of both Shi'ite and Sunni Muslims, and Ba'athist secularism is anathema to the Islamic Republic of Iran. In Ba'athist Iraq, too, it was patronage that continued the domination of the country by the Sunni Arab elite. Particularly significant was the fact that the elite forces of the Republican Guard were recruited from Sunni tribes who came from the same part of the country as the president. Nevertheless, as was seen in Chapter 4, control by the Sunni Arab minority dated back to King Faisal and the Arab officers from what were then the Ottoman provinces of Baghdad, Mosul and Basra who joined the Sharifian revolt against the Turks.

Another key element in the 'Shi'ite crescent' is the Lebanese group Hizbullah with its powerful military wing. In Lebanon, it seeks to advance the interests of the Shi'ite population. Yet in other matters it has not always acted in ways that put its Shi'ite identity first. It opposed the American-led invasion of Iraq in 2003, a stance that put it at odds with most Iraqi Shi'ites, but this is easily explained if the movement is considered primarily as an expression of Arab nationalism. As its leader, Hassan Nasrallah wrote on 14 March that year:

We tell the United States, don't expect that the people of this region will welcome you with roses and jasmine. The people of this region will welcome you with rifles, blood and martyrdom operations. We are not afraid of the American invaders, and will keep saying 'death to America'.[16]

There was a footnote to the Israeli invasion of Lebanon in the summer of 2006. At first, the governments of Saudi Arabia, Egypt, the UAE and Jordan rebuked Hizbullah. It was as though these Sunni regimes were more than happy to let Israel mortally wound the revolutionary Shi'ite movement. Yet, as before, Hizbullah proved a wily and redoubtable foe. Not only did it fight the Israelis on the ground with more than a modicum of success, but it retaliated against Israel's cold-blooded devastation of Lebanon's infrastructure with indiscriminate rocket fire against towns in northern Israel.

As civilian casualties from Israeli bombing and shelling in Lebanon steadily mounted towards one thousand dead and many more injured, the Arab regimes were compelled to change their tone in response to the moral impact of the war on their own populations. Sunni Arabs everywhere joined in applause for Shi'ite Hizbullah. Hassan Nasrallah is in theory a Shi'ite religious scholar and only secondly a politician, but he came to be seen as Nasser's successor, a true Arab patriot. His boyish yet bearded face, which does not betray his grief at the death of his son in battle against the Israelis, smiled from posters in the back streets of many Arab cities. Its alliance with the Syria of the Assads was based on pragmatism not religious solidarity.

In November 2004, two years before that Israeli invasion of Lebanon, King Abdullah II of Jordan organised a conference in Amman attended by religious scholars from across the Muslim world. It issued a declaration called 'the Amman Message' which sets out the essentials of the Muslim faith and at the same time recognises that, beyond agreed essentials, diversity of religious belief is possible within Islam. It explicitly stated that followers of the recognised Sunni, Shi'ite and Khariji schools of Sharia, as well as

Sufis and certain other groups, are to be accepted as believers by all other Muslims. It repudiated *takfir*, terrorism and extremism, and also denounced the giving of opinions by unauthorised scholars who do not adhere to the methodology of one of the accepted schools of Sharia. It was aimed at repudiating violence like that advocated by Sayyid Qutb, and at healing the Sunni/Shi'ite split.

Its endorsers included the Saudi government, which acknowledged that Shi'ites were Muslim – possibly for the first time. However, the extremists responded. In February 2006 the Askariyya shrine in Iraq, burial place of the tenth and eleventh Shi'ite Imams and traditionally the place where the Hidden Imam will reappear at the end of time, was blown up in a massive act of calculated sacrilege. The more radical Wahhabi scholars of Saudi Arabia applauded its destruction while other voices stayed silent.[17] This made it clear that Sunni–Shi'ite sectarianism was sadly all too alive and had spread its tentacles widely over the last few decades. Now Syria shows it is a demon Arab democrats need urgently to confront.

V

The Chinese Communist leader Zhou Enlai is famously reported to have said that it was 'too early to tell' how significant the French Revolution had been. Apocryphal or not, the anecdote makes an important point. The effects of revolutions can be confusing and are easily misjudged.

One encouraging sign is that all the uprisings of the Arab Spring have striven to work within constitutional frameworks. The call has always been to elect new parliaments or constituent assemblies, devise new constitutions purged of abuses, and establish freedom of speech and the rule of law. It is far too soon to examine the success of these attempts as they encounter hard political realities. However, the constitutionalism which was the concern of only a tiny, Westernised minority a century ago has put down roots across society. The discussion today is how to draft the constitution, not whether a constitution is desirable in itself.

But when crowds call for democracy, do they understand what they are asking for? Liberal commentators on Arab satellite TV channels stress to their audiences that democracy is not merely rule by the decisions of the majority; it cannot survive without respect for dissenting views and guaranteed freedom of speech, and members of parliament should represent all their constituents, not just those who voted for them. Democracy requires the establishment of a framework to which people who have lived their whole lives under an autocracy will find it hard to adapt. It also requires the USA, Israel, Iran and other foreign powers not to seek to turn events to the advantage of their own, narrow interests. For a long while to come, many army officers, officials in the security services and senior bureaucrats will remain in place because they are needed to run their countries. They will form a 'deep state' which will look after its own interests and may be hostile to reform. This is one threat to which emerging Arab democracies will remain vulnerable.

Another is the pervading culture of patronage which, as we have seen, has very deep roots and is inconsistent with true democracy. It will take decades to eradicate. There have been recent whisperings of corruption appearing among the Hamas de facto rulers of the Gaza Strip. Islamists, once in power, will seek to look after their own, as the Morsi government has shown. Arab countries need strong and competent governments to see them through the difficult times which lie ahead. There is a real risk that democratically elected governments will be weak and vulnerable to pressure from strong vested interests at home and abroad.

The democratic France of today did not begin when King Louis XVI was guillotined in 1793. In fact, France was ruled by monarchs – emperors and kings – under various constitutional settlements for more than half the period between 1793 and 1914. France's last monarch, Napoleon III, fell as a result of his defeat in the Franco-Prussian War and it was by no means certain that the Third Republic that followed him would endure. The French Revolution had split French society down the middle. Many people thought the revolution had been a tragic, destructive and bloody mistake. Others who supported it knew what they wanted abolished, but were unsure what they desired in its place. It took France a century or longer to heal the wounds the Revolution had left.

Nevertheless, the Revolution could not be rolled back. On several other occasions in the nineteenth century the population took to the streets of Europe, rallying behind the banners of liberty. The most far-reaching occasion was in 1848 in what was often called 'the Spring of Nations' or 'the Springtime of Peoples'. Uncoordinated uprisings took place across the heart of Europe from Paris to Poznan and Copenhagen to Budapest. Most of them were suppressed or, in the case of France, corrupted when the president of the new republic subsequently proclaimed himself emperor. Yet the revolutions drained legitimacy away from the continent's hereditary autocracies. Over the following decades, rulers increasingly accepted that they needed to govern by consent, and that it was better from their own point of view to make concessions to popular demands than to be engaged in a cycle of endless, and fruitless, repression.

A similar process has started with the Arab Spring. It has only just begun.

ACKNOWLEDGEMENTS

I started working seriously on this book in the summer of 2006 although the idea of writing it germinated much earlier, perhaps in early 2002, when Malcom Chapman sat me down with Bernard Lewis's *What Went Wrong* and the intractable difficulties of explaining the West and the Arab world to each other flooded through my mind. As *A Concise History of the Arabs* involved an intellectual journey as well as much study, it is no surprise that its focus and general direction changed a number of times and I constantly found myself having to rethink my path and qualify my assertions. Perhaps that was inevitable with a project of this nature, but I can only hope that I have been honest and true to myself in the final text and apologise for any errors it may contain. These are my fault alone.

I am grateful to those who read and commented in detail on the text, especially Joy Gordon, Rose Hadshar, John Stubbs and Mike Whittingham. I would also like to thank those who looked at much earlier drafts or specific sections of the manuscript: Paul Chevedden, Chloe Darke, Max Darke, Alan Fisher, Pat Fisher, Michael Haag, Mike and Sue Hunter, Don Jones, Victor Kattan, Benedict McHugo, Chris McHugo, Russell McGurk, Michael Middlehurst, John Shake-shaft, Sir Roger Tomkys, Baroness Jenny Tonge and Sir Hookey Walker. I would also like to thank Hugh and Harriet Devlin and David Devons for their comments on the original hardback edition.

I would like to thank Lynn Gaspard and her colleagues at Saqi Books for having the courage to believe in this book. I am equally grateful to my agent John Parker of Zeno for never abandoning hope that it would all come right in the end. I would also like to thank Martin Lubikowski of ML Design for producing the maps.

Finally, I have two huge debts to acknowledge. The first is to all those who taught me Arabic and Islamic studies at Oxford in the early 1970s. Without what they gave me this book could never have been written. I think especially of those giants who are sadly no longer with us: Freddy Beeston, Albert Hourani, Richard McCarthy SJ and Richard Walzer.

The second debt is to Diana for her insight, help, encouragement and understanding.

NOTES

PREFACE

1. The phrase is part of the provocative title of Samuel Huntington's famous book *The Clash of Civilizations and the Remaking of the World Order* which appeared in 1997. Huntington took the words 'clash of civilisations' from a 1990 article by Bernard Lewis called 'The Roots of Muslim Rage'. Lewis had used the expression on at least two earlier occasions, in a 1957 article 'The Middle East in World Affairs', in which he refers to 'a clash between civilisations' and in the introduction to his 1984 book *The Jews of Islam* where he states that the 'encounter [of Jews from Christendom and Jews from Islam in Israel] reprises the clash of the two civilisations from which they come, and the aim of unity will not be easy to achieve'. Lewis's work should be read with caution. His writing contains many original and valuable insights but is marred by a willingness to blame the Arabs for the West's own mistakes in the Middle East and a propensity to pander to the prejudices of Western audiences. He also stands accused of having a political agenda. See e.g. G. Achcar, *The Arabs and the Holocaust* (2010), 76. He is by no means the only Western historian against whom such charges can be laid. Neither tendency invalidates the whole of his very considerable corpus of scholarship. For 'The Roots of Muslim Rage' and 'The Middle East in World Affairs', see Lewis, *From Babel to Dragomans* (2004), pp. 397–413 and 267–96 respectively.

CHAPTER ONE: WHEN HISTORY CHANGED DIRECTION

1. Qur'an 96: 1–5; author's translation.
2. For the historiography of the life of Muhammad and the subsequent period up to 1050, see H. Kennedy, *The Prophet and the Age of the Caliphates* (1986/2004), 346–84. I have followed Kennedy in viewing the picture given by the Arabic sources as broadly correct in outline but leaving much that is confusing, contradictory and obscure. Important elements in the traditional narratives have been questioned by some historians. On the strength of Muhammad's negotiating position after the battle of the Trench, see J. Howard-Johnston, *Witnesses to a World*

Crisis (2010), 408–14, where it is argued that his adoption and reform of the pre-Islamic pilgrimage rites was a massive concession to the Meccans and an acknowledgement of his military weakness, even after the defeat of the Meccan-led siege of Medina.

3. The expression is Albert Hourani's. See A History of the Arab Peoples (1991), 29.

4. S. Griffith, The Church in the Shadow of the Mosque (2008), 159.

5. M. Cook, Forbidding Wrong in Islam (2003), 8.

6. Qur'an 42: 11; author's translation.

7. Qur'an 81: 8–9, 14; author's translation.

8. H. Kennedy, The Great Arab Conquests (2007), 86.

9. W. Kaegi, Heraclius, Emperor of Byzantium (2003), 256, 278. Note also the absence of reference to the new religion of the conquerors by Sophronius, the patriarch of Jerusalem, who surrendered the city to the Caliph Umar. See Kennedy, Great Arab Conquests (2007), 346.

10. H. Kennedy, The Court of the Caliphs (2004), 225ff.

11. Qur'an, 112: 1-4, author's translation. For Abdul Malik's coins, see N. MacGregor, A History of the World in 100 Objects (2010/2012), 251–5.

CHAPTER TWO: GROWING APART

1. Kennedy, The Prophet and the Age of the Caliphates, p. 83.

2. For a recent assessment of this, see D. Levering Lewis, God's Crucible: Islam and the Making of Europe, 570–1215 (2008).

3. A possible exception is the expulsion of Christians and Jews from Arabia by the Caliph Umar. However, they were not expelled from all Muslim territory itself and were allowed to live in lands to the north which were also under the Caliphate's rule. In the case of the Jews of Yemen at least, the expulsion seems also to have been incomplete.

4. Griffith, Church in the Shadow, 48.

5. Halm, Shi'ism, 2nd edn (2004), 46–7.

6. C. Hillenbrand, The Crusades (1999/2006), 100–1.

7. D. Gutas, Greek Thought, Arabic Culture (1995), 86–7. In the ninth century a cultural renaissance took place in Byzantium, but al-Jahiz's prejudices seem to be supported by a dearth of secular manuscript copying in Byzantium over the previous 150 years. Ibid., p. 181 and n. 57.

8. Hillenbrand, Crusades, 17–8, 50.

9. For this, and the view that the Crusades did not begin with 'a big bang' in 1095 generally, see the work of Paul Chevedden, 'The Islamic Interpretation of the Crusades', Der Islam (2004), 90–136; 'The View of

the Crusades from Rome and Damascus', *Oriens*, 39 (2011), 257–329.

10. Hillenbrand, *Crusades*, 1.
11. There are also Turkish- and Kurdish-speaking Alawis in modern Turkey.
12. J. Phillips, *Holy Warriors* (2010), 274–5.
13. On this, see Michael Cook, *Forbidding Wrong in Islam* (2003), 100. There are authorities in the Hanafi law school who argue that raisin-based alcoholic drinks are *halal*. See P. Kennedy, *The Wine Song in Classical Arabic Poetry*, p. 160. The Hanafis were the official law school of the Ottoman Empire.
14. Griffith, *Church in the Shadow*, 21, 146–7.
15. S. Griffith, 'Arabic Christian Relations with Islam', in A. O'Mahony and J. Flannery (eds), *The Catholic Church in the Contemporary Middle East* (2010), 265.
16. C. Finkel, *Osman's Dream* (2005), 84.
17. Ibid., p. 279.
18. For an admirably succinct summary of the concept of the separation of powers, see Bertrand Russell, *History of Western Philosophy* (George Allen & Unwin, 2nd edn, 1962), 613–16.
19. S. Akkach, *'Abd al-Ghani al-Nabulusi* (2007), 75. The astronomer in question was Uthman bin 'Abd al-Mannan.

CHAPTER THREE: THE WEST TAKES CONTROL

1. For an excellent and very readable account of the story of Napoleon's invasion of Egypt, see J. Cole, *Napoleon's Egypt* (2007).
2. E. Rogan, *The Arabs* (2009), 105.
3. Finkel, *Osman's Dream*, 458–9.
4. Cole, *Napoleon's Egypt*, 151.
5. Rogan, *The Arabs*, 94.
6. B. Masters, *Christians and Jews in the Ottoman Arab World* (2001), 164–5.
7. Quoted in N. Davies, *Europe: A History* (1996), 813.
8. Quote in A. Shlaim, *The Iron Wall* (2000), p. xi.
9. Quoted in J. Richmond, *Egypt 1798–1952* (1977), 151.
10. D. Newman, *An Imam in Paris* (2004), 92, 111.
11. C. Tripp, *Islam and the Moral Economy* (2006), 24.
12. J. Cole, *Colonialism and Revolution in the Middle East* (1999), 137. For Sanu' generally, see E. Ettmüller, *The Construct of Egypt's National Self in James Sanua's Early Satire and Caricature* (2012) and the chapter on him in Sadgrove's *The Egyptian Theatre in the Nineteenth Century*.

13. Ibid., pp. 155-6.
14. Ibid., p. 148.
15. M. Sedgwick, *Muhammad Abduh* (2009), 103.
16. Quoted ibid., p. 64. It should be noted that the word *thobe*, which is classical Arabic, is still used in the Gulf for the robe which is now identified as local national dress, and does not have the pejorative connotations today which Muhammad Abduh clearly associated with it.
17. J. Schacht, 'Muhammad 'Abduh', in *Encyclopedia of Islam* (1993). Abduh and his school extended the meaning of the concept of *maslaha* to the deducing of specific laws from general principles of social morality. See A. Hourani, *Arabic Thought in the Liberal Age* (1962/70), 151-2.
18. Tripp, *Islam and the Moral Economy*, 39, 127.
19. Hourani, *Arabic Thought*, 144-5.
20. Ibid., p. 167.

CHAPTER FOUR: SHARING AN INDIGESTIBLE CAKE

1. This British slogan was borrowed by Robert Fisk as the title for his massive 2005 book of reflections and reporting from many conflicts – often at considerable personal risk – in the Middle East since the 1970s. 'The Great War for Civilisation' was engraved on one of his father's campaign medals from the First World War, and Fisk notes the poignant irony of how many of the disastrous wars he has witnessed were also, ostensibly, fought 'for Civilisation'.
2. Hansard, *Parliamentary Debates*, 27 March 1923, cols. 655-6.
3. The text of the Fourteen Points may be found at avalon.yale.edu/20_century/wilson14.asp.
4. Hansard, *Parliamentary Debates*, Commons, 25 July 1921, col. 36.
5. The text of the Covenant of the League of Nations is available at avalon.law.yale.edu/20th_century/leagcov.asp.
6. Resolution of the general Syrian Congress at Damascus, 2 July 1919, Art. 19 (adopted unanimously) in Hurewitz, *Diplomacy in the Near and Middle East* (1956), 63-4.
7. Iskenderun, or Alexandretta, was the principal port for Aleppo at this time and was contained within the Mandate, but was part of the area France gradually handed back to Turkey in the late 1930s.
8. R. Storrs, *Lawrence of Arabia, Zionism and Palestine* (1940), 44.
9. Rogan, *The Arabs*, 197.
10. T. Segev, *One Palestine Complete* (2001), 33.
11. The text of the Mandate is available at avalon.law.yale.edu/20th_cen-

tury/palmanda.asp.

12. Palestine Mandate, Art. 2.

13. Ibid., Art. 6.

14. Ibid., Art. 4.

15. Covenant of the League of Nations, Art. 22.

16. Storrs, *Lawrence of Arabia*, p.53.

17. Ibid., pp. 47–8.

18. Quoted in M. Haag, *Alexandria: City of Memory* (2004), 141.

19. J. Reinharz, *Chaim Weizmann* (1993), 252.

20. Quoted in Haag, *Alexandria*, 146.

21. Reinharz, *Chaim Weizmann*, 223–4.

22. Storrs, *Lawrence of Arabia*, p. 44.

23. Ibid., p. 87.

24. 'Basha' is the colloquial Arabic for 'Pasha', an Ottoman title granted by the monarch which was also used in Egypt under the monarchy and in the Hashemite kingdoms of Iraq and Jordan. Storrs's use of the Arabic colloquial form suggests he was told this in Arabic by Arabs who could not speak English, indicating that the favourable impression Ralph Harari had made was widespread.

25. Storrs, *Lawrence of Arabia*, p. 88.

26. Quoted in Segev, *One Palestine Complete*, p. 106. Herzl was the leader and theoretician of the early Zionist movement.

27. Ibid., pp. 138–9.

28. Ibid., p. 141.

29. *Jewish Chronicle*, 11 Nov. 1921, p. 7. Quoted in Segev, *One Palestine Complete*, 187–8.

30. Segev, *One Palestine Complete*, 200.

31. Ibid., p. 326.

32. P. Mattar, *The Mufti of Jerusalem* (1988), 118.

33. Achcar, *The Arabs and the Holocaust*, 127.

34. I. Pappe, *A History of Modern Palestine* (2004), 104.

35. Achcar, *The Arabs and the Holocaust*, 137–40.

36. C. Tripp, *A History of Iraq*, 3rd edn (2007), 12.

37. Ibid., p. 48.

CHAPTER FIVE: SECULARISM AND ISLAMISM

1. J. Beinin, *The Dispersion of Egyptian Jewry* (2005), 37.

2. T. Russell, *Egyptian Service 1902–1946* (1949), 197.

3. On this, see Cole, *Napoleon's Egypt*, 238–43.

4. He was born in Tripoli, the predominantly Sunni city in what is now northern Lebanon. At the time of his birth, however, it would not have been considered part of any Lebanese entity and he would have identified himself as being from *Bilad al-Shaam*, i.e. Greater Syria.

5. Quoted in Hourani, *Arab Thought*, 234.

6. Sivan, *Radical Islam*, 101

7. Tripp, *Islam and the Moral Economy*, 127.

8. Achcar, *The Arabs and the Holocaust*, 110–11.

9. N. Delong-Bas, *Wahhabi Islam* (2005), 22–3.

10. Ibid., p. 90.

11. Ibid., p. 207.

12. Achcar, *The Arabs and the Holocaust*, 110.

13. Ibid., p. 111.

14. For a discussion of the attitude of Rashid Rida to Jews and Zionism and the influence of anti-Semitism upon him, ibid., pp. 110–18.

15. Quoted in G. Kraemer, *Hasan al-Banna* (2010), 20–1.

16. Ibid., p. 83.

17. J. Kelsay, *Arguing the Just War in Islam* (2009), 94.

18. Kraemer, *Hasan al-Banna*, 23.

CHAPTER SIX: THE WEST SEEMS TO RETREAT

1. Quoted in B. Morris, *The Road to Jerusalem* (2002), 56.

2. Quoted in Mattar, *Mufti of Jerusalem*, 91.

3. Haag, *Alexandria*, p. 298.

4. Gilbert, *Israel: A History*, 142.

5. Shlaim, *The Iron Wall*, 25.

6. V. Kattan, *From Co-existence to Conquest* (2009), 152; see also pp. 141–2.

7. Ibid., pp. 151–2.

8. Ibid., p. 166.

9. B. Morris, *1948: A History of the First Arab Israeli War* (2008), 1.

10. See Kattan, *From Co-existence to Conquest*, 189, quoting Sir O. Sargeant, FO Minute, 14 May 1948, to UK delegation in New York and Washington, FO 371/68664, Palestine, Eastern, 1948, para. 9(a).

11. B. Morris, *The Birth of the Palestinian Refugee Problem, 1947–9* (1987), p. 141.

12. Morris, *1948*, p. 182.

13. Ibid., p. 339.

14. Ibid., p. 273.

15. Ibid., p. 339.

16. P. Vatikiotis, *Nasser and his Generation* (1978), 251. Britain did not recognise the state of Israel either at this point. It would therefore also

have been the British view that Israel was not an entity on which Egypt could declare war.

17. Shlaim, *The Iron Wall*, 39.
18. Ibid., p. 77. See also p. 79.
19. Morris, *1948*, 99.
20. Kattan, *From Co-existence to Conquest*, 169; also endnotes 1–6 to p. 169.
21. Ibid., p. 233.
22. Shlaim, *The Iron Wall*, 222.
23. Ibid., p. 35.
24. B. Morris, *Israel's Border Wars, 1949–56* (1993), 36.
25. Trans. by Philip Kennedy in *Abu Nuwas: A Genius of Poetry* (2006), 69.
26. B. Lewis, *The Jews of Islam* (1984), 32.
27. Ella Shohat, 'The Invention of the Mizrahim', *Journal of Palestine Studies*, 29 (Autumn 1999), 5–20, at p. 12.
28. Both extreme Arab nationalists and Zionists who wanted to encourage Jewish emigration have been suggested as the culprits for this bombing campaign. Eli Kedourie, a respected scholar of the history of Middle Eastern politics who was himself an Iraqi Jew and certainly no fan of pan-Arab nationalism, believed the Zionists were capable of such tactics. See *The Chatham House Version* (1970), 312. For the history of the Iraqi Jewish exodus generally, see A. Shiblak, *Iraqi Jews: The History of a Mass Exodus* (1986/2005).
29. Vatikiotis, *Nasser*, 90.
30. Ibid., p. 92.
31. R. Stephens, *Nasser: A Political Biography* (1971), 347.
32. S. Aburish, *Nasser: The Last Arab* (2004), 47.
33. See the quotation from Ben Gurion's speech to the Knesset on 7 Nov. 1956 in J. Salt, *The Unmaking of the Middle East* (2008), 180.
34. G. Kraemer, *The Jews in Modern Europe, 1914–52* (1989), 215–21.
35. Beinin, *Dispersion of Egyptian Jewry*, 116–17.
36. *Ba'th* means 'rebirth' or 'resurrection' in Arabic.
37. Stephens, *Nasser*, 351.
38. See C. Kanaan, *Lebanon 1860–1960* (2005), in particular at p. 20.
39. Aburish, *Nasser*, 212.
40. Tripp, *Islam and the Moral Economy*, 75.
41. S. Qutb, *Milestones* (2001/2008-9), 111.
42. On this see B. Zollner, *The Muslim Brotherhood: Hasan al-Hudaybi and his Ideology* (2009), 52–5.
43. From a translation of S. Qutb's book *The America I Have Seen*, quoted in M. Gove, *Celsius 7/7* (2006), 20.

44. Ibid.
45. Quoted in Tripp, *Islam and the Moral Economy*, 48-9.
46. Quoted in E. Sivan, *Radical Islam* (1985/1990), 92.

CHAPTER SEVEN: THE SIX DAY WAR AND ITS CONSEQUENCES

1. Vatikiotis, *Nasser*, 251.
2. Ibid., p. 260.
3. Shlaim, *The Iron Wall*, 213.
4. Ibid., p. 226
5. Quoted in Stephens, *Nasser*, 479.
6. T. Segev, *1967: Israel, the War and the Year that Transformed the Middle East* (2007), 334.
7. On this, see A. Raz, *The Bride and the Dowry* (2012).
8. A. Shlaim, *Hussein: Lion of Jordan* (2007), 388.
9. Ibid., p. xvii.
10. Aburish, *Nasser*, 250-1.

CHAPTER EIGHT: IRAQ, ISRAEL, MILITANCY AND TERRORISM

1. Tripp, *History of Iraq*, 215.
2. Quoted in Owen, *The Rise and Fall of Arab Presidents for Life*, 39. The quote is taken from an exchange with an Iraqi citizen broadcast on Iraqi TV and repeated in a BBC documentary.
3. UN Security Council Resolution 661 (1990), 3(c).
4. On this and the sanctions regime generally, see Joy Gordon, *Invisible War* (2010).
5. S. Tatham, *Losing Arab Hearts and Minds* (2006), 184.
6. Rogan, *The Arabs*, 415.
7. A. Norton, *Hezbollah: A Short History* (2007), 104.
8. L. Freedman, *A Choice of Enemies* (2008), 515.
9. See David Gardner's account of an interview with Rabin shortly before he was assassinated in Gardner, *Last Chance: The Middle East in the Balance* (2009), 152.
10. Shlaim, *The Iron Wall*, 583.
11. Freedman, *Choice of Enemies*, 452.
12. Ibid., p. 463.
13. Lewis, *From Babel to Dragomans*, 285.
14. Morris, *Road to Jerusalem*, 80.
15. Ibid., p. 127.

16. Uris, *Exodus* (Bantam Books, 1958), 547.
17. US Department of State, *Patterns of Global Terror 2001* (2002).
18. J. Cole, *Engaging the Muslim World* (2009), 71.
19. J. Glubb, *A Soldier with the Arabs* (1957), 162.
20. F. Gerges, *The Far Enemy* (2005), 85, n. 4.
21. G. Kepel and J. Milleli (eds), *Al-Qaedah in its own Words*, tr. P. Ghazaleh (2008), 55.
22. For an account of Osama bin Laden's family life during the years leading up to 9/11, see N. bin Laden, O. bin Laden and J. Sasson, *Growing up bin Laden* (2009).
23. M. Bishara, *The Invisible Arab* (2012), 201–2.
24. Kepel and Milleli, *Al Qaedah*, 67–8.
25. Bishara, *The Invisible Arab*, 202.

CHAPTER NINE: THE AGE OF THE AUTOCRATS AND THE RISE
OF ISLAMISM

1. Owen, *Rise and Fall*, 9.
2. P. Seale, *Asad* (1988), 24.
3. Owen, *Rise and Fall*, 143; see also p. 81.
4. See F. Moffitt, 'Egypt's Economic Reform Programme: Rising Growth and Major Challenges', in N. Brehony and A. El-Desouky (eds), *British–Egyptian Relations from Suez to the Present Day* (2007), 140.
5. Galal Amin, *Egypt in the Era of Hosni Mubarak* (2011), 8.
6. Ibid., p. 55.
7. A. Arafat, *Hosni Mubarak and the Future of Democracy in Egypt* (2009/2011), 16.
8. Ibid., p. 72.
9. Ibid., p. 132.
10. This was the case in Bahrain and Qatar, where the banners of the ruling Al Khalifa and the Al Thani tribes were adopted respectively as national flags. Shi'ite pro-democracy demonstrators in Bahrain in 2011 waved the national flag, even though it was originally the flag of the ruling family which many of them detested.
11. Not to be confused with the use of the same word to refer to the 'followers' of the companions of the Prophet in the sense of the succeeding generation.
12. Percentages taken from the CIA *World Factbook* in 20012.
13. A. Allawi, *The Crisis of Islamic Civilization* (2009), 256.
14. Tripp, *Islam and the Moral Economy*, 34.

15. On this, see R. Scott, *The Challenge of Political Islam* (2010), 7.
16. Arafat, *Hosni Mubarak*, 149.
17. In the film, Hatem is not strangled by Abduh but by another man he has picked up. Another difference between the book and the film is that the latter tones down the issue of political corruption at the pinnacle of the government. If this was required by the censor, it is striking how egregiously the film still allows political corruption to be portrayed.

CONCLUSION

1. M. Provence, *The Great Syrian Revolt and the Rise of Arab Nationalism* (2005), 12.
2. J. Schacht, *An Introduction to Islamic Law* (1964), 166.
3. L. Welchman, *Women and Muslim Family Laws* (2007), 138.
4. On this, see Fatema Mernissi, *Beyond the Veil*.(1975/2011), 135–50.
5. Thus, female students at the Azhar demonstrated in 1979 against reforms to the law which improved women's rights on divorce because they 'infringed the Islamic shari'ah'. See Essam Fawzy, 'Muslim Personal Status Law in Egypt', in L. Welchman (ed.), *Women's Rights and Islamic Family Law: Perspectives on Reform* (2004), 36.
6. Welchman, *Women and Muslim Family Laws*, 78–9. This book brings out the complexities of the debate prompted by attempts to modernise Muslim family law.
7. Kelsay, *Arguing the Just War*, 85.
8. The Arabic verb for 'to conquer', *fath*, also carries the meaning of 'to open'.
9. These three scholars all live and teach in the USA. Sachedina was educated in India and Iran, al-Na'im is Sudanese and Abou El Fadl is Egyptian. For an appraisal of their work, see Kelsay, *Arguing the Just War*, 166–97.
10. Ibid., p. 179.
11. For this, see Vali Nasr, *Meccanomics: The March of the New Muslim Middle Classes* (2010; 1st publ. as *Forces of Fortune*, 2009).
12. An English transliteration and translation of the speech can be found at Blog.sami-aldeeb.com/2012/03/09/full-transcript-of-rached-ghannouchi-lecture-on-secularism-march-2-2012/, with a link to a video recording of the lecture (in Arabic) at www.upstream.tv/recorded/20827717?utm_source=Transcript+of+Rached+Ghannouchi%27s+lecture+on+Secularism+-+March+2%.

13. Quoted in A. Tamimi, *Rachid Ghannouchi* (2001), 86.
14. Ibid., p. 103. See also A. Pargeter, *The Muslim Brotherhood* (2010), 222.
15. For a discussion of this in an Egyptian context, see Scott, *Challenge of Political Islam*.
16. Norton, *Hezbollah*, 119.
17. Allawi, *Crisis of Islamic Civilization*, 122–3.

BIBLIOGRAPHY

G. Abdo, *Egypt and the Triumph of Islam*, Oxford University Press, 2000

S. Aburish, *Nasser: The Last Arab*, Duckworth, 2004

G. Achcar, *The Arabs and the Holocaust: The Arab-Israeli War of Narratives*, Saqi Books, 2010

F. Ajami, *The Dream Palace of the Arabs*, Vintage Books, 1998

S. Akkach, *'Abd al-Ghani al-Nabulusi: Islam and the Enlightenment*, Oneworld, 2007

A. Alexander, *Nasser: His Life and Times*, AUC, 2005

A. Allawi, *The Occupation of Iraq: Winning the War, Losing the Peace*, Yale University Press, 2007

A. Allawi, *The Crisis of Islamic Civilization*, Yale University Press, 2009

C. Allen, *God's Terrorists: The Wahhabi Cult and the Hidden Roots of Modern Jihad*, Da Capo, 2006

M. Allen, *Arabs*, Continuum, 2006

I. Almond, *Two Faiths, One Banner: When Muslims Marched with Christians across Europe's Battlegrounds*, I. B. Tauris, 2009

R. Alsanea, *The Girls of Riyadh*, tr. Alsanea and Booth, Penguin, 2007

G. Amin, *Egypt in the Era of Hosni Mubarak*, AUC, 2011

A. Arafat, *Hosni Mubarak and the Future of Democracy in Egypt*, Palgrave Macmillan, 2009/2011

K. Armstrong, *A History of God: The 4,000-Year Quest of Judaism, Christianity and Islam*, Ballantine, 1993

T. Asbridge, *The First Crusade: A New History*, Free Press, 2004

J. Al-Askari, *A Soldier's Story: From Ottoman Rule to Independent Iraq*, Arabian Publishing, 2003

A. Aswany, tr. H. Davies, *The Yacoubian Building*, AUC, 2004

A. Aswany, tr. J. Wright, *On the State of Egypt*, AUC, 2011

B. Baron, *The Women's Awakening in Egypt: Culture, Society and the Press*, Yale University Press, 1994

J. Beinin, *The Dispersion of Egyptian Jewry*, AUC, 2005

N. bin Laden, O. bin Laden and J. Sasson, *Growing up Bin Laden*, St Martin's Press, 2009

M. Bishara, *The Invisible Arab: The Promise and Peril of the Arab Revolution*, Nation Books, 2012

J. Bowen, *Six Days: How the 1967 War Shaped the Middle East*, Simon &

Schuster, 2003

J. Bradley, *Inside Egypt: The Road to Revolution in the Land of the Pharoahs*, Palgrave Macmillan, 2008/2012

N. Brehony, *Yemen Divided*, I. B. Tauris, 2011

R. Bulliet, *The Case for Islamo-Christian Civilization*, Columbia University Press, 2004

Z. Chehab, *Inside Hamas*, I. B. Tauris, 2007

P. Chevedden, 'The Islamic Interpretation of the Crusades: A New (Old) Paradigm for Understanding the Crusades', *Der Islam* (2004), 130-6

P. Chevedden, 'The View of the Crusades from Rome and Damascus: The Geo-strategic and Historical Perspectives of Pope Urban II and 'Ali ibn Tahir al-Sulami', *Oriens*, 39 (2011), 257-329

K. and B. Christison, *Palestine in Pieces: Graphic Perspectives of the Israeli Occupation*, Pluto Press, 2009

J. Cole, *Colonialism and Revolution in the Middle East: Social and Cultural Origins of Egypt's 'Urabi Movement*, AUC, 1999

J. Cole, *Napoleon's Egypt: Invading the Middle East*, Palgrave Macmillan, 2007

J. Cole, *Engaging the Muslim World*, Palgrave Macmillan, 2009

M. Cook, *Forbidding Wrong in Islam*, Cambridge University Press, 2003

P. Crone and M. Hinds, *God's Caliph: Religious Authority in the First Centuries of Islam*, Cambridge University Press, 1986

A. Crooke, *Resistance: The Essence of the Islamist Revolution*, Pluto Press, 2009

N. Davies, *Europe: A History*, Oxford University Press, 1996

N. Delong-Bas, *Wahhabi Islam: From Revival and Reform to Global Jihad*, Oxford University Press, 2004; AUC, 2005

M. Dumper, *The Future of the Palestinian Refugee Problem*, Lynne Rienner, 2007

E. Ettmüller, *The Construct of Egypt's National Self in James Sanua's Early Satire and Caricature*, Klaus Schwarz Verlag, 2012

M. Farouk-Sluglett and P. Sluglett, *Iraq since 1958: From Revolution to Dictatorship*, I. B. Tauris, 1987/2003

E. Fawzy, 'Muslim Personal Status Law in Egypt: The Current Situation and Possibilities of Reform through Internal Initiatives', in L. Welchman (ed.), *Women's Rights and Islamic Family Law: Perspectives on Reform*, Zed Books, 2004

C. Finkel, *Osman's Dream: The Story of the Ottoman Empire 1300-1923*, John Murray, 2005

M. Fischbach, *Jewish Property Claims against Arab Countries*, Columbia

University Press, 2008

R. Fisk, *Pity the Nation: Lebanon at War*, 3rd edn, Oxford, 1990–2001

R. Fisk, *The Great War for Civilisation: The Conquest of the Middle East*, Fourth Estate, 2005

L. Freedman, *A Choice of Enemies: America Confronts the Middle East*, Weidenfeld & Nicolson, 2008

D. Fromkin, *A Peace to End All Peace: The Fall of the Ottoman Empire and the Creation of the Modern Middle East*, Phoenix, 1989

D. Gardner, *Last Chance: The Middle East in the Balance*, I. B. Tauris, 2009

F. Gardner, *Blood and Sand*, Bantam, 2006

A. George, *Syria: Neither Bread Nor Freedom*, Zed Books, 2003

F. Gerges, *The Far Enemy: Why Jihad went Global*, Cambridge University Press, 2005

A. Ghazali, *Ihya' 'uloom al-deen*, Kitab al-sha'b, 1969 (in Arabic)

A. Ghazali, *Deliverance from Error: Five Key Texts Including his Spiritual Autobiography, al-Munqidh min al-Dalal*, tr. R. McCarthy, Twayne, 1980

M. Gilbert, *Israel: A History*, 1st edn, Black Swan, 1998

M. Gilbert, *In Ishmael's House: A History of Jews in Muslim Lands*, Yale University Press, 2010

J. Glubb, *A Soldier with the Arabs*, Hodder & Stoughton, 1957

J. Glubb, *The Great Arab Conquests*, Hodder & Stoughton, 1968

J. Gordon, *Invisible War: The United States and the Iraq Sanctions*, Harvard University Press, 2010

M. Gove, *Celsius 7/7: How the West's Policy of Appeasement has Provoked Yet More Fundamentalist Terror – and What Has to be Done Now*, Weidenfeld & Nicolson, 2006

S. Griffith, *The Church in the Shadow of the Mosque*, Princeton University Press, 2008

S. Griffith, 'Arabic Christian Relations with Islam: Retrieving from History, Expanding the Canon', in A. O'Mahony and J. Flannery (eds), *The Catholic Church in the Contemporary Middle East*, Melisende, 2010

D. Gutas, *Greek Thought, Arabic Culture: The Graeco-Arabic Translation Movement in Baghdad and Early Abbasid Society*, Routledge, 1995

M. Haag, *Alexandria: City of Memory*, Yale University Press, 2004

H. Haim, *Shi'ism*, Edinburgh University Press, 2004

J. Herrin, *Byzantium: The Surprising Life of a Medieval Empire*, Penguin, 2007/2008

C. Hewer, *Understanding Islam: The First Ten Steps*, SCM Press, 2006

C. Hillenbrand, *The Crusades: Islamic Perspectives*, Edinburgh University Press, 1999/2006

R. Hollis, *Britain and the Middle East in the 9/11 Era*, Wiley-Blackwell, 2010

A. Hourani, *Syria and Lebanon*, Oxford University Press, 1946

A. Hourani, *Arabic Thought in the Liberal Age, 1798–1939*, Oxford Paperbacks, 1962/1970

A. Hourani, *A History of the Arab Peoples*, Belknap, Harvard University Press, 1991

J. Howard-Johnston, *Witnesses to a World Crisis*, Oxford University Press, 2010

S. Huntington, *The Clash of Civilizations and the Remaking of the New World Order*, Simon & Schuster, 1997/2002

J. Hurewitz, *Diplomacy in the Near and Middle East: A Documentary Record, 1914–56*, D. Van Nostrand Co., 1956

E. Husain, *The Islamist*, Penguin, 2007

D. Ingrams, *Palestine Papers 1917–22: Seeds of Conflict*, Eland, 1972/2009

R. Irwin, *For Lust of Knowing: The Orientalists and their Enemies*, Allen Lane, 2006

P. Jenkins, *The Lost History of Christianity*, Lion, 2008

A. Julius, *Trials of the Diaspora: A History of Anti-Semitism in England*, Oxford University Press, 2010

W. Kaegi, *Heraclius, Emperor of Byzantium*, Cambridge University Press, 2003

C. Kanaan, *Lebanon 1860–1960: A Century of Myth and Politics*, Saqi Books, 2005

E. Karsch, *The Iran–Iraq War, 1980–88*, Osprey, 2002

E. Karsch, *The Arab–Israeli Conflict: The Palestine War 1948*, Osprey, 2002

E. Karsch, *Islamic Imperialism: A History*, Yale University Press, 2006

E. Karsch, *Palestine Betrayed*, Yale University Press, 2010

E. Kassab, *Contemporary Arab Thought*, Columbia University Press, 2010

V. Kattan, *From Co-existence to Conquest: International Law and the Origins of the Arab–Israeli Conflict, 1981–1949*, Pluto Press, 2009

E. Kedourie, *The Chatham House Version: and Other Middle Eastern Studies*, Weidenfeld & Nicolson, 1970

B. Keenan, *An Evil Cradling*, Hutchinson, 1992

J. Kelsay, *Arguing the Just War in Islam*, Harvard University Press, 2009

H. Kennedy, *The Prophet and the Age of the Caliphates: The Islamic Near East from the Sixth to the Eleventh Century*, Pearson Longman, 1986/2004

H. Kennedy, *The Court of the Caliphs: The Rise and Fall of Islam's Greatest Dynasty*, Weidenfeld & Nicolson, 2004

H. Kennedy, *The Great Arab Conquests: How the Spread of Islam Changed the*

World we Live in, Weidenfeld & Nicolson, 2007

P. Kennedy, *The Wine Song in Classical Arabic Poetry: Abu Nuwas and the Literary Tradition*, Oxford University Press, 1997

P. Kennedy, *Abu Nuwas: A Genius for Poetry*, One World, 2006

G. Kepel, *Jihad: The Trail of Political Islam*, tr. A. Roberts, I. B. Tauris, 2002

G. Kepel, *The War for Muslim Minds: Islam and the West*, tr. P. Ghazaleh, Belknap, Harvard University Press, 2004

G. Kepel, *Beyond Terror and Martyrdom: The Future of the Middle East*, tr. P. Ghazaleh, Belknap, Harvard University Press, 2008

G. Kepel and J. Milleli (eds), *Al-Qaedah in its own Words*, tr. P. Ghazaleh, Belknap, Harvard University Press, 2008

R. Khalidi, 'The Palestinians and 1948: The Underlying Causes of Failure', in E. Rogan and A. Shlaim (eds), *The War for Palestine*, Cambridge University Press, 2001/2007

J. Al-Khalili, *Pathfinders: The Golden Age of Arabic Science*, Penguin 2010

T. Khalidi, *The Qur'an: A New Translation*, Penguin Classics, 2008

H. Kildani, *Modern Christianity in the Holy Land*, AuthorHouse, 2010

P. Kinross, *Ataturk: The Rebirth of a Nation*, Phoenix, 1964/2001

G. Kraemer, *The Jews in Modern Egypt, 1914–52*, University of Washington Press, 1989

G. Kraemer, *Hassan al-Banna*, One World, 2010

R. Lacey, *Inside the Kingdom: Kings, Clerics, Modernists, Terrorists and the Struggle for Saudi Arabia*, Hutchinson, 2009

E. Lane, *Manners and Customs of the Modern Egyptians*, East West Publications, 1836/1978

D. Levering Lewis, *God's Crucible: Islam and the Making of Europe, 570–1215*, W. W. Norton, 2008

B. Lewis, *The Jews of Islam*, Routledge & Kegan Paul, 1984

B. Lewis, *The Middle East: 2000 Years of History from the Rise of Christianity to the Present Day*, Weidenfeld & Nicolson, 1995

B. Lewis, *Semites and Anti-Semites*, Phoenix Grant, 1986/1997

B. Lewis, *The Crisis of Islam: Holy War and Unholy Terror*, Phoenix, 2003

B. Lewis, *From Babel to Dragomans: Interpreting the Middle East*, Phoenix, 2004

M. Lings, *Muhammad: His Life Based on the Earliest Sources*, The Islamic Texts Society, 1983/1991

S. Longrigg, *Syria and Lebanon under French Mandate*, Oxford University Press, 1958

A. Maalouf, *The Crusades through Arab Eyes*, tr. J. Rothschild, Saqi Books,

1984/2006

C. MacEvitt, *The Crusades and the Christian World of the East: Rough Tolerance*, University of Pennsylvania Press, 2008

N. MacGregor, *A History of the World in 100 Objects*, Penguin, 2010/12

R. McGurk, *The Senussi's Little War: The Amazing Story of a Forgotten Conflict in the Western Desert, 1915–17*, Arabian Publishing, 2007

A. MacLeod, *Accommodating Protest: Working Women, the New Veiling and Change in Cairo*, AUC Press, 1991

I. Manji, *The Trouble with Islam Today*, St Martin's Press, 2004

B. Masters, *Christians and Jews in the Ottoman Arab World: The Roots of Sectarianism*, Cambridge University Press, 2001

P. Mattar, *The Mufti of Jerusalem: Al-Hajj Amin al-Husayni and the Palestinian National Movement*, Columbia University Press, 1988

J. Mearsheimer and S. Walt, *The Israel Lobby and US Foreign Policy*, Penguin, 2007

F. Mernissi, *Beyond the Veil: Male–Female Dynamics in Muslim Society*, Saqi Books, 1975/2011

T. Mitchell, *Colonising Egypt*, Cambridge University Press, 1988

F. Moffitt, 'Egypt's Economic Reform Programme: Rising Growth and Major Challenges' in N. Brehony and A. Desouky (eds), *British–Egyptian Relations from Suez to the Present Day*, Saqi Books, 2007

B. Morris, *The Birth of the Palestinian Refugee Problem 1947–9*, Cambridge University Press, 1987

B. Morris, *Israel's Border Wars, 1949–56*, Oxford University Press, 1993

B. Morris, *The Road to Jerusalem: Glubb Pasha, Palestine and the Jews*, I. B. Tauris, 2002

B. Morris, 'Revisiting the Palestinian Exodus of 1948', in E. Rogan and A. Shlaim (eds), *The War for Palestine*, Cambridge University Press, 2001/2007

B. Morris, *1948: A History of the First Arab Israeli War*, Yale University Press, 2008

T. Mostyn, *Egypt's Belle Epoque*, Tauris Parke Paperbacks, 2006

V. Nasr, *Meccanomics: The March of the New Muslim Middle Classes*, One World, 2010

K. Nelson, *The Art of Reciting the Qur'an*, AUC, 2001

D. Newman, *An Imam in Paris: Account of a Stay in France by an Egyptian Cleric (1826–31)*, Saqi Books, 2004/2012

A. Norton, *Hezbullah: A Short History*, Princeton University Press, 2007

A. O'Mahony and J. Flannery (eds), *The Catholic Church in the Contemporary Middle East*, Melisende, 2010

T. Osman, *Egypt on the Brink: From Nasser to Mubarak*, Yale University Press, 2010

R. Owen, *The Middle East in the World Economy, 1800–1914*, Methuen, 1981

R. Owen, *State, Power and Politics in the Making of the Modern Middle East*, Routledge, 2000

R. Owen, *Lord Cromer: Victorian Imperialist, Edwardian Proconsul*, Oxford University Press, 2004

R. Owen, *The Rise and Fall of Arab Presidents for Life*, Harvard University Press, 2012

I. Pappe, *A History of Modern Palestine*, Cambridge University Press, 2004

I. Pappe, *The Ethnic Cleansing of Palestine*, One World, 2006

A. Pargeter, *The Muslim Brotherhood: The Burden of Tradition*, Saqi Books, 2010

D. Pearl and W. Menski, *Muslim Family Law*, A. M. Shakoori, no date

J. Phillips, *The Fourth Crusade and the Sack of Constantinople*, Pimlico, 2005

J. Phillips, *Holy Warriors: A Modern History of the Crusades*, Vintage Books, 2010

M. Provence, *The Great Syrian Revolt and the Rise of Arab Nationalism*, Austin, 2005

D. Pryce-Jones: *The Closed Circle: An Interpretation of the Arabs*, Paladin, 1990

Y. Qaradawi, *Fiqh al-jihad*, Maktabat Wahba, 2009 (in Arabic)

S. Qutb, *Milestones*, tr. anon., Islamic Book Service, 2001/2008-9

S. Qutb, *A Child from the Village*, tr. J. Calvert and W. Shepard, Syracuse University Press, 2004

S. Qutb, *The Sayyid Qutb Reader: Selected Writings on Politics, Religion and Society*, ed. A. Bergesen, Routledge, 2008

T. Ramadan, *Islam, The West and the Challenges of Modernity*, tr. S. Amghar, The Islamic Foundation, 2001

A. Raz, *The Bride and the Dowry: Israel, Jordan and the Palestinians in the Aftermath of the June 1967 War*, Yale University Press, 2012

J. Reinharz, *Chaim Weizmann: The Making of a Statesman*, Oxford University Press, 1993

J. Richmond, *Egypt 1798–1952*, Methuen & Co., 1977

M. Rodinson, *Europe and the Mystique of Islam*, tr. R. Veinus, I. B. Tauris, 2006

E. Rogan, *The Arabs: A History*, Allen Lane, 2009

E. Rogan and A. Shlaim (ed.), *The War for Palestine*, 2nd edn, Cambridge University Press, 2007

T. Royle, *Glubb Pasha: The Life and Times of Sir John Bagot Glubb, Commander of the Arab Legion*, Little Brown, 1992

T. Russell, *Egyptian Service, 1902–46*, John Murray, 1949

P. Sadgrove, *The Egyptian Theatre in the Nineteenth Century, 1799–1882*, Ithaca University Press, 1996

A. Safieh, *The Peace Process: From Breakthrough to Breakdown*, Saqi Books, 2010

E. Said, *Orientalism*, Routledge & Kegan Paul, 1978

J. Salt, *The Unmaking of the Middle East: A History of Western Disorder in Arab Lands*, University of California Press, 2008

P. Sands, *Lawless World*, Penguin, 2005/2006

R. Satloff, *Among the Righteous: The Holocaust's Long Reach into Arab Lands*, Public Affairs, 2006

J. Schacht, *An Introduction to Islamic Law*, Oxford University Press, 1964

J. Schacht, 'Muhammad 'Abduh', in *Encyclopedia of Islam*, Brill, 1992

J. Schneer, *The Balfour Declaration: The Origins of the Arab–Israeli Conflict*, Bloomsbury, 2010

R. Scott, *The Challenge of Political Islam: Non-Muslims and the Egyptian State*, Stanford University Press, 2010

P. Seale, *Asad: The Struggle for the Middle East*, I. B. Tauris, 1988

M. Sedgwick, *Muhammad Abduh: A Biography*, AUC, 2009

R. Segal, *Islam's Black Slaves*, Farrar, Strauss & Giroux, 2001

T. Segev, *One Palestine Complete*, tr. H. Watzman, Abacus, 2001

T. Segev, *1967: Israel, the War and the Year that Transformed the Middle East*, tr. J. Cohen, Little, Brown, 2007

J. Shaheen, *Reel Bad Arabs: How Hollywood Vilifies a People*, Arris Books, 2003

N. Sharansky (with Ron Dermer), *The Case for Democracy: The Power of Freedom to Overcome Tyranny and Terror*, Public Affairs, 2004/2006

A. Shiblak, *Iraqi Jews: The History of a Mass Exodus*, Saqi Books, 1986/2005

A. Shlaim, *The Iron Wall*, Penguin, 2000

A. Shlaim, *Lion of Jordan: The Life of King Hussein in War and Peace*, Allen Lane, 2007

A. Shlaim, 'Israel and the Arab Coalition in 1948', in E. Rogan and A. Shlaim (eds), *The War for Palestine*, Cambridge University Press, 2001/2007

E. Shohat, 'The Invention of the Mizrahim', *Journal of Palestine Studies*, 29 (Autumn 1999), 5–20

E. Sivan, *Radical Islam: Medieval Theology and Modern Politics*, Yale University Press, 1985/1990

A. Soueif, *Cairo: My City, Our Revolution*, Bloomsbury, 2012

R. Stephens, *Nasser: A Political Biography*, Penguin Press, 1971

R. Storrs, *Lawrence of Arabic, Zionism and Palestine*, Penguin, 1940

A. Stratton, *Muhajababes*, Constable, 2006

A. Tamimi, *Rachid Ghannouchi: A Democrat within Islam*, Oxford University Press, 2001

A. Tamimi, *Hamas: Unwritten Chapters*, Hurst, 2007

S. Tatham, *Losing Arab Hearts and Minds*, C. Hurst & Co., 2006

C. Tripp, *Islam and the Moral Economy*, Cambridge University Press, 2006

C. Tripp, *A History of Iraq*, 3rd edn, Cambridge University Press, 2007

US Department of State, *Patterns of Global Terror, 2001*, US Department of State, 2002

L. Vaglieri, 'Ghadir Khumm', in *The Encyclopedia of Islam*, 2nd edn, Brill, 1965

P. Vatikiotis, *Nasser and his Generation*, Croom Helm, 1978

P. Vatikiotis, *The Modern History of Egypt*, 2nd edn, Weidenfeld & Nicolson, 1980

L. Welchman (ed.), *Women's Rights and Islamic Family Law: Perspectives on Reform*, Zed Press, 2004

L. Welchmann, *Women and Muslim Family Laws: A Comparative Overview of Textual Development and Advocacy*, Amsterdam University Press, 2007

B. Whitaker, *What's Really Wrong with the Middle East*, Saqi Books, 2010

J. Wilkinson, *Arabia's Frontiers: The Story of Britain's Boundary Drawing in the Desert*, I. B. Tauris, 1991

B. Zollner, *The Muslim Brotherhood, Hasan al-Hudaybi and Ideology*, Routledge, 2009

SUGGESTIONS FOR FURTHER READING

I have read right through the overwhelming majority of the works in the bibliography from cover to cover, and a few of them twice. The following suggestions are for those readers who are new to the history of the Arabs and would like a few pointers as to how they can begin to explore the matters covered by this book.

The definitive English language history of the Arabs which deals with the entire period under consideration and towers above all others is Albert Hourani's *A History of the Arab Peoples*. Also to be highly recommended is Eugene Rogan's very readable *The Arabs: A History*, which deals with the entire Arab world from the conquest of the Egyptian Mamluks by the Ottoman Sultan Selim the Grim in 1516-7 onwards.

For the early period, from the Prophet Muhammad to the Abbasid Caliphate, I have relied first and foremost on the scholarship of Hugh Kennedy, especially *The Prophet and the Age of the Caliphates*. For the life and career of Muhammad, I have also used the translations of extracts from early historians by Martin Lings in *Muhammad: His Life Based on the Earliest Sources*.

For the encounter between Christianity and Islam which followed the Arab conquests, my main source is Sydney Griffith's groundbreaking *The Church in the Shadow of the Mosque*. For the Crusades, I have used Caroline Hillenbrand's *The Crusades: Islamic Perspectives*, Jonathan Phillips' *Holy Warriors: A Modern History of the Crusades* and Thomas Asbridge's *The First Crusade*. Paul Chevedden builds a convincing case for his revisionist thesis that the Crusades did not begin with a big bang in 1095. This can now be found in *Crusade Creationism versus Pope Urban II's Conceptualization of the Crusades* (in *The Historian* 75, Spring 2013). For an introduction to the achievements of philosophers and scientists writing in Arabic during the Middle

Ages, I recommend Jim Al-Khalili's *Pathfinders: The Golden Age of Arabic Science* and Dimitri Gutas's *Greek Thought, Arabic Culture*.

I have made great use of Caroline Finkel's *Osman's Dream* for the narrative history of the Ottoman Empire from its inception to its demise. For Greater Syria in the late Ottoman period (focussing in particular on sectarian matters), *Christians and Jews in the Ottoman Arab World* by Bruce Masters has been invaluable, as have two books by Juan Cole with regard to nineteenth-century Egypt: *Napoleon's Egypt* and *Colonialism and Revolution in the Middle East*, his study of the country in the decades leading up to the British occupation.

For the issue of Palestine and the creation of Israel, I have relied very heavily on Avi Shlaim's *The Iron Wall*, Tom Segev's *One Palestine Complete* (for the period of the Mandate), Benny Morris's *1948: A History of the First Arab Israeli War* and Victor Kattan's *From Co-existence to Conquest*. *The Iron Wall* continues the narrative up to the 1990s and can be read in tandem with Shlaim's biography of King Hussein, *Lion of Jordan*. Avi Raz's *The Bride and the Dowry* provides a fascinating study of Israeli policy in the period immediately after the Six Day War.

For American policy in the Middle East in recent decades, I have relied on Sir Lawrence Freedman's *A Choice of Enemies*. It should perhaps be read in conjunction with Robert Fisk's *The Great War for Civilisation*, a vast book based on his eye-witness and battle-hardened experiences as a journalist reporting on conflicts in and around the Arab world from the 1970s onwards.

For Iraq since 1918, I have relied almost entirely on Charles Tripp's *A History of Iraq*. For Syria, I have found Patrick Seale's *Asad* (a biography of Hafez al-Assad) a very valuable source. There is also Michael Provence's in-depth study of the 1925 rebellion against the French, *The Great Syrian Revolt and the Rise of Arab Nationalism* which deserves to be better known at this tragic time for that country. For Nasser and his era, I found the biography by Robert Stephens, *Nasser*, extremely helpful.

For Arab Jews in the twentieth century, the best studies I have found are Abbas Shiblak's *Iraqi Jews: A History of a Mass Exodus*, Joel Beinin's *The Dispersion of Egyptian Jewry* and Gudrun Kraemer's *The Jews in Modern Egypt 1914–1952*.

Turning to the realm of ideas, my starting point has been Hourani's *Arabic Thought in the Liberal Age 1798–1939* for the intellectual encounter with the modern West. I have supplemented my knowledge of that period in particular with Mark Sedgwick's *Muhammad Abduh: A Biography*, Kraemer's *Hasan al-Banna*, and Daniel Newman's *An Imam in Paris*, a study and translation of Tahtawi.

For the development of Islamism over the last fifty years or so, I have relied on the trilogy of books by Gilles Kepel, especially *Jihad: The Trail of Political Islam* but also *The War for Muslim Minds: Islam and the West* and *Beyond Terror and Martyrdom: The Future of the Middle East*. Two other very helpful books in the same area are *The Far Enemy: Why Jihad Went Global* by Fawaz Gerges and *Radical Islam: Medieval Theology and Modern Politics* by Emmanuel Sivan. The two works which require the reader to wrap his or her head in a towel but repay careful consideration are Tripp's *Islam and the Moral Economy* and Barbara Zollner's *The Muslim Brotherhood, Hasan al-Hudaybi and Ideology*. Gilbert Achcar's *The Arabs and the Holocaust* should also be mentioned here as it shines much needed light on an area that was in danger of being completely obscured by partisan tracts. I also recommend Ali Allawi's thoughtful study, *The Crisis of Islamic Civilization*.

For the years leading up to the Arab Spring, I have found *Egypt in the Era of Hosni Mubarak* by Galal Amin, *On the State of Egypt* by Alaa Al Aswany, *Hosni Mubarak and the Future of Democracy in Egypt* by Alaa al-Din Arafat, David Gardner's *Last Chance: The Middle East in the Balance* and (with regard to Muslims and Christians in Egypt) Rachel Scott's *The Challenge of Political Islam* particularly helpful.

INDEX

Abbas
uncle of Prophet Muhammad
53
Abbas, Mahmoud 252–3
foreign policy of 253–5
Abbasid Caliphate 53–5, 57–8, 61,
66, 70, 106, 172, 233
Abbasid Revolution (AD 750)
54, 59
Abd al-Raziq, Ali 307–8
Abduh, Muhammad 106–7,
158–9, 209, 307–9
Chief Mufti of Egypt 105
Abdul Hamid II, Sultan 89, 108,
158, 263
reign of (1876–1909) 88
Abdul Malik, caliph 46–7, 49
Abdullah I of Jordan 172–3, 180,
183
assassination of (1951) 188, 225
Abdullah II of Jordan 318
Amman Message (2004) 318–19
Abraham 32, 258–9
construction of Ka'aba 26
family of 26
Abu Bakr 34, 43, 56
family of 33, 37, 40
First Caliph 33, 42
Shi'ite view of 44
Abu Dhabi 267
Abu Sufyan
family of 30, 39
Governor of Yemen 39
Acre 77
Aden 97, 191, 207, 215, 262, 293
al-Afghani, Jamal-al-Din 104–5, 287

Afghanistan 230, 283, 288
Operation Enduring Freedom
(2001–) 262
Soviet Invasion of (1979–89)
228, 230–1
Aflaq, Michel
co-founder of Ba'ath Party 201
Agadir 293
Aghlabids
territory controlled by 54
Aisha
wife of Prophet Muhammad 33,
41, 56
Alaric the Visigoth
Sacking of Rome (AD 410) 22
Alawis 69, 202, 268, 270, 317
Shi'ite and Sunni opposition to
66, 317
territory inhabited by 122, 316
Aleppo 20, 63–4, 67, 93, 120, 123,
144, 191, 300
Alexandria 36, 80–1, 95, 114, 133,
172
Algeria 16, 73, 85, 108, 266, 288–9
French colonisation of (1830–
1962) 91, 96, 101, 127, 215
independence of (1962) 198,
215
Jewish population of 192
War of Independence (1954–62)
198
Algiers 77
Ali ibn Abi Talib, Imam 43, 316
Fourth Caliph 40, 42
family of 40
murder of (AD 661) 42

Amazigh 16
Amman 120, 318
Amritsar massacre (1919) 99
Anatolia 34, 80–1
    Armenian population of 85
    Greek population of 85
    Kurdish population of 85
    Turkish settlement of 62, 121
Ancient Greece 19–20, 22, 74
Andalucía 50
Anglo-Egyptian Treaty (1936) 171,
    194
Anglo-French Declaration (1918)
    115
Anglo-Iraqi Treaty (1930)
    signing of 147
Anglo-Ottoman Convention (1913)
    90
Ankara 121
Ansar 40
Aoun, General Michel 244
al-Aqsa Mosque
    fire (1969) 226
Arab-Israeli War (1947–9) 16, 181,
    185–6, 198, 216
Arab League (League of Arab
    States) 176, 217, 249
    aims of 180
    members of 173, 298
    role in founding of PLO 220
    support for PLO 220, 242
Arab Revolt (1916–18) 112–13, 145
Arab Socialist Union 277
Arab Spring 13, 257, 265–6, 293,
    321
    Bahraini Uprising (2011–) 298
    Egyptian Revolution (2011) 13,
    165, 296, 299, 304
    Libyan Civil War (2011) 13, 258, 298
    role of women in 306

Syrian Civil War (2011–) 244,
    258, 268–70, 272, 298, 300–1,
    316
Tunisian Revolution (2010–11)
    14, 293, 296, 299
use of social media in 295
Yemeni Revolution (2011–12)
    298–9
Arabic (language) 15–17, 19–20, 46,
    49, 51–2, 55, 60–1, 66, 73, 75,
    77–8, 83, 85, 95, 101–2, 108–9,
    111, 114–16, 133, 145, 150, 154,
    190, 202
    as official state language 129
    terminology of 44, 57–60
    use by Christians 52, 69, 93–4
Arafat, Yasser 235, 250
    president of PLO 220, 228, 249,
    252
Aristotle 59, 74
    Topics 59
Armenians 125
Asia Minor 22
al-Askari, Ja'far 90, 148
al-Assad, Bashar 272–3
    family of 268, 271, 317
    President of Syria 272, 299–300
al-Assad, Hafez 223, 243, 269–70,
    273
    death of (2000) 272
    family of 268, 270–1, 317
al-Assad, Maher 272
al-Assad, Rif'at
    family of 270
Assassins 64
al Aswany, Alaa
    The Yacoubian Building (2002)
    290–2
Ataturk, Mustafa Kemal 121–2,
    139, 158, 305

Austria 77
Austro-Hungarian Empire 94
Avars 22
Aws
    conversion to Islam 24
Ayn Jalut 67
al-Azma, Yusuf
    Syrian Defence Minister 122

Baal 29
Ba'ath Party 223, 232
    founding of 201
    ideology of 201–2, 268, 270, 317
    Iraqi 232, 268, 317
    Syrian 268, 301, 316
Badr, battle of 25–6
Baghdad 53, 55, 57, 61, 77, 88, 118,
    120, 144–5, 170, 192, 233, 235,
    240, 317
Bahrain 16, 97, 113, 215, 279, 315
    Uprising (2011–) 298
Baker, James
    US Secretary of State 245
al-Bakr, Hasan
    coup led by (1968) 232
Ba'lbek 19
Balfour, Arthur
    British Foreign Secretary 127
Balfour Declaration (1917) 122,
    127–8
    political impact of 134, 136–7,
    139–40
    provisions of 113, 116, 128, 139
Bani Hashim 38
Bani Umayya 38, 44
al-Banna, Hassan 164–5, 167, 207, 261
    assassination of 193
    founder of Muslim Brotherhood
    164
    influence of 165–6

Banque Misr 154
Baring, Evelyn (Earl of Cromer)
    British Consul-General of Egypt
    97–8
Bashir II
    Ottoman Governor of Mount
    Lebanon 67
Basij 233–4
Basra 39, 77, 90, 145, 317
Bedouin 227, 283
    territory inhabited by 176
Begin, Menachem 224
Beirut 95, 120, 123, 241–2
Benghazi 298
Ben Gurion, David 169, 183–4,
    188, 216
    Israeli Defence Minister 199
    Israeli Prime Minister 180, 182,
    199
Berbers 16, 54
    conversion to Islam 50
Berlin 90
Bevin, Ernest
    British Foreign Secretary 175
bin Laden, Osama 231, 259–63
    assassination of (2011) 261
    expulsion from Sudan (1996)
    261–2
    ideology of 263, 306
    media presence of 262–3
Bitar, Salah al-din
    co-founder of Ba'ath Party 201
Blum, Leon
    administration of 126
Bolsheviks 113
Bonaparte, Napoleon
    conquest of Egypt (1798) 77–9,
    85, 91, 95, 107, 157
Bouazizi, Muhammad
    suicide of (2010) 293, 295

Bourghiba, Habib
    abolition of polygamy (1956) 306-7
Bulgaria 88
Bush, George H. W.
    foreign policy of 245
Bush, George W.
    foreign policy of 238-9, 249
al-Bustani, Butrus 95
Byzantine Empire 22, 34-6, 45-7
    Fall of (1453) 70-1
    Persian invasion of 35

Cairo 55, 77, 80-1, 88, 99, 102-3, 132, 151, 155, 161, 164-5, 172, 191, 194, 199, 204, 290-1, 295, 309
Camp David Accords (1978) 225
Canada
    opposition to Palestinian non-member observer status in UN (2012) 255
Carter, Jimmy
    foreign policy of 224
Catholicism 66, 71, 73, 95
    Arab 91
Champollion, Jean-François 36
Chancellor, Sir John
    British High Commissioner of Palestine 140
Chechnya 230
China 60
Churchill, Winston 141
Circassians
    territory inhabited by 118
Christianity 17, 19-20, 23, 31, 33-4, 36-7, 46, 51-2, 60, 75, 86, 92, 105, 189-90, 202, 305, 313, 315
    Bible 28-9, 37, 46

Coptic 140, 151
Greek 58
Incarnation doctrine 69
Latin 58, 74
Orthodox 37, 46, 70, 74, 89, 123-4, 131, 141, 201, 259
persecution of 92, 190
roots of 27-8
Cilicia 18
Clinton, Bill
    foreign policy of 246, 248
Coalition Provisional Authority 239
Cold War 196, 220, 245
Communism 138, 142
Constantinople 17, 20, 36, 49, 63, 70-1, 73, 77, 83, 88, 90, 93, 121
Copernicus 60
Cordoba 54, 60-1
Crimean War (1853-6) 87
Cromer, Lord
    see Baring, Evelyn
Crusades 61-3, 78, 108, 127, 157
    First Crusade (1096-9) 62
    Sacking of Constantinople (1204) 63
Cyprus
    Maronite Christian population of 66
Czech Republic
    opposition to Palestinian non-member observer status in UN (2012) 255

Damascus 20, 34-5, 49-50, 55, 63-4, 67-8, 77, 90, 92-3, 118, 120, 122-4, 135, 172, 188, 201, 219, 242, 272, 300-1, 309
    Umayyad Mosque 20
Danube, River 22, 50-1, 73

Dhu'l-Hijjah 32
Diana of the Ephesians 29
al-Din, Nur 68
Dreyfus Affair 162
Druze 66–7, 91–2, 202
    territory inhabited by 122–3, 223, 317

Eden, Sir Anthony 198
Egypt 19, 34, 36, 39, 41, 45, 51, 64, 66, 81, 83–4, 86, 97, 102, 139–40, 145, 150–3, 173, 191, 198, 217, 266, 281–4, 288, 290–1, 315
    British Occupation of (1882–1952) 84–5, 95, 97–9, 111, 279, 301
    Coptic Christian population of 36, 140, 151, 289–90, 314
    corruption in 276
    Dinshaway incident (1906) 99
    economy of 82–3, 274–6
    Free Officers coup (1952) 195–7, 200, 207, 221, 291, 314
    General Assembly 99
    government of 98, 182, 193, 318
    Italian Invasion of (1940) 170
    Jewish population of 133, 192, 200–1
    Legislative Council 99
    military of 83–4, 126, 151, 198–9, 203, 218, 222
    Muslim population of 290
    Napoleonic conquest of (1798) 77–9, 85, 91, 95, 107, 157
    National Assembly 218
    Nubian population of 17
    presidential election (2012) 296–7
    Revolution (1919) 151–2
    Revolution (1952) 200
    Revolution (2011) 13, 165, 296, 299, 304
    Supreme Council of the Armed Forces (SCAF) 296–7
    Young Egypt 155
Egypt-Israel Peace Treaty (1979) 225, 228, 241
Elijah 29
Enlightenment 75, 102
Entente Cordiale 111
Eshkol, Levi
    Israeli Prime Minister 217
Ethiopia
    Italian Invasion of (1935) 154
Euphrates, River 77, 119
European Union (EU) 254

Facebook 295
El Fadl, Khaled Abou 308
Faisal I of Iraq, King 122, 135, 145–7, 172–3, 317
    death of 148–9
    family of 112, 120, 148
    role in Arab Revolt (1916–18) 112
Faisal II of Iraq, King 204
    murder of 204
Faisal of Saudi Arabia, King 216
    accession of (1964) 226
Falluja 239–40
Farouq 173, 193
fascism 142, 155
Fatah
    conflict with Hamas 253
    Palestinian nationalist movement 180
Fatiha 28
Fatima
    daughter of Prophet Muhammad 23
Fatimid Caliphate 62, 66
    territory of 55

Fayoum 35

Fez 242

First Intifada (1987-93) 245, 249, 251

First World War (1914-18) 90, 93, 96, 99-100, 111, 125, 127, 145, 150, 155, 157, 272
belligerents of 111-12, 163, 168
Gallipoli Campaign (1915-16) 121
Paris Peace Conference (1919) 132, 151

fitna 43, 212, 316

Ford, Gerald 225

France 15, 78, 83-4, 91, 97, 108, 112, 122, 156, 168, 197, 215, 234, 320-1
Popular Front 126
Revolution (1789-99) 78, 319-21

Franks 51, 63-4, 68, 75

Gaddafi, Muammar 267, 273
removal from power and death of (2011) 298
rise to power (1969) 281

Gaza Strip 182, 198, 217, 250, 253
Israeli occupation of 187, 225, 246
refugee population of 187

Gemayyal, Amin 242-4

Gemayyal, Bashir
assassination of (1982) 242

Geneva Convention (1949)
Article 49(6) 254-5

Germany 111, 163, 168, 170

Ghannouchi, Rached 264, 309-10, 312
ideology of 310-12, 315
president of Nahda Party 309

Ghazali 28

Ghazi I 148
accession of (1933) 148

Glubb Pasha 173, 181, 259
Commander of Jordanian Arab Legion 168, 180-1

Golan Heights 222
Israeli occupation of 219, 241

Goldstein, Baruch
attack on shrine of Abraham (1994) 258-9

Granada 70

Greater Syria 18-20, 23, 36, 39, 45, 51, 62, 66-7, 73, 80, 93, 95, 108, 118, 120-1, 167
Christian population of 34, 59, 84-5, 93
invasion of 36
Maronite Christian population of 66
Muslim population of 93
Ottoman occupation of 92-3, 100
Shi'ite population of 85

Greece 19
Christian population of 87
Italian Invasion of (1940-1) 171
War of Independence (1821-32) 80, 87, 91-3

Grey, Viscount Edward
British Foreign Secretary 113-14

Gulf Co-operation Council (GCC) 299
formation of (1981) 280

Habash, George 259
founder of PLFP 259

Habsburg Empire 83

Hacohen, Mordechai Ben-Hillel 133

hadith 56, 70, 132, 160, 163, 209

Hadramawt 261
Hadrian's Wall
Hagana 143, 179
Haifa 123
Hajj 32-3
al-Hakim, Fatimid caliph
    demolition of Church of Holy
    Sepulchre (1009-10) 62
al-Hakim, Ayatollah Muhsin
    supporters of 232
al-Hallaj, Hussein bin Mansour
    execution of (AD 922) 57
Hamas 249, 251, 289, 320
    conflict with Fatah 253
    electoral performance of 252
    opposition to Oslo Peace Process
    252
Hama 124, 300
Hamza
    uncle of Prophet Mohammad 30
Hariri, Rafiq
    assassination of (2005) 244
Harvey 60
Hassan
    grandson of Prophet
    Muhammad 42, 44
    death of 44
Hebrew (language) 138
    as official state language 129
Hebron 126, 134, 139, 180, 247-8,
    258
Hejaz 55
Heraclius 36-7
Hind
    wife of Abu Sufyan 30, 39
Hitler, Adolf 122, 142, 198
Hittin, battle of 64
Hizb al-Nur 302
Hizbullah 243, 252-3, 289, 318
    members of 317

    presence in Lebanon 317
Holocaust 163, 174-5, 255
Homs 35, 63, 123
al-Hoss, Selim 244
Hubal
    worship of 23, 30
Hulagu 61
Hungary 73, 90
    Ottoman Hungary (1541-1699)
    75
Hussein, Imam 42, 44
    death of 44-5, 53, 144, 258
    shrine of 161-2
Hussein of Jordan, King 220,
    222-3, 246
    family of 204
    removal of PLO from Jordan
    (1970) 223, 288
Hussein, Saddam 231-3, 235-6,
    243-5, 261, 273, 282, 307
    engagement with UN Oil-For-
    Food Programme 238
    removal from power (2003) 289
Hussein, Taha 208-10
al-Husseini, Abd al-Qadir 179
    death of 180
al-Husseini, Hajj Amin
    Grand Mufti of Jerusalem 141,
    143, 170, 175, 180

Ibn Abdul Wahhab, Muhammad
    160
    founder of Wahhabism, 159-61
Ibn Buwayh, Ahmed 55
Ibn Saud, Abdul Aziz 156-7, 173,
    263, 267
    conquest of Hejaz (1924-6) 142,
    161-2
    death of (1953) 267
Ibn Taymiyya 69, 212

Ibn Tulun, Ahmed
  Abbasid Governor of Egypt 54
ijtihad
  concept of 105, 160
imperialism 96
India 79, 109, 122
  independence of (1947) 194
  Partition (1947) 194
Indonesia
  Bali bombing (2002) 260
International Court of Justice 254
International Islamic Front against Jews and Crusaders 262
International Monetary Fund (IMF) 274
Iran 14, 59, 73, 144, 226, 232, 315, 317, 320
  government of 258
  Islamic Revolution (1979) 229, 231, 243, 285
Iran-Iraq War (1980-8) 231, 233-4, 237
Iraq 16, 19, 36, 41, 51, 53, 60, 118, 122, 139-40, 169, 173, 175, 196, 198, 226, 239, 267, 281-4, 288, 307, 315, 319
  British Mandate of (1920-32) 116, 119-20, 126, 145-7, 240, 279, 301
  Christian population of 59, 85, 145-6, 313
  economy of 240
  Farhud (1941) 192
  government of 146
  insurgency activity in 239-40, 264
  Jewish population of 145-6, 191-2
  July Revolution (1958) 203-4, 284
  Kurdish population of 16, 118-19, 145, 147, 233
  military of 146
  oil reserves of 234
  Operation Iraqi Freedom (2003-11) 210, 231, 238-9, 256-7, 317
  Republican Guard 235, 317
  Shi'ite population of 85, 144-5, 232-3, 316
  Sunni population of 145-6, 240, 317
  Turkoman population of 145
  Yezidi population of 145
Iraqi Communist Party
  establishment of first central committee (1935) 149
Islam 14-17, 19, 30-1, 37, 42-3, 45, 51, 55-6, 58, 62, 74, 86, 89, 100, 104-5, 107, 161, 188-9, 202, 210, 227, 230, 236, 257-8, 285, 309-11, 319
  conversion to 24, 27, 36, 49-51, 53
  political 305
  roots of 27-8, 32
Islamism 14, 208, 230-1, 288, 290, 297, 302, 320
  pan-Islamism 98, 104, 157
Ismail Pasha 81-3, 84, 161
  Ottoman Khedive of Egypt 83, 161, 196
Israel 14, 17-18, 112, 174, 182, 217, 224, 245, 255, 263, 268, 295, 320
  formation of (1948) 180-1, 184-5, 216
  personal status laws of 314-15
  settlement movement 225
Israeli Defence Force (IDF) 219, 250

Istanbul 17, 20, 90
(*see also* Constantiniple)
Italo-Turkish War (1911–12) 97, 154
Italy 91, 97, 170

Jaffa 123, 136–7, 180
Jahiliyya 209–10
al-Jahiz of Basra 60
Japan 100
Jerusalem 35, 49, 62–4, 68, 71, 126, 131, 134–5, 138, 143, 179–81, 186–7, 219, 224, 248
Jesus Christ 30, 32, 262
Jewish Agency 129–30
jihad 57–8, 61–2, 157–8, 230, 259
translations of 58
Jordan 16, 18, 120, 140, 172–3, 180, 188, 200, 204, 215, 217, 222, 246, 266
Christian population of 313
government of 318
refugee population of 187, 240, 300
removal of PLO from (1970) 223, 251, 288
Jordan, River 116, 119, 217
Judaism 17, 20, 22–3, 31, 33–4, 52, 86
Ashkenazi 84
persecution of 133–4, 136, 190
roots of 27–8
Sephardic 133–4
Torah 28, 133

Ka'aba 22–4, 26, 31
Kabul 231
Kailani, Rashid Ali 192
Iraqi Prime Minister 170
Kashmir 230
Kenya

US embassy bombing (1998) 262
Kerbala 44, 144, 161–2, 316
Khadijah
wife of Prophet Muhammad 23, 33
Kharijites 41–2
Sharia variant of 318
al-Khateeb, Hamza
death of (2011) 300
al-Khattab, Umar Ibn 37, 56
Second Caliph 34, 42, 89
Shi'ite view of 44
Khazraj
conversion to Islam 24
Khomeini, Ayatollah Ruhollah 229
theory of '*velayat-e faqih*' 229
Kibbutz movement 138
Kissinger, Henry
US Secretary of State 222
Kitchener, Earl Herbert 99
Koreish 39–41
worship of Hubal 23
Kufa 39, 44–5
Kurdish Democratic Party 205
Kurdistan 240
Kurds 234
language of 145
territory inhabited by 16, 85, 118–19, 145, 233, 236–7, 240
Kuwait 16, 96, 113, 215, 236, 279, 315
Iraqi Invasion of (1990) 231, 235, 243, 245, 261

League of Nations 147
Covenant of 115–16, 128, 176
Mandates 115–16, 176
Lebanon 16, 18, 25, 66, 124, 143, 169, 172–3, 181, 188, 204, 220,

241, 295, 315, 317
Alawi population of 126
borders of 268
Civil War (1975–90) 221
Druze population of 123, 126
French Mandate of (1920–43) 116, 119, 122, 126
government of 223, 244
independence of (1943) 172
Israeli Invasion of (1982) 241–2
Israeli Invasion of (2006) 318
Jewish population of 192
Muslim population of 123
refugee population of 250, 300
Shi'ite population of 258
South Lebanon Conflict (1982–2000) 243
Lebanon Conflict (1860) 91–2
Libya 16, 85, 266–7
Civil War (2011) 13, 258, 298
Italian Colony/Protectorate (1912–43) 97, 154, 168, 215
resistance movement 125, 157
Likud Party
electoral performance of (1977) 224
Litani, River 181
Locke, John 74–5
London 17, 137, 139–40, 241

Ma'arrat Nu'man 108
Macedonia 79
Mahdi
Sudanese religious leader 97
al-Mahdi, Muhammad
disappearance of (AD 874) 45
Shi'ite veneration of 45
Makhlouf, Rami 272
Mamluk Empire 62, 68, 77–8, 101, 273

territory of 145
victory at Battle of Ayn Jalut (1260) 67–8
Manama 298
Manji, Irshad
concept of 'Desert Islam' 29, 302
al-Mannan, Uthman bin Abd 75
Manzikert, battle of 57
Maronite Christians 66–7, 91–2, 95, 241, 243, 314
territory inhabited by 66–7, 92, 95, 123, 223
Marseilles 165
Martel, Charles
victory at Battle of Poitiers (AD 732) 50
Mauritania 16
Mawdudi, Abul Ala 209
Mecca 22–6, 30–1, 38, 49, 57, 157, 162, 173, 209, 281, 308
Medina 24–5, 27, 30, 32, 37–40, 90, 162, 173, 281, 308–9, 312
Mehmet II, Sultan 71
Mongols
defeat at Battle of Ayn Jalut (1260) 67–8
Sacking of Baghdad (1258) 61, 67, 88
Montesquieu 74–5, 102
Montevideo Convention (1933) 184
provisions of 254
Morocco 16, 114, 266, 283, 315
French Protectorate of (1912–56) 96–7, 111
government of 296
independence of (1956) 215
Jewish population of 193
Spanish Protectorate of (1913–56) 96, 112

Morsi, Muhammad
President of Egypt 296-7
Moses 32, 135
Mosul 120, 317
Mount Lebanon 123
Mu'awiya 39, 41-2, 44
death of (AD 681) 49
Mubarak, Hosni 273-4, 277-9, 290, 292, 297
economic policies of 274-5
removed from power (2011) 1, 295, 297, 302
Mughal Empire 62
Muhammad, Prophet 24-5, 34, 38-9, 53, 88, 106, 157, 160, 173, 202, 210, 281, 286, 309-10
birth of (c. AD 570) 22
death of 24, 27, 31, 33, 38, 44, 50, 57, 308
family of 23, 30, 33, 40-3, 53, 56, 162, 258
pilgrimage of (AD 632) 27
revelation of Qur'an to 23-4, 303, 308
speech at Ghadir Khumm 43-4, 56
Muhammad Ali Pasha 81, 84, 86, 92, 101, 126, 156
death of (1849) 79
Ottoman Khedive of Egypt 79-80, 145
mujahid 125
Muslim Brotherhood 166-7, 194, 210, 212, 243, 270, 278, 288-9
branches of 251
founding of (1928) 164
ideology of 305
members of 182, 193-4, 199, 305, 310
repression of 207

Mussolini, Benito 161, 198
regime of 142, 154

Nadir 25
al-Nafis Ibn 60
Nahas Pasha
Egyptian Prime Minister 171
head of Wafd Party 171
al-Na'im, Abdullahi 308
Najaf 144, 239, 316
Nasrallah, Hassan
head of Hizbullah 317-18
Nasser, Gamal Abdul 195, 199, 202-4, 215, 218, 220, 267, 276, 284
death of (1970) 221, 289
economic policies of 227
foreign policy of 207
President of Egypt 196-7
National Democratic Party (NDP) (Egypt) 277-8
nationalism 86, 89, 102, 132-3, 135, 142, 153, 157, 170, 194, 198, 228-9
Arab 91, 95, 138, 144, 148, 154, 156, 168, 172, 190-1, 206, 216, 223, 226, 236, 299, 317
Austrian 83
economic 205
Egyptian 81, 97, 99-100, 154, 191, 205
Iraqi 149
Jewish 132-3, 136
Palestinian 169, 180-1
secular 231, 260
Turkish 112
Nazism
anti-Semitism of 141, 169
Nehru, Jawaharlal 196
Netanyahu, Benjamin 247-8
Nile, River 80-1, 150, 154, 195,

197, 273
Nixon, Richard 225
Noah 32
Nokrashi Pasha
    assassination of (1948) 193
Non-Aligned Movement
    members of 196
North Atlantic Treaty Organization
    (NATO) 298
Norway
    Oslo 246
Nour, Ayman 278
Nubia 68
Nubians
    territory inhabited by 17
Nuwas, Abu
    'The Jewish Wine Seller'
    189–90, 313

Obama, Barack 255
Oman 16, 215, 266–7, 279
    One Arab Nation 201
Operation Cast Lead (2009) 253
Operation Summer Rains (2006)
    253
Operation Susannah (1954) 198,
    216
    political impact of 199–201
Organisation of the Islamic
    Conference
    formation of (1969) 226–7
Organisation of Petroleum
    Exporting Countries (OPEC)
    226
    founding of (1959) 226
    oil embargo (1973) 226
Oslo Peace Process 246, 249
    opposition to 252
Ottoman Empire 17, 62, 67, 70–1,
    76–7, 85–6, 96, 102, 135, 139,

144, 169, 263, 268
    military of 79, 86, 93, 125, 145,
    301
    millet system of 140
    tanzimat 91, 93
    territory of 75, 85, 89–90, 100,
    116, 118, 154, 172, 317
    Young Turk Revolution (1908)
    90–1, 112

Pahlavi, Muhammad Reza 228–9
Pakistan
    independence of (1947) 194
Palestine 20, 113, 120, 157, 168–9,
    172–3, 188, 237, 268
    Arab Revolt (1936–9) 142–3, 156
    Bedouin population of 176
    British Mandate of (1920–48),
    16, 116, 119, 123, 126–31, 136,
    140–1, 173–4, 177, 180–1, 183,
    239, 279, 301
    Christian population of 126–7,
    140, 184, 313
    Jewish population of 126–7,
    133–4, 136–9, 186
    Legislative Council 140
    Muslim population of 140, 184
    Nablus 126
    Occupied Territories 18, 187,
    219, 224, 241, 245–7, 249–51,
    253–4
    Shi'ite population of 126
    Sunni population of 126, 141,
    258
Palestine Liberation Organisation
    (PLO) 228, 241–2, 246–7, 249,
    252
    formation of (1964) 220
    removal from Jordan (1970) 223,
    251

removal from Lebanon (1982) 251
US recognition of 245
Palestine National Authority (PNA) 247, 250-1, 253-4
corruption in 252
Palmyra 19, 20
pan-Arabism 201, 216, 241
Paris 17, 80, 101, 103, 309
Peace of Westphalia (1648) 73-4
Peel Commission (1936-7) 143
Pentagon 249
Persian (language) 59
Persian Empire 22-3, 34
Persian Gulf War (1990-1) 235
Iraqi Invasion of Kuwait (1990) 231, 235, 243, 245, 261
political impact of 235-6
Philippines 230
Popular Front for the Liberation of Palestine (PFLP) 259
Dawson's Field hijacking (1970) 260
Port Said 199
Protestantism 73, 91
Psalms 28
Pyrenees 50

Qaboos, Sultan 296
al-Qa'ida 14, 261, 263-4
affiliates of 264, 299
members of 260, 264
Qala'at Sima'an 19
Qalb Lozeh 19
al-Qaradawi, Yusuf 313
Qasim, Brigadier Abd al-Karim 204, 267
death of (1963) 205
land reform policies of 204-5
Qatar 16, 97, 215, 279

Qaynuqa' 25
Quneitra 222
Qur'an 18, 24, 27-32, 38, 41, 46, 53, 56-7, 69-70, 106-7, 159-60, 167, 208-10, 232, 284, 287-8, 308, 311
Qurayzah 25
Qutb, Sayyid 207, 209-12, 225, 231, 260-1, 288, 319
A Child from the Village 208
execution of (1966) 210, 213
Milestones 210

Rabin, Yitzhak
assassination of (1995) 247
Israeli Chief of Staff 217
Israeli Prime Minister 222, 246, 250
Ramadan 31-2
Ramadan, Tariq 313
Rashidun 43, 49
Sunni view of 44
Reagan, Ronald 245
Republic of Ireland 136
Rhine, River 20, 22, 50-1
Rida, Rashid 158-9, 207, 209, 287
influence of 165
support for Wahhabism 162-3
Riyadh 202
'Road Map' (2003) 255
Roman Empire 19-20, 22, 74
sacking of Rome (AD 410) 22
Romania 87
Rome 17, 20, 22, 50-1, 91
Rommel, Erwin 171
Russian Empire 77, 88-9, 96, 100, 112
Russo-Japanese War (1904-5) 100
Russo-Turkish War (1877-8) 88

Sachedina, Abdulaziz 308
Sadat, Anwar 221, 224, 276, 289
    assassination of (1981) 210, 225,
    273
    visit to Jerusalem (1977) 224
al-Sadr, Muqtada
    Mahdi Army 239
Safad 126
Safavid Empire 62, 144
Said, Khaled
    death of (2010) 295
Said, Nuri 170
    Iraqi Prime Minister 169
St John of Damascus 36, 47
St Mark 36
St Paul 29
al Sakakini, Khalil 169
Saladin 68, 161, 199, 226
    victory at Battle of Hittin (1187)
    64
Salafism 286
    political 302
Saleh, Ali Abdullah
    President of Yemen 299
Samu 218
Samuel, Sir Herbert
    British High Commissioner of
    Palestine 136
Sanu', Ya'qoub (James Sanhua)
    102–4, 191
Saudi Arabia 13, 97, 159, 173,
    226–7, 261, 279, 283, 285, 296,
    305, 315, 319
    government of 318
    proclamation of (1932) 162, 263
Second Intifada (2000–5) 248
Second Lebanon War (2006) 318
Second World War (1939–45) 96,
    98, 126, 147, 155, 167, 171, 180,
    215

Italian Invasion of Egypt (1940)
    170
    Italian Invasion of Greece
    (1940–1) 171
    Pearl Harbor Attack (1941) 169
Selim the Grim 88–9
Seljuk Empire 62
    removal of Buwayhid from
    Baghdad (1055) 55
Sharia 32, 56, 68, 102, 159–60,
    166, 190, 209, 280, 286, 303–4,
    306, 309, 315, 318
Sharif Hussein of Mecca 112–13
Sharon, Ariel 221–2, 249
    construction of West Bank
    barrier 251
    Israeli Defence Minister 241
    Israeli Prime Minister 250
    visit to al-Aqsa Mosque (2000)
    248
Shenouda III, Pope 314
Sidon 123
Shi'ites 43, 45, 53, 55–6, 89, 118,
    144–5, 161, 202, 206, 228,
    230, 232–3, 240, 289, 315–16,
    318–19
    core beliefs of 43–4
    holy sites specific to 316
    opposition to Alawis 66, 317
    Sharia variant of 318
    view of significance of Ghadir
    Khumm 43–4
    'Twelvers' 45
Shohat, Ella 191
Sicily 50, 52, 62
    Norman conquest of 61
Sidqi, General Bakr 148–9
    assassination of (1937) 148
    coup led by (1936) 148
Siffeen, barrle of 41

Sinai 199–201, 216, 218, 225
 Israeli occupation of 188, 222
Six-Day War (1967) 203, 217, 256
 political impact of 220, 225–6
 territory occupied by Israel
 following 187, 219, 253–4
socialism 138, 154, 228, 287
 Arab 215, 228
Sohar 296
Soviet Union (USSR) 176, 203,
 206, 234
 collapse of (1991) 15, 231
 Invasion of Afghanistan (1979–
 89) 228, 230–1
Spain 50, 52, 57, 62, 112
 Civil War (1936–9) 156
 Jewish population of 71
 Muslim population of 71
 Reconquista 62, 70–1
 Stevens, Christopher 264
Storrs, Sir Ronald 131, 134, 141
 British Governor of Jerusalem
 and Judaea 130
Sudan 16, 82, 193, 197, 215, 266
 expulsion of Osama bin Laden
 (1996) 261–2
 Nubian population of 17
Suez Canal 13, 80–1, 153–4, 168,
 194, 197–8, 200
Suez Canal Company
 nationalisation of 197
Suez Crisis (1956) 198–200, 205,
 216, 218
Sufism 56–7
 brotherhoods of 166
suicide bombing 258
Sulayman, Hikmat 148–9
Sunna 28, 31, 53, 70, 107, 311
Sunnis 33, 43, 45, 56, 63, 67, 89,
 123–4, 141, 201, 206, 230, 239,
 258, 269, 289, 315, 318–19
 core beliefs of 56
 opposition to Alawis 317
 view of Rashidun 44
Sykes-Picot Agreement (1916) 113
 provisions of 112
Syria 16, 18–19, 26, 39, 41, 112,
 125, 144, 169, 172–3, 192, 217,
 245, 266–7, 272, 283, 288, 315
 Alawi population of 126, 316
 borders of 144, 268
 Christian population of 35, 124,
 126, 313, 317
 Civil War (2011–) 244, 258,
 268–70, 272, 300–1, 316
 Druze population of 124, 126,
 317
 Emergency Law (1966) 271
 French Mandate of (1924–46)
 119–20, 122–6, 239–40, 268–9,
 301
 government of 258
 Great Syrian Revolt (1925–7)
 142
 independence of (1946) 172
 Kurdish population of 16,
 118–19
 military of 49, 203
 refugee population of 240
 Sunni population of 269
Syrian National Congress 120–2,
 135

Taha, Mahmud Muhammad 309
 execution of (1985) 308
al-Tahtawi, Rifaʻa 101
 influence of 102, 165
Taif 244
Taif Agreement (1989) 244
takfir 319

Taliban 262, 283
  capture of Kabul (1996) 231
  ideology of 283, 306
  opposition to education of women 283
  removed from power (2001) 262
de Talleyrand-Périgord, Charles 79
Tanzania
  US embassy bombing (1998) 262
Tawfiq Pasha 83-4
  Ottoman Khedive of Egypt 83
Tawheed 161
Tchad 16
Tel Aviv 137, 179
Third Reich (1933-45) 142
  Afrika Corps 171
  impact on European Jewish migration 142, 175
  supporters of 143
Thirty Years' War (1618-48) 73
Tiberias 126
Tigris, River 77, 119, 144
Timurid Empire 62
Tito, Josip Broz 196
Tobruk 169
Toledo 60
Torah 28
Trench, battle of 26
Tripoli (Lebanon) 123
Tripoli (Libya) 77, 298
Tunis 55, 77
Tunisia 16, 54, 85, 293, 310, 312
  French Protectorate of (1881-1956) 96
  independence of (1956) 215
  Jewish population of 193
  Nahda Party 309
  Revolution (2010-11) 14, 293, 296, 299

Turkey 18, 83, 90, 97-8, 115, 120, 139, 150, 152, 173, 300
  borders of 268
  economy of 88
  family law of 305-6
  refugee population of 300
Turkish (language) 83
Tyre 123

Uhud, battle of 26, 30, 33, 39
Umayyad Caliphate 44-5, 49, 53, 62
  disintegration of 61
Umma 104, 210
Uniates 91
United Arab Emirates (UAE) 16, 97, 113, 279
  formation of (1971) 215
  government of 318
United Arab Republic (UAR)
  formation of (1958) 203
  Syrian secession from (1961) 203, 205
United Kingdom (UK) 15, 78, 83-4, 91, 112, 122, 156, 168, 183, 197, 216, 229, 237, 254, 281
  Foreign and Commonwealth Office 177
  government of 82, 143
  imperial territory of 97-8, 152
  Labour Party 194
  military of 85, 151, 194
  Parliament 113-14, 140
  White Paper (1939) 144, 169-70
United Nations (UN) 176, 183, 218, 235-6, 253, 255, 282, 307
  Arab Human Development Report (2005) 285
  Charter 176
  General Assembly 176, 179, 255

Oil-For-Food Programme 238
Palestine Commission 177
Partition Plan for Palestine (1947) 176-7
Relief and Works Agency for Palestinian Refugees (UNRWA) 187
    personnel of 200, 239
Security Council 237, 254, 298
United States of America (USA) 13, 16, 75, 91, 95-6, 114, 119, 121, 151, 156, 169, 176, 197, 203, 206, 226, 229, 237, 241, 254, 320
    9/11 attacks 14, 238, 249, 256, 260, 262-3
    Civil War (1861-5) 82
    Congress 115
    military of 263, 297
    navy of 114
    opposition to Palestinian non-member observer status in UN (2012) 255
    State Department 257
    World Trade Center bombing (1993) 260
Urabi Pasha 103
Urban II, Pope
    launch of First Crusade (1095) 62
Uthman 38-40, 56
    murder of 40, 42, 45
    Shi'ite view of 44
    Third Caliph 38, 42
Uris, Leon
    Exodus (1958) 256

Vandals
    Crossing of Rhine (AD 406) 50
    Sacking of Rome (AD 455) 50
Venezuela

    founding member of OPEC 226
Vienna 73, 75

Wafd Party 151, 153, 171, 290
Wahhabis 80, 161
Wahhabism 160, 261, 319
    core beliefs of 160-1
    supporters of 159
Al Waleed, Khalid Ibn 33-4
Washington DC 246
Weizmann, Dr Chaim 132, 163
    head of Zionist Commission 131
West Bank 181, 184, 187-8, 219, 247-8, 253
    Israeli occupation of 187, 222, 250
    refugee population of 187
Western Roman Empire
    collapse of (AD 480) 22
Wilson, Woodrow
    Fourteen Points (1918) 114-15, 126

Yarmouk, battle of 39
Yarmouk, River 119
Yemen 16, 39, 55, 73, 90, 97, 173, 216, 266, 283
    independence of South Yemen (1967) 281-2
    North Yemen Civil War (1962-70) 206, 267
    Revolution (2011-12) 298-9
    USS Cole bombing (2001) 262
Yezid, son of Mu'awiya 44
Yezidis 118
    territory inhabited by 145
Yiddish (language) 137
Yom Kippur War (1973) 269
    belligerents of, 14-15, 221
Young Turks 90, 112

YouTube 295
Yugoslavia 196, 230

Zaghloul, Sa'd 151
    death of (1927) 153, 225
Zai'm, Husni 183, 226
Zangi, Nur al-Din 64
Zarqa' 259-60
al-Zarqawi, Abu Musab 260
al-Zawahiri, Ayman 260

Zionism 17, 128, 130-1, 137-8, 140,
    162, 174-5, 179, 183-4, 191, 247
    concept of 127, 132-3
    opposition to 135
    political 134
Zionist Commission 132, 141
    aims of 133-4
    members of 131
    visit to Jerusalem (1918) 131
Zoroastrianism 22